I have always been a fan of Dr. Joe's impromptu analogies (such as 5L's or L.I.F.E) that I have heard on his keynotes and in his podcasts. However, his book Numbers to Narratives is a masterclass providing a framework along with practical tools and techniques giving life to boring data converting them into powerful stories that drive action. With his signature blend of passion, expertise, and practical insights, he empowers readers to extract actionable insights, build trust through data integrity, and inspire change with compelling visuals. This book is an essential read for those who want to transform their data into a powerful tool for innovation and business success.

Arvind Murali, Chief Data Officer

"From Numbers to Narratives" covers the crucial topic of how we communicate the story from data. We learn to perform analysis, but the storytelling part is often overlooked, and this is where we can make valuable recommendations and drive decisions if we're persuasive. After graduating from university with an MS in Applied Statistics, learning how to communicate with the business was one of the most painful experiences in my career. From meetings that went awry to good ideas that were forgotten but could have had an impact had I presented information differently. "From Numbers to Narratives" allows you to learn from real-world case studies and compelling narratives to get a jumpstart on honing your storytelling craft instead of taking years and learning through trial and error. I would absolutely recommend this book to anyone, especially those who have just completed a technical degree.

Kristen Kehrer, Head of Decision Science and AI

Dr. Joe is a highly appropriate author for this book. He has a unique and rare knack for taking the audience on a journey and regaling stories in a way that comes across as both enigmatic and engaging. Having seen him present first hand, it's clear that Perez is right at home with the subject matter of crafting engaging stories with data. His frameworks are enjoyable and easy to follow, but also demonstrate a fluency and simplicity that makes the user WANT to ask the next question. Ultimately, that's what data storytelling pangs for us to do, and Dr. Joe is an exemplary guide on the path to perfecting your data narratives.

Brian Booden, Trusted Analytics Advisor, Managing Director

Nothing is more demoralizing than discovering that the data visualizations you've painstakingly worked on—acquiring the data, cleaning it, and creating the visuals—are left unexamined and unused. This is where Dr. Joe Perez's book shines. It shows how to turn numbers into compelling stories that connect us to our audiences (executives, users, or customers). Dr. Joe provides study questions at the end of each chapter to help us refine our thoughts on data storytelling, upping our storytelling game! By engaging our audiences, we can transform data from mind-numbing numbers into strategic changes that drive real impact. This book is a must-read for anyone who wants their data visualizations to connect with audiences and inspire action. I can't wait to read the rest of the book!

Felicia Joyner, Speaker, Senior Executive Business Analyst

"From Numbers to Narratives" is a transformative journey that brilliantly bridges the gap between raw data and compelling storytelling. Dr. Joe Perez masterfully unveils a comprehensive framework that empowers readers to turn complex information into actionable insights. His unique blend of practical tools, real-world case studies, and engaging narratives makes this book an indispensable resource for anyone looking to harness the true potential of data. Whether you're a seasoned data professional or a business leader seeking to drive impactful change, this book will equip you with the skills and inspiration to become a data alchemist in your own right.

Nicholas Kelly, Author, Analytics Consultant,
Data Visualization Expert

If you wish to talk about Data Visualization, the man to talk to is Dr. Joe Perez. In his latest installment, "From Numbers to Narratives that Transform Businesses," he illustrates the power of storytelling with data to support business decision making. Dr. Joe informs readers how to creatively craft compelling data visualizations that transforms static numbers into captivating narratives that drive impactful change. Unleash the magic of data to use it as a storytelling tool to inform data-driven decisions within your organization. In this book, Dr. Joe walks readers through the L.I.F.E. pillars of relevant data and more, giving you full confidence to unlock the full potential of data to transform your business. Each chapter ends with thought-provoking questions to drive home key concepts that enables readers to relate these concepts to their own data-related challenges. Numbers to Narratives is an engaging read that is an actionable framework to transform data visualizations into data storytelling.

Aaron Whittenberger, CBAP, AAC, CPOA, ICP-APO, A-CSPO

Dr. Joe Perez's "From Numbers to Narratives" is the guide we've all been looking for that transforms the way we think about data. With a perfect blend of analytical rigor and creative storytelling, this book empowers readers to unlock the true potential of their data. Dr. Joe's approach focuses on creating visually appealing charts as well as diving deep into the art of crafting compelling narratives that fuel decision-making and drive business transformation. His unique L.I.F.E. framework (Legacy, Integrity, Fervency, Efficiency) ensures that data becomes more than just numbers. This book is a great read for anyone looking to turn data into a powerful tool for change.

George Firican, Data Governance & Business Intelligence Director

Being able to tell stories with our data is a key skill in the world we currently live and work in. So, I am really excited about Dr. Joe's latest book. "From Numbers to Narratives" offers a great approach to data storytelling, taking readers on a journey from raw data to compelling narratives that drive business growth. Dr. Joe blends analytical rigor with creativity, providing a roadmap for crafting effective data visualizations and making informed, data-driven decisions. I love the idea of the L.I.F.E. principles (Legacy, Integrity, Fervency, and Efficiency) and how they drive an understanding of how to enrich data for maximum impact. Whether you are a seasoned data professional or just beginning to explore the world of data visualization, this book equips you with practical tools, engaging stories, and actionable strategies to turn data into a catalyst for innovation and meaningful change. If you are looking to unlock the full potential of your data then you must read this book!

Nicola Askham, Data Governance Expert, Speaker

Dr. Joe Perez's "From Numbers to Narratives" is a mirror of his decades of experience and his dynamic, energetic nature. This book transforms data into compelling stories, making it a versatile and academically profound guide for professionals across industries. Recognizing that not everyone is a natural communicator, Dr. Perez speaks to those who struggle with expressing their ideas, analyzing their audience, or using data as evidence. In this book, he provides invaluable insights and practical techniques that speak to both novices and seasoned professionals, offering fresh perspectives and empowering readers to turn data into meaningful, impactful stories.

Nagim Ashufta, Founder/CEO, DRIVA

"From Numbers to Narratives" is a different kind of visualization book that weaves together data storytelling, actionable insights, and the transformative "L.I.F.E." pillars of relevant data – Legacy, Integrity, Fervency, and Efficiency. Dr. Joe's signature enthusiasm shines forth on every page, and the reader can't help but be infected by his deep love for the subject matter. With FERVENT energy, he provides practical tools and real-world case studies that show how to inform and influence data-driven decisions with compelling visualizations and an accompanying data story. After years in the data industry trenches, JOE KNOWS what pays the bills, and this book wastes zero time getting right to the heart of the matter. "From Numbers to Narratives" is a worthy addition to the greats of the genre, offering a fresh perspective on using data as a catalyst for business success.

Albert Bellamy, CEO, Senior BA Instructor, USMC Veteran

Dr. Joe has taken something that can be hugely complex, and turned it into an interesting, informative, and enjoyable read from which I have learned so much. This book really is tailored towards people rather than the process, and is so easy to understand that even I, who works in data but not in visualization, can understand it. From the practical frameworks to the useful tools and techniques, "From Numbers to Narratives" is a great book, with case studies and study questions in every chapter to challenge my knowledge, which I really love.

Susan Walsh, The Data Classification Guru

"From Numbers to Narratives" by Dr. Joe Perez is an exceptional resource for data professionals and business leaders alike. This book doesn't simply explain data concepts; it masterfully weaves metaphors, real-world examples, and thought-provoking questions to engage readers of all learning styles. Whether you are an experienced analyst or just starting to explore data visualization, you'll find something valuable here. Dr. Joe, a well-known data thought leader, practitioner, and dynamic speaker, brings his unique energy into the pages, making complex topics accessible and actionable. With its blend of practical tools, inspiring stories, and interactive prompts, this book equips you with the tools and strategies helping you to understand data and to turn it into a powerful force for business transformation. It's a must-read for anyone looking to elevate their data storytelling and decision-making capabilities.

Dora Boussias, Data & Tech Executive, Thought Leader

Data communication has arrived in the mainstream – there are no news articles, no business decisions and not even debates between friends that don't include facts and figures to make a point, and that make crafting compelling narratives and visualizations around data more important than ever. Dr. Joe Perez not only masterfully guides us through the art of data visualization and storytelling through case studies and best practices, but he makes it highly accessible and memorable through frameworks like "Bringing Data to L.I.F.E.." Dr. Joe's passion for data built on his decades of experience can be felt through every word, and that makes this book a highly engaging and inspiring read. "Numbers to Narratives" is a must-read for any data professional, data leader, and anyone who communicates with data.

Tiankai Feng – Author of "Humanizing Data Strategy"

Dr. Joe is a rare powerhouse speaker, bringing a dynamic, evangelical energy to data conferences and beyond. In "Numbers to Narratives," he takes the same electrifying content from his renowned keynotes and transforms it into a practical how-to guide. His signature style—blending pithy alliterations, sharp, memorable phrases, historical anecdotes, and creative frameworks— brings you on a delightful journey from raw data to real business value. A must-read for data leaders, it's sure to earn a permanent place on your bookshelf.

Scott Taylor, The Data Whisperer

I've known Dr. Joe as an amazing speaker, whose passion for data captivates a broad expert audience. He continues to build momentum in this field. By reading his books, I realized how closely my own perspective on data storytelling aligns with his! Dr. Joe truly makes data easy to understand, providing a comprehensive framework that can be applied pragmatically wherever you are in your data journey. This book, in particular, is a powerful tool that will help you leap forward, whether you're just starting out in your data journey or are already an expert. It offers a refreshingly genuine perspective, which is quite remarkable. Thank you, Dr. Joe, for serving the cause of data!

Christelle Patriarca, Data/Agile Advisor, Certified Coach, Founder of Data Is Life Consulting

You know that feeling when something finally clicks? That's what Dr. Joe Perez delivers in "From Numbers to Narratives." He takes data—something that often feels dry and distant—and turns it into a tool for growth, both personally and professionally. It feels like sitting down with a trusted mentor who's ready to flip how you think about data on its head and show you how to turn it into stories that speak, connect, and drive action. The most powerful takeaway? Data isn't just numbers—it's the story you haven't told yet. This book is a must-read for anyone who's tired of boring charts and ready to bring their data to life in a way that makes a difference.

Terence Sathyanarayan, MBA, CIO, Entrepreneur

Dr. Joe Perez's "From Numbers to Narratives" is an essential read for all business employees navigating today's data-driven landscape. As data storytelling becomes increasingly crucial for conveying the business value of data, Dr. Joe offers a structured framework for transforming raw numbers into compelling narratives that resonate with diverse audiences. This book emphasizes the importance of data literacy across an organization, not just for data professionals, but for all business users who are now expected to work with data in their decision-making. Dr. Joe's dynamic writing style, rich with relevant examples from pop culture and history, brings this often-complex topic to life. His engaging writing approach – similar to his captivating presentation style – makes data storytelling accessible and highlights its importance for readers at all levels of expertise. "From Numbers to Narratives" is a must-read for anyone looking to master the art of communicating data's value. Dr. Joe's passion for storytelling is evident on every page, making this book an enjoyable and informative resource for data professionals and business users alike. Highly recommended!

Peggy Tsai, Chief Data Officer, BigID

Despite many decades working with data of all types and sizes, I'm an idiot when it comes to visualizing data. I still think a donut chart is edible. I'm dumb like that. Turns out, that's not a good approach for visualizations. Dr. Joe's book, "From Numbers to Narratives," not only taught me the best steps in visualizing data for stakeholders, but how to make it simple enough to dolts like myself can understand it. It's a great book; a must-read!

**Joe Reis, Best-Selling Author, Instructor,
Data Engineer, Recovering Data Scientist**

From Numbers to Narratives That Transform Businesses

This book shows the reader how to transform cold numbers into captivating narratives that drive business success. Master the art and science of data storytelling, blend logic with creativity, and turn insights into action. Learn to craft stunning visuals, navigate data-driven decisions, and infuse your data with key principles for maximum impact. This book is your roadmap to turning data from mere information into a powerful catalyst for transformation.

Dr. Joe Perez is Senior Systems Specialist and Team Leader at the NC Department of Health & Human Services and a former Business Intelligence Specialist at NC State University.

From Numbers to Narratives That Transform Businesses

Harnessing the Power of Data Visualization

Dr. Joe Perez

CRC Press
Taylor & Francis Group
Boca Raton London New York

CRC Press is an imprint of the
Taylor & Francis Group, an **informa** business

Designed cover image: Joe Perez

First edition published 2025
by CRC Press
2385 NW Executive Center Drive, Suite 320, Boca Raton FL 33431

and by CRC Press
4 Park Square, Milton Park, Abingdon, Oxon, OX14 4RN

CRC Press is an imprint of Taylor & Francis Group, LLC

© 2025 Dr. Joe Perez

ISBN: 9781041032946 (hbk)
ISBN: 9781041032939 (pbk)
ISBN: 9781003623212 (ebk)

DOI: 10.1201/9781003623212

Typeset in Minion
by Newgen Publishing UK

Contents

PART III **Bringing Data to L.I.F.E. and Life to Data**

Foreword

I CAN VIVIDLY RECALL THE first time I ever met Dr. Joe Perez in person. It was mid-July in 2023, and I was attending the annual CDOIQ symposium in Cambridge, Massachusetts, during a rather intense New England summer heat wave. Both Dr. Joe and I were scheduled to speak at the event, and being the consummate networker that Dr. Joe is, he contacted me on LinkedIn several weeks in advance of the event to remind me he was speaking, and to personally invite me to attend his session.

Dr. Joe and I had been supporting each other's content on LinkedIn for over a year and we had developed a virtual rapport, but until that time, I had never interacted personally with him. Given his dedication to creating compelling content and his support for my efforts, I agreed to attend his CDOIQ session – and I'm extremely glad I did.

When it comes to the best timing for a conference presentation – Dr. Joe unfortunately got the shortest end of the stick on that hot summer day. His presentation was scheduled to be the very last of the conference after three full days of sessions. Turnout for sessions always wanes the longer a conference lasts regardless of the topic or the speaker, so given it was the end of day three, I knew Dr. Joe would probably be facing an uphill battle on audience attendance and participation. Still, I wanted to go and support him, as he had been supporting me.

As it turns out, about 20 devoted CDOs and data professionals attended Dr. Joe's session, and within minutes of opening his mouth, it appeared to me that he had almost all of them in the palm of his hand – including me. I learned very quickly that day in Cambridge that Dr. Joe is an extremely powerful and engaging speaker, who has an incredible gift for storytelling. His timing, body language, and delivery are all perfectly suited for public oration – and the icing on the cake is Dr. Joe's velvet voice. Dr. Joe was recently a guest on my Podcast, CDO Matters, where I correctly noted that Dr. Joe's voice is like chocolate cake for your ears, and I meant it.

On that steamy day next to the MIT campus, "Dr. Joe" (as he is better known) delivered an impassioned and insightful presentation to a room of 20 people like a true champion. Looking back, I don't think Dr. Joe's delivery, or the audience experience, would have been any different if there were 5000 people in that room, which is a testament to his passion. I was beyond impressed with his skill and professionalism that day, and I've been a fan ever since.

As a speaker and storyteller, Dr. Joe clearly has the goods – but he's also got the goods when it comes to his content. When you listen to Dr. Joe share his insights on data and analytics, it's clear he's learned his lessons by doing, since what he shares is both insightful and actionable – a rare combination of skills and experience at a time when influence often seems to matter more than substance.

That's why I was beyond thrilled when Dr. Joe asked me to write the foreword to this book. What you will read in these pages are a series of stories and insights on the transformative power that visual representations play in the world of data. I have zero artistic bones in my body and struggle to draw stick figures (and my wife is convinced I'm partially colorblind) – but given Dr. Joe's innate storytelling skills – it only took him about a half a chapter to make me a true believer of the importance of effective data visualizations. Like the first time I listened to Dr. Joe deliver his message in public, within minutes of starting this book, I was absolutely hooked.

His passion for the subject oozes through every page, and that's a big reason why Dr. Joe's message is so powerful. You'll want to read more, and with every word you consume, you'll be more of a believer in his message – and you'll be better equipped to tell an impactful data story in a way that you've never told one before. Throughout the book, Dr. Joe uses helpful and approachable mnemonics to help you remember all of the main messages of each chapter, and he uses highly relatable and recent stories and real-world use cases to ground his ideas and his message.

This book is for any data professional who is passionate about building compelling, meaningful, and impactful data products for their customers. It will be highly useful for data product managers, leaders, analysts or anyone else who works closely with data customers in defining requirements for analytical insights. It will also be highly beneficial for any data team looking to more deeply integrate more compelling and engaging visual elements into the design of their analytical solutions. Data leaders and CDOs will benefit from this book by learning how visual treatments of data can provide more impact for their customers, and how emotions play a critical role in how the consumers of analytical insights get value from them.

Yes, this is a book about visualizations – but ultimately, it's also a book about our emotional responses to data – something not discussed nearly enough in the data world. I can't think of any better way to summarize my key takeaway from this book than to quote Dr. Joe himself, which is that this book is about "transforming cold numbers into stories that stir the soul." It's an inspiring message delivered by an inspiring human, and I invite you to turn the page and be moved by a master storyteller. Enjoy!

Malcolm Hawker
Chief Data Officer, Profisee

Preface

UNLEASH THE MAGIC OF data! *From Numbers to Narratives* converts raw data into engaging stories that propel business growth. Acquire the skills to master data storytelling, merging analytical thinking with creative flair to translate insights into actionable strategies. Discover how to create compelling visuals, make informed data-driven choices, and enrich your data with L.I.F.E. for optimal effectiveness. This book is your roadmap to turning data from mere information into a powerful catalyst for transformation.

Overall Objectives: (laying the groundwork and setting the pace) In this book, the reader will:

- Craft data visualizations that captivate audiences, transforming static numbers into captivating narratives that drive action and change.

- Navigate data-driven decisions with confidence, demystifying complex information and extracting actionable insights to fuel informed strategies and achieve tangible results.

- Infuse data with L.I.F.E., weaving legacy, integrity, fervency, and efficiency into every analysis, unlocking the true potential of information and driving impactful change.

- Become a data alchemist, transmuting raw information into valuable insights, overcoming cognitive biases to identify opportunities and propel innovation forward.

- Unlock the magic within their data, wielding it as a storytelling tool to inspire action, shape the future, and transform their organization into a data-driven powerhouse

Acknowledgments

Dr. Joe and Dianna Perez, 2024.

FOR AS LONG AS I can remember, I've been a fan of data storytelling. Years before the term was coined, decades before software tools to facilitate it were invented, I was looking for insight to be derived from information, an underlying story to be told from facts, and meaning to be pulled from patterns. Saying words or writing them down has never been enough for me; there always had to be inflection in my voice, passion in my tone, color in my descriptions, and a spark of inspiration in my mind. Whatever or whomever would encourage me to make the story, the report, or the message more compelling would be someone I'd see as an instrument to further equipping me along my journey.

And what a journey it has been; as an educator, a technology professional, an international keynote speaker, and now, an author. Many individuals and organizations come to mind that fit this description of "instrument," both in the abstract and the specific. From the hundreds of students I have taught, to the thousands of audience members in my presentations, to the countless colleagues and others who have heard me speak and urged me to compile my thoughts and ideas into a book, I express deep gratitude for lighting the fire that has culminated in the work you are now reading. To be honest, I wish I could remember the first person who, after telling me how one of my data-related keynotes inspired them, said, "Dr. Joe, you have got to write a book on this topic!"

Going even farther back, my middle school teachers recognized my potential for storytelling and encouraged me to develop my skills. They saw the way I could find patterns in everyday items and use them to create compelling narratives. This early encouragement sparked the fire within me that has fueled my passion for data storytelling and ultimately led to the writing of this book.

But to be more specific, when I was building the presentation that would form the basis of Part I of this book, two colleagues from the NC Department of Health & Human Services were of invaluable help. Dr. Jessie Tenenbaum (then Chief Data Officer) and Haley Young (currently acting Chief Data Officer in 2024) took their valuable time to provide me with constructive suggestions, positive feedback, and helpful advice, transforming a rough speech into a highly polished presentation. In fact, this talk (now called "Leveraging Beauty and Brains for Effective Data Storytelling") has become one of my signature keynotes as I continued to improve upon it over the following five years. I am deeply grateful for the kindness those two brilliant ladies showed me, and the intensity of their passion for actionable data has enhanced my own.

Then there are the dozens of conference organizers who have graciously invited me to speak at their events, several of whom have had me return multiple times. All of them have been incredibly supportive of my work as a speaker, even suggesting that I write a book based on my data-related topics. One such organizer is Pio Marolla, CEO of ThinkLinkers in Europe. I've had the pleasure of collaborating closely with Pio on several events. His professionalism and expertise in master data management are exceptional. He's a strong leader who ensures that everything runs smoothly, from planning to execution. Pio's passion for master data management is evident in his work, and he has a remarkable ability to connect with his audience. His support and guidance have been invaluable, and I'm grateful for the opportunity to work with him.

Tiffani Neilson, Chief Marketing Officer at IoT Marketing, has been a valuable collaborator and supporter throughout my journey as an author. Our work together as co-hosts on Mind2Mind, our monthly podcast, has significantly contributed to refining my writing skills. Her insights and feedback have been invaluable in shaping my approach to data storytelling in "Numbers to Narratives." Tiffani's dedication and professionalism are a constant source of inspiration. I've had the pleasure of speaking at several events produced by her and her team, and I've always been impressed by their ability to execute flawless events. Tiffani's expertise and leadership are evident in everything she does.

Another organizer for whom I've spoken several times is John Ward, Portfolio Director at Worldwide Business Research. I've been impressed by his dedication to creating unforgettable events and his ability to foster a collaborative environment. I've learned quite a bit from his expertise in engaging audiences and delivering impactful presentations, which has directly influenced my approach to data storytelling in this book, specifically as it relates to data-driven decision-making, the theme of Part II of this book. In fact, John's insights and support have been instrumental in my journey as a data storyteller, and I'm grateful for his contributions to this project.

The heart of a developer will be evident as you read "Numbers to Narratives," and no conference organizer embodies that better than Neringa Young, CEO of Build Stuff, a European conference where I've had the privilege of speaking several times on the main stage. "People will read anything you write, Dr. Joe," she once said to me. Her dedication to excellence is evident in everything she does, from organizing conferences to creating a welcoming atmosphere for speakers and attendees. Her leadership and attention to detail have inspired me to strive for excellence in my own work, including my writing. I'm grateful for her support and encouragement, which have played a significant role in the development of this book.

Fellow keynote speakers and authors have also been an incredible source of encouragement throughout my writing journey. Several of them have generously contributed endorsements to this book, and you'll hear from some of them in the Preface (including one who even wrote the Foreword).

When data analytics and data governance giants like George Firican, Nicola Askham, Harpreet Sahota, Joe Reis, and Chris Tabb couldn't wait to have me on their podcasts, it was a clear sign that my work was resonating with the data community. When outstanding, top-notch authors and data storytelling experts like Brent Dykes, Lea Pica, Kate Strachnyi, and Tiankai Feng expressed their admiration for my work, it was a validation that I was on the right track. One of them, Lea, even included a shoutout to me in her book.

And when phenomenal powerhouses like Peggy Tsai, Scott Taylor, Adita Karkera, Malcolm Hawker, and Kristen Kehrer (whom I consider my "data heroes" like all the others) were so excited to take a selfie with me (as though I were the celebrity and not them), it was a clear indication that my work was making an impact. Their enthusiasm and support have been essential and profoundly appreciated.

There are countless other conference organizers, fellow speakers, colleagues, and friends who have inspired and supported me throughout my writing journey; their positive input has been invaluable. While I can't mention everyone by name in this section, I want to express my sincere gratitude to all of those who have encouraged and supported me. Their contributions have helped shape this book and make it a reality. If this were a separate chapter, I could dedicate pages to acknowledging each person individually. The multifaceted mindset that enabled me to write "Numbers to Narratives" is a result of the positive input from a multitude of brilliant people.

However, I would be remiss if I were to overlook the significant influence of my family. My brother, Oscar, who played a crucial role in my previous book, "The Madness Behind the Method," also offered consistent encouragement and support. My two grown sons, Joshua and Andrew, have always been staunch advocates for their father, impressed as they were by all the data storytelling videos I've created. They were equally amazed when they grasped the magnitude of the work I was undertaking with this book. I could never thank them enough, and no father could be prouder of the fine young men of integrity, hard work, and faith these two have become.

And then there's my lifelong companion, soulmate, girl of my dreams, love of my life, and mother of my children: my dearest wife Dianna. She is the ultimate confidant, encourager, proofreader, and provider of helpful feedback. I couldn't ask for a better partner.

She is so much more than I could possibly deserve. I am grateful beyond words for all the countless times I've run concepts by her and she has patiently listened to me, even though data storytelling isn't her strong suit and technology isn't her favorite subject. Despite her lack of expertise in these areas, her intelligence and insightful observations have been both amazing and refreshing. Her inner beauty shines through in everything she does, and her extraordinary outer beauty is only surpassed by her inner strength and character. She has always exceeded expectations, never complained, and been my biggest cheerleader every step of the way.

I will forever be grateful for her undying love and never-ending support. She is the best wife a man could ever want. As my tribute song to her says, she's "My Dianna; my sweetheart and my friend!" I thank God for blessing me with Dianna.

Finally, as a Christian, I must express my gratitude to my Lord and Savior, Jesus Christ. Any success you see in me or in any of my work, whether spoken or written, is completely by the grace of God. The Lord told His disciples in the latter part of John 15:5, "Without Me ye can do nothing." Truer words were never spoken, as I am indeed nothing without Him.

Although this book is not a religious work by any means, I acknowledge that God is the Source of all truth and knowledge. He has blessed me with the talent to speak at conferences and write books, and He has fueled my passion for striving for excellence in everything I do. My goal is to make a positive impact on others and ultimately glorify Him. As the Apostle Paul wrote in 1 Corinthians 10:31, "Whether therefore ye eat, or drink, or whatsoever ye do, do all to the glory of God." I strive to live my life according to this principle, and I hope that my work reflects my dedication to glorifying God in all that I do, even while showing excellence when authoring a book about data storytelling.

I couldn't possibly thank God enough for His blessings on me. I trust that some of that blessing will make a positive impact on you as you read the rest of this book.

I

Leveraging Beauty and Brains for Effective Data Storytelling

INTRODUCTION

Anyone can make a pretty bar graph, but can you make sound decisions based on your graphical reports? How do you turn a flashy concept into an actionable visualization? Can your ideas become reality?

American mathematician John Tukey once said, "The greatest value of a picture is when it forces us to notice what we never expected to see." What value do you see in your data, and what ideas do you have when you see it? Are you relying only on nice-looking graphics to accomplish this or on the raw scientific data behind those graphs? Or should it be done by some leveraged combination of the two?

In this section, to both capitalize on that value and explore those ideas, we will cover the five "Stages of the Spectrum" for data storytelling in action. By leveraging beauty and brains, balancing art and science, and combining form and function, the author's goal is that the reader will discover the difference between impact and influence, and how that plays into making data actionable.

DATA IN ACTION

Early on a February morning in 1991, a massive ground assault by an American-led coalition began against Iraq in a military operation that has been heralded as one of the shortest and least costly of America's military victories. This monumental feat could not have been accomplished, however, without actionable data – more accurately, without the brilliant application of deceptive actionable data.

Iraq had attacked and invaded Kuwait several months earlier, placing American and other socioeconomic interests in jeopardy, not to mention those of the Kuwaitis themselves, thus requiring a response in kind. The enemy needed to be driven out and stability restored to the region. The original plan to do so called for a heavy frontal assault, but General Norman Schwarzkopf, commander of the multinational coalition, challenged the military strategists and others to come up with a more creative plan that would result in fewer casualties on all sides in a prolonged conflict. The resulting new plan involved deceiving the enemy into thinking the coalition would execute an amphibious attack from the east and south, leaving their west flank virtually undefended. Troops would then swoop in from the west, catch them off guard, and outflank them with what would later be called the Left Hook.

This strategy involved following what is known as Magruder's Principle, a military form of deception based on the idea that it is much easier to exploit your enemies' beliefs than to change them, thus reinforcing any preconceptions they might have. The Iraqis were already thinking the Americans would attack from the Persian Gulf, so why not make them plan for it? The enemy used the data they derived from the misinformation the Americans fed them to drive their decisions and inform their strategy. Getting into the intricate details of this elaborate ruse is beyond the scope of this chapter, but essentially, it worked.

As a result, the data derived from the Iraqis' reactions gave coalition leadership the insight needed to answer the incessant questions and make those tough decisions. The data ultimately enabled the American-led forces to exceed the general's challenge: The ground offensive achieved all of its objectives in less than one hundred hours with fewer casualties than expected. This is a true testament to actionable data.

Techopedia defines actionable insight as "information that can be acted upon or information that gives enough insight into the future that the actions that should be taken become clear for decision makers."[1] Stated in an alternate way, it can be defined as meaningful data that is useful for making a decision, answering a question, or solving a problem.

These are the three essential tenets or characteristics of actionable data that will surface multiple times in this section. It distinguishes data that can improve the overall situation from data that serves as nothing more than fancy window dressing or interesting trivia (i.e., totally useless data from a practical standpoint). When one considers the staggering amount of data that is created in a single day (more than 2.5 quintillion bytes worldwide according to a recent Forbes estimate),[2] it becomes even more astounding to know that perhaps less than one half of 1% of this data is actually analyzed and used.[3] Consider this: not many years ago, at the beginning of 2020, the number of bytes in the digital universe was 40 times bigger than the number of stars in the observable physical universe.[4]

So how do you turn your own actionable data into a reality as we begin this journey into the realm of data alchemy? Create a *data storytelling journey*. The Data Warehouse Institute defines data storytelling as "the practice of building a narrative around a set of data and its accompanying visualizations to help convey the meaning of that data in a powerful and compelling fashion."[5] And with every data visualization, there is always a starting point. The developer or designer typically commences with an idea or a concept that exists only in their mind. As the end goal, this person will typically envision a completed data visualization containing one or more graphs.

But to make your data a reality, view your data's story as an imaginary horizontal line (from left to right) that includes five Stages of the Spectrum (i.e., best practices) for getting from the idea/concept on the left to the completed visualization and direction on the right (Figure 0.1). Those five stages – Conception, Inception, Perception, Inspection, and Direction – comprise the five chapters that will be expounded upon throughout Part I of this book.

The way Figure P1.1 depicts these stages might cause the reader to assume the author intends for them to occur sequentially. While that may be the tendency under normal circumstances, it is also possible for stages

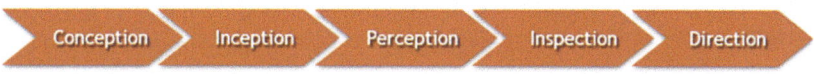

FIGURE 0.1   The five Stages of the Spectrum.

to share concurrency or even overlap to a certain extent. In any case, it is essential to approach them in the light of a holistic strategy and with a positive mindset so it is an enjoyable activity for the developers, data scientists, decision-makers, and other information technology professionals who share a passion for actionable data. In this process, the professional observer will likely come to this conclusion: Before a concept can become reality, it needs to be visualized, and it must stand up to scrutiny.

NOTES

1 "Actionable Insight." Techopedia, 2016. Accessed December 4, 2023, www.tec hopedia.com/definition/31721/actionable-insight

2 Jaime D'Agord. "How You Communicate with Data: Be More Effective & Influential." Zencos, April 22, 2019. www.zencos.com/blog/identify-audience-message-methods-data

3 TechRepublic. "Why Less than 0.5% of all Data Is Ever Analyzed." Accessed December 11, 2023, www.techrepublic.com/article/why-less-than-0-5-of-all-data-is-ever-analyzed/

4 Branka Vuleta. "How Much Data Is Created Every Day?" SeedScientific, October 28, 2021. https://seedscientific.com/how-much-data-is-created-every-day/

5 "What Is Data Storytelling?" TDWI Glossary. Accessed December 4, 2023, https://tdwi.org/portals/what-is-data-storytelling-definition.aspx

CHAPTER 1

Conception

Start the Race

START THE RACE

Having established the ground rules, along with the realization that the data storytelling journey along the spectrum from concept to reality involves passing through five discrete – but sometimes overlapping – stages, this chapter will cover the first of the five stages: Conception.

Each of the five stages has a name (e.g., "Conception"), an imperative (e.g., "start the race"), and a key word. When commencing an endeavor that has an end goal in mind, such as a data storytelling journey, viewing it as a race is an appropriate metaphor, because they both have a starting point, a progression, and a finish line indicating completion. While there may or may not be an element of competition, there must still be a good beginning – where the concept or idea is conceived – that articulates the need; thus, the key word for this first stage is *articulate*.

Know the Audience

In articulating the need, it is important to understand the audience. These are the individuals who are going to be consuming the data (often referred to as key stakeholders, users, customers, clients, business partners, or some other similar term). Visualization consultant Jaime D'Agord once wrote,

DOI: 10.1201/9781003623212-2

"Your audience determines the depth of your data communication and the presentation method."[1] For example, it would not make any sense to articulate the need to a room full of DBA's and programmers in the same way as to a group of business intelligence specialists, nor to unit auditors in the same way as to university faculty members. Since each of these groups has differing needs, agendas, and viewpoints, one must consider these factors and vary their approach to accommodate them. It is essential to speak to them using terms they understand and from a relatable perspective. Otherwise, there will be no connection with the intended audience.

Know the Data

Of equal importance is to know the data: Understanding the source, the variables, the units in which it is measured, whether or not it has been aggregated (and how) are all components to an essential starting point. In fact, the most important characteristic to be articulated is the purpose for the data. That is, one must answer the question, "What am I trying to show?"

Dr. Andrew Abela, chairman of the Department of Business & Economics at the Catholic University of America in Washington, DC, created a graphics tool that masterfully articulates the need and sets the pace with four categories that he identified for data storytelling (Table 1.1).[2] Although designed more than a decade ago, this tool has stood the test of time. To use these four categories, the question, "What am I trying to show?" becomes, "Am I showing comparison, distribution, composition, or relationship?" The answer to that question determines the type of visualization that is most appropriate and effective in telling the data's story, which in turn leads to even more questions that guide the person

TABLE 1.1   The Four Categories of Data

Category being shown	Question to be asked	Key
Comparison	Am I comparing among *items* or over *time*?	Behavior
Distribution	Among *how many* variables is this being distributed?	Dimension
Composition	Does it *change* over time, or is it *static* over time?	Structure
Relationship	How many variables are being *related*?	Class

analyzing the data to refine their approach along the way in a hierarchical methodology.

Choose the Data

Abela's Chart Chooser (Figure 1.1) allows the analyzer to arrive at the appropriate type of graph that is considered "best practice" for the situation in question.

For example, Figure 1.1 illustrates how one might take "Composition" and answer the questions in the chart to inform their decision regarding the type of data visualization that is the most appropriate for the given situation. This being the case, one would start by asking the question, "Does the data in question change over time, or is it static over time?" If the data changes over time, then you proceed down to ask the next question: "Are there many time periods involved in the data or few time periods?" If there are many time periods involved, you continue along to the next question: "Are the differences in those time periods relative, or are they relative and absolute?" At that juncture, one has reached the end, at which point, depending upon the answer to the final question, the choice is made for the appropriate data visualization.

All stories must have a beginning, and in the Conception stage of the spectrum, we have seen the importance of knowing your audience, knowing your data, and choosing your data as you start the race to help your stakeholders make a decision, answer a question, or solve a problem.

Case Studies

As we close the door on the Conception stage in Chapter 1, where we've identified the need for clarity and relevance in shaping our data stories, it's crucial to remember that these abstract principles translate into tangible action when faced with real-world challenges. Let's take a leap from theory to practice by examining two compelling case studies, one from the public health arena and the other from business.

First of all, let's look at the New York City Department of Health's data-driven approach to combating COVID-19 misinformation and boosting vaccination rates in a diverse city. This example will shed light on how "knowing your audience" and "choosing your data" become the linchpins of successful data storytelling, demonstrating the transformative power of tailored communication in the face of a complex public health crisis.

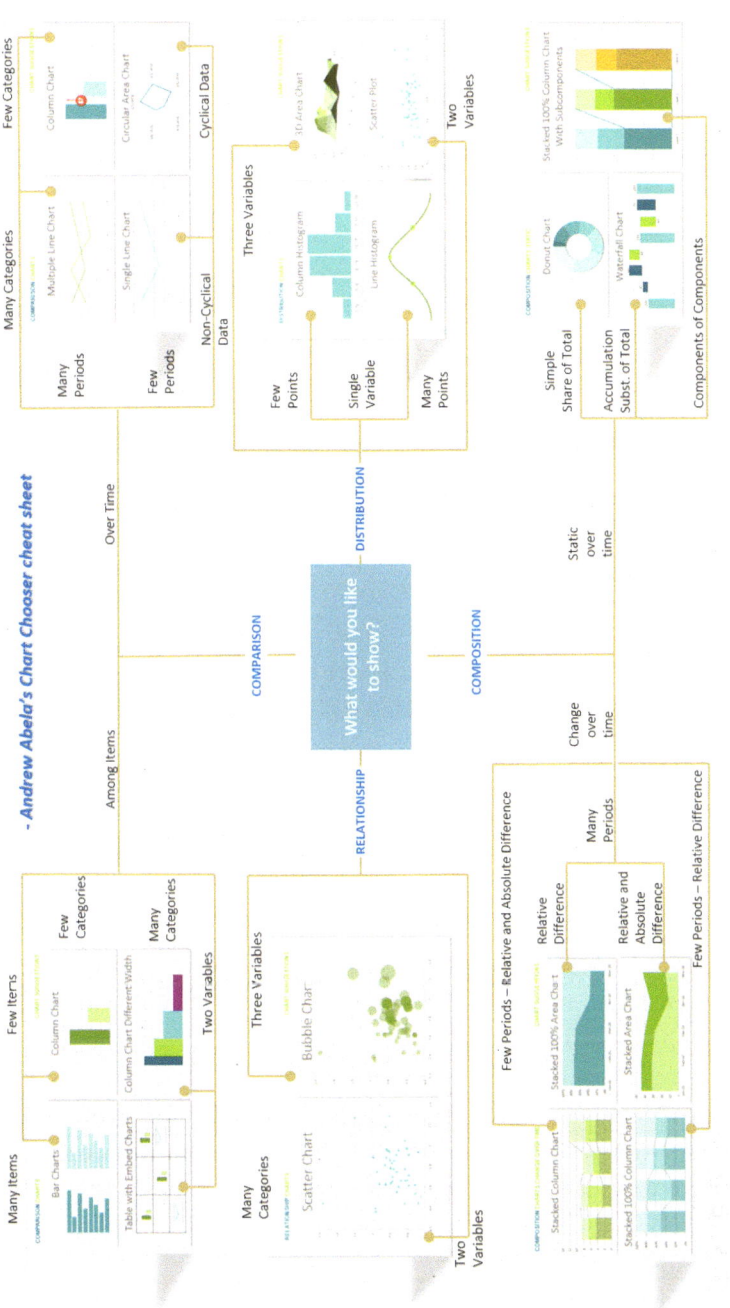

FIGURE 1.1 Abela's Chart Chocser. (©Dr. Andrew V. Abela, 2021, www.extremepresentation.com.)

CASE STUDY 1: NYC'S DATA-DRIVEN APPROACH TO COVID-19 COMMUNICATION[3]

hj**Articulating the Need for Diverse Audiences**: The COVID-19 pandemic presented a unique challenge for public health officials – communicating complex information to a diverse population with varying levels of health literacy and cultural backgrounds. In 2020, the New York City Department of Health (NYC DOH) faced this head-on, recognizing the need to tailor their messaging to resonate with different communities. They embarked on a data-driven approach, leveraging data visualization to break down complex information in a clear, accessible, and culturally relevant manner.

Understanding the Data and Audience: The NYC DOH team deeply explored public health data, analyzing infection rates, demographics, and vaccine uptake across different neighborhoods and cultural groups. This data-driven understanding allowed them to identify specific needs and concerns within each community, such as language barriers, vaccine hesitancy, and misinformation.

Designing Culturally Relevant Visualizations: Moving beyond traditional graphs and charts, the NYC DOH team embraced innovative data visualization techniques. They created culturally specific infographics and video messages featuring relatable icons and imagery that resonated with different communities. For example, one infographic used a culturally relevant map of the city to highlight the disproportionate impact of COVID-19 on certain neighborhoods, while another video message featured a local religious leader debunking vaccine myths in his native language.

Charting the Course to Success: The NYC DOH's data-driven approach yielded significant results. Their culturally relevant data visualizations reached millions of individuals across the city, increasing vaccination rates and fostering trust in public health initiatives among diverse communities. This case study exemplifies the power of articulating the need for data storytelling through "knowing your audience" and "choosing your data" in a way that resonates with diverse populations.

While public health initiatives like the NYC DOH campaign exemplify the power of data storytelling in addressing societal challenges, the private sector also stands to gain immense value from harnessing the transformative potential of data. Let's shift gears and explore a compelling case study from the business world – a large retail chain's data-driven journey toward rekindling customer engagement and driving growth. This example will shed light on how data can be transformed into actionable insights, guiding strategic decision-making and propelling businesses toward success.

CASE STUDY 2: RETAIL REVITALIZATION THROUGH DATA-DRIVEN STORYTELLING[4]

Articulating the Need for Growth: A prominent retail chain, facing declining sales and dwindling customer engagement, found itself at a crossroads. The executive team recognized the need for a drastic shift in strategy, requiring a deep understanding of the root causes and actionable insights to chart a new course.

Diving Deep into the Data: Embracing a data-driven approach, the chain plunged into its vast repository of purchase data, customer demographics, and website traffic patterns. This comprehensive analysis unearthed hidden trends and correlations, shedding light on customer behavior, product preferences, and store performance.

Crafting Compelling Narratives: Moving beyond sterile spreadsheets and technical jargon, the team transformed the data into captivating stories. Interactive dashboards, heat maps, and data-driven reports brought complex insights to life, highlighting connections between customer behavior, product categories, and store locations. These narratives enabled executives to visualize trends, identify opportunities, and make informed decisions.

From Insights to Action: Armed with data-driven insights, the chain implemented a series of strategic changes. Personalized marketing campaigns targeted specific customer segments, product offerings were optimized based on local preferences, and store layouts were revamped for improved customer experience. These data-driven initiatives yielded impressive results, leading to a significant rise in sales, customer engagement, and market share.

STUDY QUESTIONS: SPARKING NEW THOUGHT ON DATA STORYTELLING

1. **Conceptual Connections**: Compare and contrast the five stages of data storytelling you outlined with similar frameworks or models for communication or project management. What unique insights does your framework offer, specifically in the context of data-driven narratives?

2. **Audience Alchemy**: Consider the diverse audiences encountered in the NYC DOH and retail chain case studies. Analyze how each case study tailored its approach to resonate with its specific audience. Can you think of other examples where tailoring data storytelling for diverse audiences has been successful?

3. **Beyond Charts and Graphs**: This chapter emphasizes "choosing your data" as a crucial element. Imagine you're crafting a data narrative for a non-technical audience. What unconventional data sources or storytelling methods could you employ to engage and inform them effectively?

4. **Ethical Storytelling**: Data can be wielded in powerful ways, with potential for both positive and negative impact. How can data storytellers ensure their narratives are ethical, unbiased, and promote responsible interpretation of information?

5. **Personal Transformation**: This chapter highlights the potential for data storytelling to empower individuals. In your own field or area of interest, how could you leverage data storytelling to enhance your personal or professional development?

6. **Future Visions**: Look ahead to the future of data storytelling. What technological advancements or societal shifts do you anticipate in the coming years that will reshape the way we tell stories with data?

7. **Measuring Momentum**: Evaluating the success of a data story is crucial. Beyond traditional metrics like audience engagement, suggest additional benchmarks or frameworks for measuring the impact of data storytelling, particularly in driving long-term change.

8. **Storytelling Crossroads**: Imagine you encounter a situation where data points appear to contradict established narratives or deeply held beliefs. How can you approach this conflict ethically and effectively, utilizing the principles of data storytelling to navigate potential biases and foster constructive dialogue?

NOTES

1 Jaime D'Agord. "How You Communicate with Data: Be More Effective & Influential." Zencos, April 22, 2019. www.zencos.com/blog/identify-audience-message-methods-data

2 "Free Abela's Chart Chooser PowerPoint Template," SlideModel.com. Accessed December 4, 2023, https://slidemodel.com/free-powerpoint-templates/free-abelas-chart-chooser-powerpoint-template/

3 New York City Department of Health. "NYC COVID-19 Data and Trends." April 1, 2020. www.nyc.gov/site/doh/covid/covid-19-data-trends.page

   J. Kim and Y. Seock. "COVID-19 and the Digital Divide: Implications for Health Equity and Communication Strategies." *Journal of Communication*, 74(3), 2020, pp. 301–322. doi:10.1093/joc/jcaa067

   New York City Department of Health. "NYC COVID-19 Public Education and Outreach Campaign." January 14, 2021. https://infohub.nyced.org/reports/students-and-schools/school-quality/information-and-data-overview

4 H. Smith and M. Jones. "Data-Driven Retail Transformation: A Case Study in Customer Engagement and Growth." *Journal of Retail Management*, 48(2), 2023, pp. 123–138. doi:10.1016/j.jretman.2022.12.006

CHAPTER 2

Inception

Make the Case

MAKE THE CASE

After starting the race, the next stage is when the analytics professional must make the case for expressing the concept visually; "advocate" is the associated key word.

Mike Parkinson, CEO and founder of Billion Dollar Graphics, advocates that humans are affected by graphics in two ways: cognitively and emotionally. Regarding the cognitive aspect, Parkinson said, "Graphics expedite and increase our level of communication. They increase comprehension, recollection, and retention. Visual clues help us decode text and attract attention to information or direct attention increasing the likelihood that the audience will remember."[1]

To illustrate the cognitive affect, imagine this: You've secured approval and funding for your dream project – a state-of-the-art Analytics Data Center at a major university. Construction begins, but excitement quickly gives way to concern. Cost overruns loom, and your desk overflows with expense reports: hundreds of rows and columns, a swirling vortex of numbers threatening to drown you in data. Traditional spreadsheets become daunting fortresses, demanding hours of deciphering before yielding any semblance of insight. Ibuprofen sales skyrocket.

DOI: 10.1201/9781003623212-3

In this data deluge, wouldn't you welcome a life preserver? Enter the power of visual representation. A well-crafted set of graphs offers clarity like a beacon, cutting through the fog of numbers and illuminating the path to understanding. No more squinting at endless rows; instead, color-coded bars and insightful trends leap from the page, pinpointing problem areas with laser precision. Suddenly, cost overruns aren't abstract figures, but a stark visual narrative, revealing patterns and anomalies begging to be investigated.

This is the transformative power of data visualization. It's not just about aesthetics; it's about cognitive liberation. As Parkinson alluded to, visuals unlock meaning from the data prison, replacing spreadsheets with intuitive maps, guiding your analysis with precision and clarity. No more ibuprofen-fueled nights; visual insights empower you to act quickly, confidently, and effectively, ensuring your dream project stays on track and within budget.

Regarding the emotional aspect of graphics, Parkinson also said, "Pictures enhance or affect emotions and attitudes. Graphics engage our imagination and heighten our creative thinking by stimulating other areas of our brain (which in turn leads to a more profound and accurate understanding of the presented material)."[2]

Continuing with the previous analogy, suppose you are committed to promoting computer literacy among economically disadvantaged children in your state, and you have been working with the National Science Foundation to set up Code Camps for those children. However, measuring the impact of your new programs proves elusive. Spreadsheets offer nothing more than bland pronouncements, failing to capture the essence of your endeavor. Hours spent squinting at rows and columns once again leaves you frustrated, longing for a deeper understanding.

Then, a single chart transforms the landscape. A soaring bar representing increased student coding proficiency leaps from the page, a visual display of success. The emotional impact is immediate and visceral – a surge of pride, a validation of your efforts, a tangible testament to the Code Camp program's transformative potential. No table of numbers, no dry statistical report could ever evoke such a powerful response.

This shift from data fatigue to emotional resonance is the magic of data visualization. It doesn't simply inform; it ignites. It taps into our deepest emotional values, transforming cold numbers into stories that stir the soul. Witnessing children conquer coding challenges through the lens of a compelling graph evokes a deeper sense of purpose, fueling your commitment to the cause. Data becomes more than mere statistics; it becomes a vibrant tapestry woven with hope, perseverance, and the joy of making a difference.

In the battle against information overload, graphs are not just analytical tools; as Parkinson attested, they are emotional weapons. They forge a connection between data and action that spreadsheets can only dream of achieving. By translating passion into visual narratives, data visualization unlocks transformative potential, inspiring action and leaving a lasting impact on both your audience and your own journey.

To summarize these two assertions about the cognitive and emotional effect of compelling visuals, graphics get a hold of both our brains and our hearts. Any educational endeavor that manages to touch both the brain and the heart is bound to be successful.

Beyond the cognitive and emotional benefits (as illustrated in Figure 2.1), consider the strategic advantage compelling visuals wield. Imagine battling budget concerns for your university data center. Static charts may inform, but a dynamic dashboard equipped with predictive analytics paints a far more persuasive picture. Stakeholders can not only track cost trajectories but also explore contingency plans and assess the impact of potential interventions. This proactive approach transforms your presentation from a reactive defense into a proactive strategy, earning trust and fostering buy-in from even the most skeptical investors.

Visuals can also become collaboration catalysts. Think of your Code Camp initiative. Instead of one-way presentations, envision interactive heatmaps showcasing geographic areas with the highest demand for coding

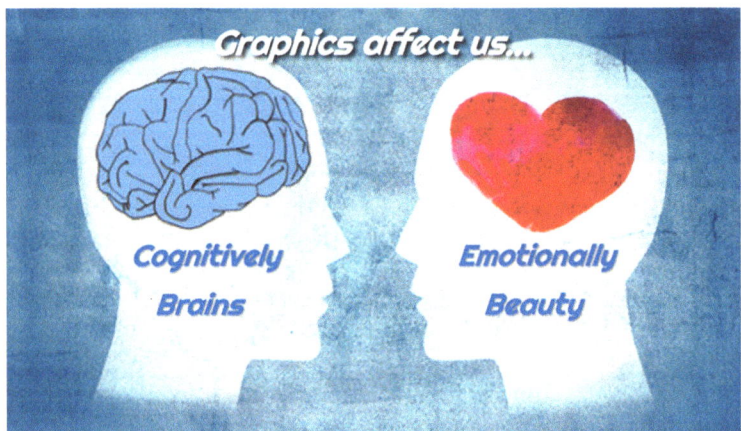

FIGURE 2.1   How graphics affect us.

programs. Local educators, community leaders, and potential funders can all engage with this data, identifying underserved communities and co-creating targeted solutions. This collaborative approach leverages the social intelligence within your network, amplifying the impact of your data story beyond your own capabilities.

Furthermore, remember the transformative power of empathy. Data visualizations have the unique ability to translate abstract statistics into relatable human stories. Imagine your Code Camp infographic featuring not just code snippets but also photos of children proudly displaying their creations. This emotional connection transcends mere data points, prompting viewers to envision the program's transformative impact on individual lives. This fosters a sense of shared purpose and motivates viewers to become active participants in the cause, creating a powerful network of advocates and champions.

Finally, consider the ripple effect of virality. In a world bombarded with information, shareable and impactful visualizations break through the noise, sparking conversations and igniting imaginations. Picture your Code Camp infographic shared across social media platforms, each retweet and "like" carrying your message to new audiences. This organic reach can snowball into a nationwide movement, inspiring other communities to replicate your program and creating a lasting legacy of positive change.

To illustrate the strategic strength of visual storytelling, consider a study published in the *Harvard Business Review*. Research indicates that companies leveraging data visualization in their marketing campaigns can achieve significant benefits. For example, Scott Berinato's work emphasizes the importance of smart data visualizations for decision-makers. These visualizations lead to a 30% increase in customer engagement and a 25% boost in conversion rates. Managers who effectively communicate insights through data visualization gain a competitive edge in today's data-driven landscape.[3] This research not only validates the persuasive power of visuals but also highlights their tangible business benefits.

By embracing the cognitive, emotional, and persuasive power of data visualization, you can transform your data stories from mere presentations into catalysts for action. So, the next time you face a mountain of data, remember, you don't need a pickaxe – you need a paintbrush. (We will talk more about the "Right tool, right job" concept in Chapter 3.) Let your visualizations captivate minds, ignite hearts, and inspire change, one pixel at a time.

Making the Case with Graphics

Before we even dip our toes into the vast ocean of data, consider this: our brains possess a remarkable superpower, a built-in turbocharger for information processing. According to Walter and Gioglio in their book *The Power of Visual Storytelling*, humans, allegedly, can process visuals a staggering 60,000 times faster than text.[4] Imagine the information highway – data whizzes by in a blur, but visuals act like neon billboards, grabbing our attention in an instant. This innate preference isn't a mere quirk; it's a testament to the efficiency and power of visual communication. When we encounter data presented as a captivating chart or a compelling graph, understanding blossoms, insights flash, and decisions are made with newfound clarity. It's in this fertile ground of human perception that data visualization truly flourishes, transforming cold numbers into stories that ignite our minds and shape our actions.

As British data journalist David McCandless so aptly put it in his 2010 TED Talk, "Sight, by far, has the highest bandwidth of any of the five senses... About 80% of the information we take in is by eye."[5] The amazing and wondrous complexity of the human eye (Figure 2.2), coupled with the lightning-fast processing speed for visuals, underscores the profound potential of data visualization to revolutionize the way we interact with information and the world around us.

Additional research in the years since McCandless' statement suggests that that number is likely closer to 90%.[6] Two European research professors,

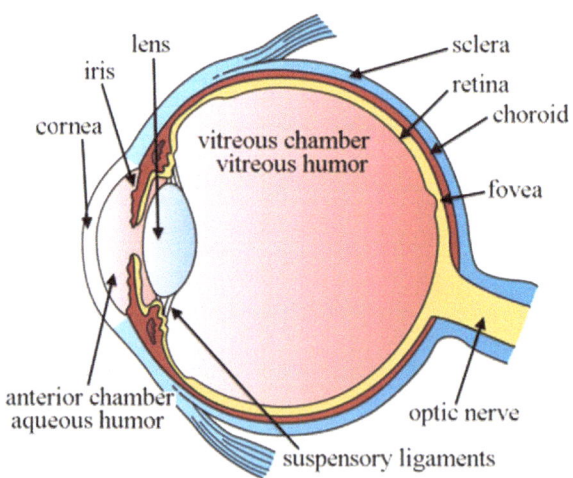

FIGURE 2.2   The human eye.

Robin Hogarth and Emre Soyer, teamed up on an experiment in which three groups of economic professionals were asked the same question regarding a specific data set, the results of which appear to bring credence to McCandless' claim.[7]

The first group of economists was given the data and an accompanying analysis. Seventy-two percent of them answered the question incorrectly. A second group was given the data, the analysis, and a graph, and although they did better than the first group, 61% of those economists were still incorrect in their answer. A third group was provided only a graph (no data, no analysis), and a mere 3% of this group got the answer wrong.

These results make the case for visual representation of data and, as such, should be advocated for the inception of effective business intelligence and analytics reporting strategy.

Furthermore, consider two groups of participants assigned with the task of identifying fake news articles. One group receives purely textual articles, while the other group is provided with the same articles alongside a "misinformation radar" visualization, highlighting suspicious words and phrases. A 2020 study by Cao, Qi, Sheng, Yang, Guo, and Li involving more than 100 participants revealed that the visual group consistently identified fake news articles about 20% faster and with 15% higher accuracy compared to the text-only group.[8] These findings underscore the potency of visual data representations in aiding our understanding and decision-making, even in complex tasks such as fake news detection.

Crafting the Narrative

While Mike Parkinson and David McCandless paint a compelling picture of visual prowess, advocating for data visualization demands a sharper focus than captivating hearts and brains alone. In a world flooded with competing priorities, decision-makers crave actionable insights, not just aesthetic thrills. To secure their buy-in, we must build an unbreakable case rooted in strategic purpose, not fleeting emotional connection. Here's how to craft a narrative that compels action:

From Confusion to Clarity: The Antidote to Data Overload. Imagine struggling to navigate a city with only a cryptic text description. Data, similarly, can overwhelm with its sheer volume and complexity. Visuals act as GPS, bringing order to the chaos. A well-designed graphic transforms numbers into intuitive patterns, revealing hidden relationships and trends that text alone could never expose. In an age of information overload, clarity is power, and visuals hand decision-makers the reins to navigate the data landscape with confidence.

From Insights to Inspiration: Igniting the Spark of Action. Data, while informative, often lacks the emotional punch to propel us forward. Compelling visuals bridge this gap, transforming cold statistics into stories that resonate with our deepest human emotions. A powerful image juxtaposed with a striking data point can spark outrage, empathy, or even hope, propelling viewers beyond passive understanding into active engagement. Remember, data that stirs the soul is data that fuels action, inspiring lasting change across the organization.

From Expertise to Empowerment: Breaking Down the Data Wall. Jargon-laden reports and cryptic charts often erect invisible walls between analysts and decision-makers. Visuals, however, act as the battering ram, democratizing data and making it accessible to everyone. Interactive dashboards, engaging infographics, and clear-cut charts empower stakeholders at all levels to explore the data, ask questions, and participate in meaningful discussions. This encourages a collaborative environment where data drives decision-making throughout the organization, not just within the privileged circle of the data experts.

From Analysis to Innovation: Unleashing the Creative Kraken. Data visualization isn't just about presenting what we know; it's about sparking the flame of creative problem-solving. When confronted with a captivating visual, viewers are more likely to break free from the shackles of conventional thinking and embrace unconventional solutions. The visual journey of exploring an interactive chart that reveals unexpected correlations can lead to brainstorming sessions and breakthrough ideas that mere numbers alone could never inspire. In a data-driven world, visuals unlock the door to creative exploration, paving the way for innovation and transformative change.

From Presentation to Legacy: Leaving a Footprint in the Sands of Time. Information delivered solely through text is fleeting, fading like yesterday's news. Visuals, however, leave an indelible mark on memory. A powerful image or a data-driven story can stay etched in minds long after the presentation ends, serving as a constant reminder of the message and driving sustained action. By leveraging the power of visual storytelling, you ensure your data's impact transcends the presentation room and leaves a lasting legacy, shaping the narrative of your organization for years to come.

Case Studies

So, while endeavoring to show how to "Make the Case" with the second stage of the spectrum in this chapter, we've established the undeniable power of visual communication, our brains wired to process vibrant imagery at lightning speed compared to the pedestrian pace of text. But how does this translate into real-world impact and enhance our quest for transforming numbers into narratives? Let's dive into two compelling case studies that showcase the transformative potential of data visualization, bridging the perception gap and igniting meaningful action.

CASE STUDY 1: FROM DATA DELUGE TO PUBLIC HEALTH HERO: THE POWER OF MAPS IN TRACKING THE COVID-19 PANDEMIC[9]

In the early 2020s, the COVID-19 pandemic plunged the world into uncharted territory, demanding immediate action and critical decision-making in the face of a rapidly evolving crisis. Data, once again, became our lifeline, but drowning in spreadsheets and raw numbers (as was the case with the fictional examples cited earlier in this chapter) offered little solace. Enter the power of maps.

Johns Hopkins University's Coronavirus Resource Center, through its interactive COVID-19 Dashboard, transformed the data deluge into a visual narrative. Color-coded maps pinpointed hotspots, revealing the geographic spread of the virus with stark clarity. Trends emerged, prompting targeted interventions and resource allocation. Public awareness soared as individuals could track the pandemic's trajectory in their own communities, creating a sense of collective responsibility and adherence to public health measures.

This case study exemplifies how data visualization transcends mere information dissemination. It becomes a powerful tool for public engagement and action, empowering individuals to understand the pandemic's impact at a personal level and driving collective action toward containment and mitigation.

CASE STUDY 2: FROM SALES SLUMP TO SOARING SUCCESS: HOW DATA VISUALIZATION RESCUED A RETAIL CHAIN[10]

Imagine a retail giant, once a beacon of consumer delight, facing a downward spiral in sales. The culprit? A disconnect between product offerings and customer preferences, hidden within mountains of sales data. Traditional reports offered little insight, leaving executives grappling with a sense of frustration and uncertainty.

Then, a data visualization revolution swept through the company. Interactive dashboards replaced static reports, showcasing customer demographics, purchase patterns, and regional trends in vibrant charts and heatmaps. Suddenly, the data spoke volumes. Executives discovered a mismatch between popular products in certain regions and their limited availability, leading to lost sales opportunities.

Armed with these visual insights, the company implemented targeted inventory adjustments and personalized marketing campaigns. The results were dramatic. Sales soared, customer satisfaction skyrocketed, and the retail giant reclaimed its lost ground. This case study demonstrates how data visualization can transform even the most complex data into actionable insights, driving strategic decision-making and propelling businesses toward success.

STUDY QUESTIONS: MAKING THE CASE

1. **Beyond Aesthetics: Creativity or Clarity?** This chapter emphasizes both the cognitive and emotional power of visuals. Do you think prioritizing artistic flair in data visualization can sometimes compromise its clarity and effectiveness? When, if ever, would prioritizing creative expression over immediate understandability be justified?

2. **Visual Literacy Revolution: Closing the Gap?** With data increasingly informing everyday decisions, what role do you see data visualization playing in closing the gap between data specialists and the general public? What steps can be taken to make data visualization more accessible and empowering for non-experts?

3. **Emotional Resonance: Friend or Foe?** While this chapter highlights the potential of visuals to ignite emotions, could this power be misused? Can certain types of data visualization manipulate or exploit viewers' emotions for unintended purposes? How can we ensure ethical and responsible use of emotion in visual storytelling?

4. **Action, Reaction, or Inaction?** This chapter discusses using visuals to inspire action. However, could certain visualizations, without proper context or analysis, lead to misinformed decisions or even inaction? How can we prevent visualizations from becoming misinterpreted or misused to drive the wrong actions?

5. **The Future of Vision: Augmented Analytics?** With advancements in technology, imagine a future where data visualization becomes interactive and personalized. How might this "augmented analytics" reshape the way we interact with data, make decisions, and understand the world around us? What potential benefits and challenges could this present?

6. **Storytelling vs. Science: Striking a Balance?** Data visualization often walks the line between scientific accuracy and compelling storytelling. Can we strive for both objectives without compromising scientific integrity? How can we ensure that visual narratives present data accurately while still captivating viewers?

7. **Data Visualization Democracy: Accessible to All?** This chapter advocates for democratizing data through visuals. However, certain tools and technologies may still present barriers to access. How can we ensure that everyone, regardless of expertise or background, has the opportunity to benefit from data visualization?

8. **The Legacy of Visualization: Beyond Presentations?** While this chapter mentions leaving a lasting impact with visuals, consider the ethical implications of data visualization becoming permanent fixtures in society. How can we ensure that visual narratives don't perpetuate biases or misinformation in the long term?

NOTES

1 Troy Larson. "Powerful Facts About Visual Communication." MindManager Blog, November 18, 2011. www.mindjet.com/blog/2011/11/powerful-facts-about-visual-communication/

2 Troy Larson. "Powerful Facts About Visual Communication." MindManager Blog, November 18, 2011. www.mindjet.com/blog/2011/11/powerful-facts-about-visual-communication/.

3 Scott Berinato. *Good Charts: The HBR Guide to Making Smarter, More Persuasive Data Visualizations*. Harvard Business Review Press, 2023.

4 Ekaterina Walter and Jessica Gioglio. *The Power of Visual Storytelling: How to Use Visuals, Data, and Stories to Explain Why Things Matter*. Wiley, 2015.

5 David McCandless. "The Beauty of Data Visualization." TEDGlobal 2010, July 2010. www.ted.com/talks/david_mccandless_the_beauty_of_data_visualization

6 James T. Enns. *Visual Perception and the Visual System*. Oxford University Press, 2020, pp. 123–125.

7 Stephen Ziliak. "Visualizing Uncertainty: On Soyer's and Hogarth's 'The Illusion of Predictability.'" *International Journal of Forecasting*, 28(3), 2012, pp. 712–714. https://ssrn.com/abstract=1998149

8 Juan Cao, Peng Qi, Qiang Sheng, Tianyun Yang, Junbo Guo and Jintao Li. "Exploring the Role of Visual Content in Fake News Detection." In *Disinformation, Misinformation, and Fake News in Social Media*, edited by K. Shu, S. Wang, D. Lee, and H. Liu. Springer, 2020, pp. 141–161.

9 Johns Hopkins University Coronavirus Resource Center. Coronavirus COVID-19 Dashboard. December 17, 2023. https://coronavirus.jhu.edu/

10 Brent Maloney. "Data Visualization of Online Retail Sales in Tableau." Medium, May 31, 2023. https://medium.com/@maloney.brent/case-study-data-visualization-of-online-retail-sales-in-tableau-3af21e51f6e7

CHAPTER 3

Perception

Motivate the Base

MOTIVATE THE BASE

In our journey from concept to reality, having started the race and made the case in the first two chapters, it is now time to motivate the base with **perception**, the third stage of the spectrum. With this stage, the key word is **educate**. Progress in the data storytelling journey is not likely if either the target audience or the stakeholders are not on board, so they must be educated (i.e., **learn** that they are stakeholders in this process). These individuals are not likely to take ownership nor provide the necessary backing (financially or otherwise) if they do not understand what is being presented; cannot see its value when applied to their own agenda(s); or if the data visualization does not help them to make a decision, answer a question, or solve a problem (i.e., the three basic tenets of actionable data mentioned in Chapter 1).

Understanding and adhering to basic principles is foundational to any educational initiative and a major consideration in the data storytelling journey, as we often hear comments like: "They're all talk and no action," or, "This project is nothing but form without function." Function is what

DOI: 10.1201/9781003623212-4

is being done with the data, whereas form is how to express functional outcomes in the best way. Or stated another way, "Does it look good?" (form) or, "Does it work?" (function). There are some best practices that should be kept in mind to ensure function gets the right priority over form in data storytelling so you can educate and motivate your base effectively. The following are common examples of when form has been prioritized over function.

Clearly Presenting Your Data

Many have a love-hate relationship with pie charts. When used correctly, pie charts are an effective way of showing how the parts of a whole relate proportionately to the whole. Unfortunately, not everyone understands this concept, as shown in Figure 3.1, derived from a 2012 television news report: (1) The numbers in the pie chart add up to 193% (a number that is obviously greater than 100%, which is representative of the whole), and (2) the slices are disproportional (i.e., though 70 is greater than 63, the latter number appears larger).

Though the survey questions used to assemble this pie chart allowed for multiple choices (respondents were able to choose more than one option) – hence the awkward percent total – a pie chart clearly should not have been used in this case, because it is misleading. A bar graph would instead be better suited to present the data accurately (Figure 3.2).

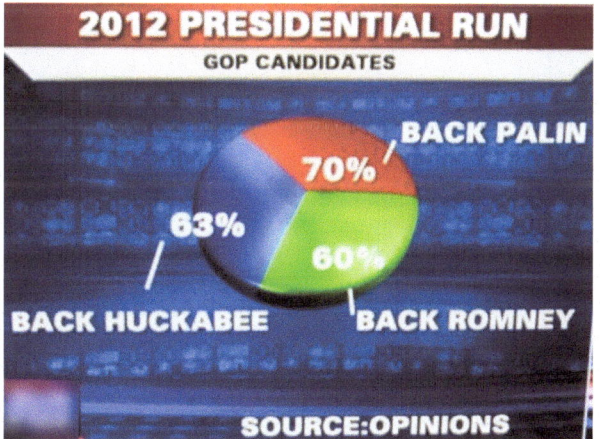

FIGURE 3.1   Screenshot from 2012 news report with inaccurate pie chart.

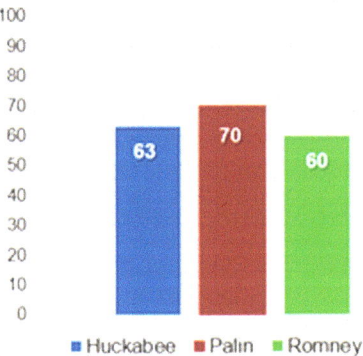

FIGURE 3.2   Bar graph illustrating the correct use of the data in Figure 3.1.

Avoid Visual Manipulation

For line graphs and bar charts, ensure that the vertical axis has a consistent scale. In Figure 3.3, the sample line chart on the left, adapted from the *2021 Global Business Ethics Survey*,[1] shows the percentage of employees who observed ethical misconduct in their organization and how that percentage has changed over time. A cursory glance might lead to the assumption of a huge increase between 2003 and 2005; however, a closer look will show that the vertical axis is scaled from 44% to 54%, thus making the change between those years appear to be more drastic than it really is.

By contrast, the line graph on the right (also shown in Figure 3.3) shows the same data, but with the vertical axis scaled to start from zero – a more realistic depiction of the employee ethical observation trend over that same 20-year period.

Many organizations purposefully represent their graphics in a particular way with no regard for statistical accuracy. In fact, specific misrepresentation of data occurs in many cases for self-serving purposes; that is, the only interest is to make the graph "look good" and convey the message they want it to convey, rather than letting the data speak for itself. They will engage in unethical manipulation of data to make their preconceived point.

Data analytics professionals should hold themselves to a higher standard of accuracy and integrity. That said, it does not necessarily mean that the Y-axis scale should always be forced to start at zero. Sometimes, when comparing multiple data sets that have multiple series (especially when numbers are very close together), the only way one can see a difference is to adjust the scale. However, it is best to employ consistent methodologies

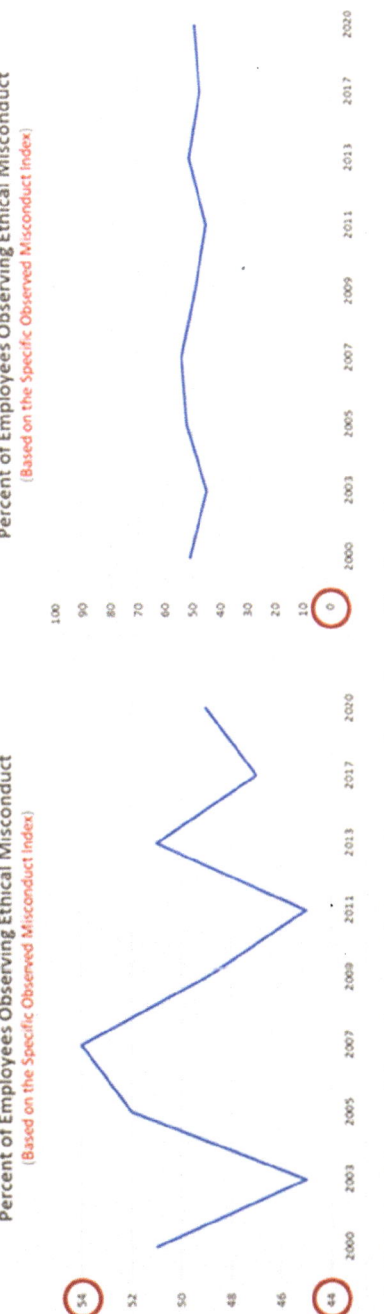

FIGURE 3.3   Line and bar charts with inconsistent and consistent Y-axis scale.

across the board to avoid making the data appear to be more dramatic than it really is.

Proper Labeling

Not only should the Y-axis be scaled consistently, but it should also be labeled properly. As shown in Figure 3.4 (taken from a South American television newscast during the COVID-19 pandemic showing COVID testing rates per million inhabitants of the six countries depicted), the chart is missing the label on the Y-axis. Although this may not seem important on the surface, a closer look reveals that at least three of the bars are disproportional to the quantities they represent (note the circled values). For example, the value shown for the EEUU bar (7,000) is much greater than 330, the value shown for the Argentina bar. However, the EEUU bar appears only slightly taller than the Argentina bar.

Likewise, the 14,100 value in the Italia bar is twice the value of the EEUU bar, so the Italia bar should be twice the height of the EEUU bar instead of being only slightly taller. The absence of the label for the Y-axis accentuates the fact that the bars are disproportionate to the quantities they represent. Even if the Y-axis were present, the distorted perspective being displayed (or at least implied) cannot be denied, as it portrays the false impression that the differences in testing rates among the six countries depicted are insignificant. This is clearly not the case; therefore, the chart is misleading.

FIGURE 3.4   Bar chart with missing label on Y-axis.

Ditch the Distortion

Data visualization, a shimmering beacon of insight in the ocean of information, can, in the wrong hands, morph into a devious siren, luring us onto
treacherous reefs of misinformation. Imagine a financial report where key
metrics perform a disappearing act, their true values swallowed by the abyss
of a manipulated Y-axis, similar to the example shown above. Or picture a
scientific study boasting statistically improbable results, achieved through
a sleight of hand with error bars and p-values. These deceitful examples
paint a sobering truth: unethical data visualization isn't just a statistical
faux pas, it's a recipe for disastrous decisions.

Consider the following whimsical scenarios:

The Cartographer's Conundrum: Picture yourself traversing a dense rainforest, relying on a meticulously hand-drawn map. Each twist of the path,
each gnarled branch, is faithfully rendered, guiding you safely through the
verdant labyrinth. Now, picture a mischievous cartographer, a trickster with
ink and brush, subtly tampering with the map. A vital tributary disappears,
a treacherous ravine shrinks to a harmless dip. With each step, you veer
further from your intended destination, ensnared in a web of deceit woven
on parchment. This, dear reader, is the treacherous landscape of unethical
data visualization, where facts are subtly contorted and narratives reshaped
to suit self-serving agendas.

The Mirage of Miracles: The consequences of such cartographic chicanery
reach far beyond a misstep in the jungle. Misleading graphs warp decision-
making, steering investments toward mirages of opportunity and burying
inconvenient truths beneath layers of visual artifice. Imagine a healthcare
policy championed by a chart showcasing a dramatic decline in disease
rates, only to discover later that the Y-axis was cleverly truncated, obscuring
a plateauing, not diminishing, trend. The repercussions of such deception
are measured not in lost bearings, but in lives and resources squandered on
a false hope.

The Bar Chart Ballet: Ethical data visualization, like an honest map,
demands meticulous attention to scale and accuracy. Just as a cartographer
wouldn't distort the size of a river to exaggerate its importance, a data analyst shouldn't manipulate scales to make trends appear more dramatic
than they are (as did the example chart above showing employee ethical
misconduct). Remember, a graph isn't a stage backdrop; it's a compass,

guiding us through the complexities of information. Its beauty lies not in embellishments but in the clarity with which it reveals the terrain ahead.

The Shrinking Competitor: Let's consider the humble bar chart, often the workhorse of presentations. In the hands of a responsible data wrangler, it stands upright, each bar a faithful representation of the values it conveys. But in the grip of a manipulative charlatan, the bars become contortionists, stretching and shrinking to tell a predetermined story. Imagine a sales report where bars representing competitor products are artificially shrunk, casting the presenter's offering in a falsely dominant light. Such optical illusions might win momentary applause, but they leave behind a lingering unease, a suspicion that the truth has been stretched beyond recognition. We will see a real-life example of this as depicted by the Apple Corporation momentarily.

Ultimately, data visualization built on a foundation of truth, like a sturdy bridge spanning a churning river, inspires trust and fosters informed action. The temptation to embellish, to nudge the needle ever so slightly in favor of a desired outcome, is ever-present in the world of information presentation. But such practices, like a cartographer intentionally misplacing a vital landmark, lead us astray on the path to informed understanding. Misleading visuals distort public perception, shaping decisions based on faulty narratives rather than the unvarnished truth.

To summarize, the essence of ethical data visualization lies in its meticulous commitment to accuracy and integrity. Just as a cartographer wouldn't inflate the size of a city to exaggerate its significance, a data analyst shouldn't manipulate scales or tweak axes to make trends appear more dramatic than they are. Remember, a graph isn't a PR tool; it's a compass, guiding us through the complexities of information. Its value lies not in embellishments, but in the clarity with which it reveals the terrain ahead.

Other Best Practices for Influencing Perception

- **Chronology**: When plotting chronological elements, they should be depicted from left (the past) to right (the present and future) along the X-axis.

- **Quantity**: When measuring quantities and other numerical items, plot them along the Y-axis, with the smaller numbers at the bottom and the larger numbers at the top.

- **Color**: Colors should be used consistently, keeping in mind that there are some universally accepted constants; the most familiar ones of which are that red means stop, danger, decline, whereas green means go, safety, growth, etc. Although there is a rising view that a more muted palate should be employed (for accessibility concerns), the overriding principle still applies. Contrasting colors can effectively differentiate among groups, while varying shades of the same color can communicate the relative strength or weakness of a value, according to data visualization principles.[2]

- **Shapes**: Graphical elements used in visualizations should be kept proportional to each other. Master statistician and Yale professor Edward Tufte advocated not exceeding what he called the Lie Factor.[3] It states that the representation of numbers, as physically measured on the surface of the graphic itself, should be directly proportional to the quantities represented. As a mathematical equation, it is often expressed like this: The size of the effect shown in the graphic divided by the size of the effect shown in the data should never be greater than one.

To illustrate, in one of the iterative product releases for an iPad model, Apple touted its greater battery capacity over its predecessor – a 17% increase in battery capacity. However, Figure 3.5 is misleading. The battery icon on the right, representing the capacity of the new iPad, appears to be three or four times larger than the one on the left representing the predecessor – disproportionately more than a 17% increase.

FIGURE 3.5   An Apple ad/data visualization that exceeds Tufte's Lie Factor.

While color can be a powerful tool for communication, relying solely on it can exclude audiences with visual impairments, estimated to be about 2.2 billion people globally, or 27% of the world's population (World Health Organization, 2023).[4] Imagine presenting crucial healthcare data (e.g., birth rates) using only a red-green color scheme. For someone with red-green colorblindness, interpreting such a visualization would be incredibly difficult, potentially leading to misinterpretations and missed information.

Therefore, consider incorporating alternative means of visual differentiation alongside color. Using different patterns, textures, shapes, and sizes can provide redundancy and ensure inclusivity for viewers with color vision deficiencies. Remember, data presented clearly and with accessibility in mind empowers everyone to make informed decisions based on meaningful insights.

Right Tool, Right Job

Data visualization, a potent tool for transforming statistics into actionable insights, can lose its impact if paired with the wrong instrument. Would a person in their right mind use a chainsaw to carve a turkey or a sledgehammer to crack a walnut? The answer is obvious.

This is where the art of selecting the most suitable visualization tool comes into play. Abela's chart chooser becomes your trusted guide, navigating the vast arsenal of visual options, each with its own strengths and limitations. Just like a skilled artist selects the perfect brush based on the desired texture and effect, aligning your data with the most appropriate visualization is crucial for crafting a compelling and actionable narrative.

Pie charts, for instance, excel at showcasing parts of a whole, especially when employing common-sense best practices. The concept of "common sense" is certainly a world apart from the example cited earlier from the 2012 newscast. When used properly, pie charts far exceed those expectations. However, two pie charts displayed side-by-side can easily become a visual recipe for confusion, as is the case with Figure 3.6. While mathematically accurate, they often fail to answer the critical question: are they effectively communicating anything meaningful?

This is a case in which the designer for these pie charts should have consulted Abela's chart chooser. To clarify: each chart by itself intends to show how the five countries depicted compare among themselves and to what extent they contribute to the whole. The two charts together show how that overall makeup changed from one point in time (on the left) to the next point in time (on the right). The specific timeframe under consideration here or the nature of the components being compared are less relevant in this example. The real challenge lies in the limitations of human perception.

Our brains, while adept at processing information, struggle to decipher intricate details when presented with multiple dimensions simultaneously. This limitation is confirmed by a 2023 study from Van Orden and Stone, which found memory performance for multiple object-property dimensions declined sharply as the number of dimensions increased, highlighting the challenges of deciphering intricate details in complex visuals.[5]

In the case of Figure 3.6, overlapping pie slices, like tangled brushstrokes in a painting, obscure the subtle variations that hold the key to understanding the story. Hence, while these pie charts might be statistically valid, they fail the "actionability" test – the ultimate measure of success for any data visualization. That is, do they help the viewer to make a decision, answer a question, or solve a problem (the three tenets of actionable data introduced in Chapter 1)?

The obvious answer to that question is a resounding "NO!" – because you cannot decipher the intended message by simply "looking" at the pies. A "visual" perception does not produce results. This presents an interesting

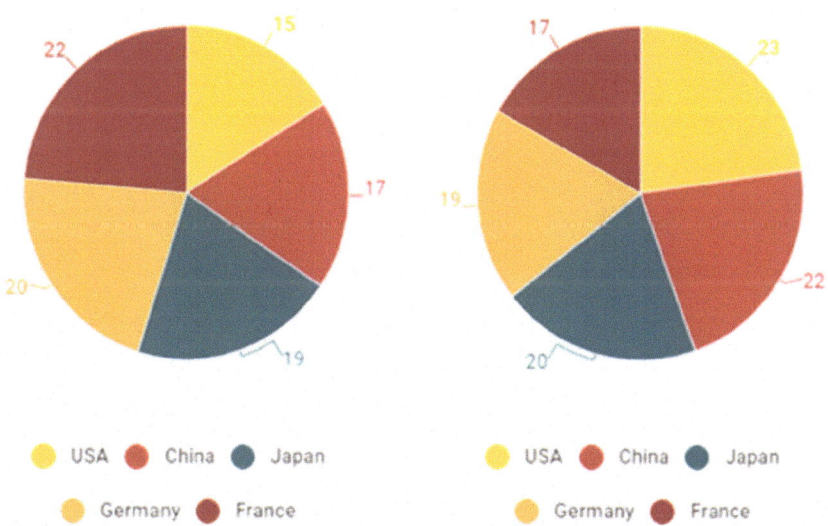

FIGURE 3.6   Two side-by-side pie charts comparing five countries over two time periods.

play on words, for one cannot spell the word "visualization" without spelling the word "visual."

Actionability means the visual empowers you to make informed decisions, answer questions with confidence, and ultimately, solve problems. These side-by-side pie charts, however, leave you staring at the canvas, yearning for clarity. Isn't the "visual" in "data visualization" the very essence of its power? If you need extensive verbal explanation to untangle the picture, the message has been tragically lost in translation.

But fear not, data storyteller! With a simple switch of the brush – replacing the pies with side-by-side bar graphs – the scene transforms, as depicted in Figure 3.7.

Suddenly, the data leaps off the canvas, and the narrative unfolds with breathtaking clarity. The trend they were trying to convey – the complete reversal of the countries' order from one timeframe to the next – shines like a beacon in the previously muddled landscape.

This is the magic of using the right tool. Bar graphs, like precise chisels, excel at carving out comparisons, revealing shifts and differences with laser-like accuracy. The message becomes not just audible but undeniable, propelling you toward informed decisions, insightful answers, and effective problem-solving.

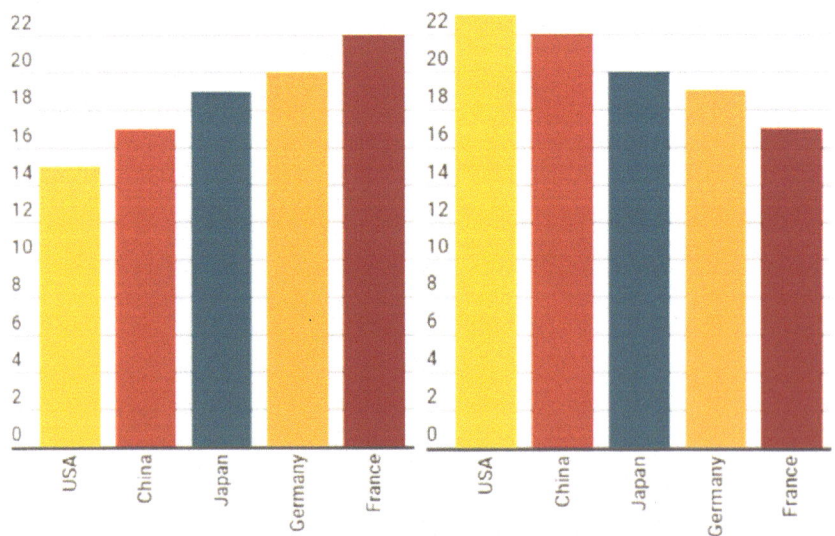

FIGURE 3.7   Side-by-side bar graphs clearly illustrating the point.

Remember, choosing the right visualization tool is like selecting the perfect brush for a painting. It's not merely about technical expertise; it's about understanding the data's inherent story and finding the visual language that allows it to resonate with your audience. So, ditch the imprecise tools for the delicate task and watch your data blossom into actionable insights, one well-chosen instrument at a time.

Brief Recap

Data storytelling thrives on collaboration. To bridge the gap between your insights and informed action, Chapter 3 empowers you to motivate your base, thus educating your stakeholders, audience, and anyone who needs to be on board with your data-driven narrative. By educating your audience and embracing these principles, you become a data storyteller who not only informs but also inspires. Go forth, motivate, and educate! Remember, perception paves the way for action-driven data success.

To recap our data-driven journey along the spectrum from concept to reality, in the conception stage, we learned to "start the race" by knowing both the data and the audience. In the inception stage, we saw the importance of "making the case" for expressing your data visually. In the perception stage, we have "motivated the base" by educating ourselves on the best practices involving consistency of scale, proper labeling, chronology, quantity, color, and shapes.

CASE STUDIES

Case Study #1: Misleading Charts in Super Bowl Ads[6]

The 2023 Super Bowl, a massive cultural event with millions of viewers, unfortunately served as a platform for several examples of unethical data visualization in advertisements. One particularly egregious case involved a snack company promoting its new line of "healthy" chips.

The ad: The ad opens with a vibrant pie chart showcasing the chip's ingredients. Each slice represented a different component, with large segments allocated to "whole grains" and "protein," suggesting a nutritious snack. Smaller slices depicted "fiber" and "healthy fats," further reinforcing the health-conscious message.

The deception: Upon closer inspection, viewers with a keen eye might notice discrepancies. The pie chart totaled over 100% (like the pie chart from the 2012 presidential election campaign), a clear violation of basic mathematical principles. Additionally, the "whole grains" section, seemingly the largest, actually represented a blend of grains containing refined flours and sugars, not the whole-grain goodness implied by the visuals.

The consequences: This deceptive data visualization not only misled viewers about the actual nutritional content of the chips but also undermined trust in the brand. Social media erupted with criticism, and the company faced potential legal repercussions for false advertising. This case perfectly illustrates the dangers of prioritizing form over function in data storytelling and the importance of ethical practices for maintaining audience trust.

Case Study #2: Clarity through Data Viz in Climate Change Communication[7]

Climate change, a complex and often overwhelming issue, can be challenging to communicate effectively to the public. However, the non-profit organization "Climate Central" has mastered the art of using data visualization to educate and inspire action.

The project: Climate Central's "Rising" project uses interactive maps and graphs to depict the real-time and projected impacts of climate change on specific locations. Users can enter their zip code and see how rising sea levels, extreme weather events, and changing temperatures will affect their communities.

The effectiveness: The interactive visualizations, employing clear labeling, consistent scales, and appropriate color palettes, present complex data in a readily understandable format. This approach not only educates viewers about the urgency of climate change but also personalizes the issue, making it relatable and sparking local action.

The impact: "Rising" has been widely acclaimed for its innovative approach to data storytelling. The project has garnered millions of views, engaged diverse audiences, and fueled local climate action initiatives. This case demonstrates the power of ethical and well-designed data visualization to not only inform but also inspire positive change.

STUDY QUESTIONS: MOTIVATING THE BASE

1. **Beyond Pie Charts**: Imagine you're tasked with visualizing the growth of different social media platforms over the past decade. Instead of the typical pie charts, propose two alternative visualization methods that would provide a clearer and more insightful picture for your audience. Explain the rationale behind your choices.

2. **Ethical Dilemma**: You're creating data visualizations for a company about to launch a new product. They request you to slightly adjust the scales or colors to make the data appear more impressive. How would you navigate this ethical conflict? What alternative solutions could you propose to effectively showcase the data without compromising integrity?

3. **Accessibility Beyond Sight**: In Chapter 3, we discussed color as a key element in data visualization. How can you cater to audiences with visual impairments while maintaining the integrity and clarity of your visuals? Explore alternative methods or design considerations to ensure inclusivity in your data storytelling.

4. **Form and Function Fusion**: Can aesthetics ever play a role in driving action through data visualization? If so, how can you strike a balance between eye-catching design and functional communication in your visuals? Provide concrete examples to illustrate your point.

5. **Storytelling Symphony**: How can you leverage the principles of effective storytelling (narrative structures, character development, conflict resolution) to craft data visualizations that engage and motivate your audience? Discuss specific techniques or examples to demonstrate your answer.

6. **Dynamic Data, Dynamic Visuals**: Imagine you're creating visuals for a real-time dashboard tracking website traffic. How would you design your visualizations to effectively communicate the constantly changing data while avoiding overload and maintaining clarity?

7. **Data Detective**: Analyze the visuals presented in Chapter 3. Identify examples of both effective and ineffective visualization practices. Explain your reasoning and propose alternatives for the less effective ones.

8. **Future Forecast**: As data volumes and visualization tools continue to evolve, what do you anticipate will be the future of data storytelling?

Predict potential challenges and opportunities that may arise in effectively educating and motivating audiences through data in the years to come.

OTHER SOURCES CONSULTED

- Moore, Mike. "An Introduction to Analysis and Data Visualization using Tableau Software." Western Michigan University, 2019.

- Brady, Timothy Francis, et al. "Real-World Objects Are Not Represented as Bound Units: Independent Forgetting of Different Object Details from Visual Memory." Journal of Experimental Psychology: General, vol. 142, no. 3, 2013, pp. 791–808.

- Hooper, Lydia. "Bad Infographics: The Worst Infographics of 2020." Venngage, 26 Jan. 2021, 4.

- Sobczak, Spencer. "Data Culture Matters (part 1)." LinkedIn, 8 Jan. 2019, www.linkedin.com/pulse/data-culture-matters-part-1-spencer-sobczak/.

- Sobczak, Spencer. "Data Culture Matters – Part 2." LinkedIn, 18 Jan. 2019, www.linkedin.com/pulse/data-culture-matters-part-2-spencer-sobczak/.

NOTES

1 Ethics & Compliance Initiative. "Global Business Ethics Survey." Accessed December 13, 2023, www.ethics.org/global-business-ethics-survey/#non-mem ber-download

2 Mike Moore. *An Introduction to Analysis and Data Visualization using Tableau Software*. Western Michigan University, 2019.

3 Edward R. Tufte. *The Visual Display of Quantitative Information*. Cheshire: Graphics Press, 2001.

4 World Health Organization. "Visual Impairment and Blindness." July 18, 2023. Accessed December 13, 2023, www.who.int/news-room/fact-sheets/detail/blindness-and-visual-impairment

5 K. O. Van Orden and J. V. Stone. "Visual Memory for Multiple Object-Property Dimensions: Individual Differences, Resource Limitations, and Model Comparison." *Journal of Experimental Psychology: General*, 152(4), 2023, pp. 710–734.

6 Ingrid Adamow. "Ethics and Super Bowl Ads: Take the Good with the Bad." The Quad, 2013. www.buquad.com/2013/02/06/ethics-and-super-bowl-ads-take-the-good-with-the-bad/

7 "Sea Level Rise: Risk and Resilience." Climate Central, https://sealevel.climate central.org/; "Coastal Risk Screening Tool." Climate Central, https://coastal.cli matecentral.org/; "The Facts About Sea Level Rise." Climate Central, https://sealevel.climatecentral.org/#:~:text=The%20Facts%20About%20Sea%20Le vel,line

CHAPTER 4

Inspection

Give It Space

GIVE IT SPACE

After having "started the race" with the first stage of Conception, "making the case" (the second stage of Inception), and "motivating the base" (the third stage of Perception), it is now time to "give it space" with the fourth stage of the spectrum, Inspection (key word: "investigate"). Ask yourself, does your data stand up to scrutiny?

To put it another way, the first three stages of our data odyssey have ignited a spark, built a case, and captivated an audience. Yet, before going any farther, we must step back, not in retreat, but with purpose. This chapter invites us to enter a sanctuary of scrutiny, a deliberate pause where our captivating narrative breathes and reveals its true depth.

Think of it like launching a rocket. The raw energy of conception propels us, the thrust of inception guides us, and the emotional thrust of perception ignites the final countdown. But just as a rocket wouldn't launch without a stable platform, our data visualizations need space to stand on their own, to withstand the scrutiny of inquisitive minds. It's in this "space" that we ensure every brushstroke of our visual story has integrity, every pixel aligns with truth, and every message resonates with authenticity.

DOI: 10.1201/9781003623212-5

This meticulous examination isn't about nitpicking flaws, but revealing hidden strengths. Like a sculptor stepping back to assess a masterpiece, we too must scrutinize our data creations, giving them room to breathe and unveil their true potential. This resonates with a recent joint study by Sungkyunkwan University and the University of Washington, which investigated the impact of data visualization design on decision-making.[1] The researchers found that participants who were presented with visualizations that had undergone thorough inspection, with clear axes, consistent color palettes, and concise annotations, were significantly more likely to make accurate and informed decisions compared to those presented with visually captivating but poorly scrutinized visualizations.

In this stage, we're not dimming our spark, but refining its brilliance. We're not silencing our story, but amplifying its voice with the chorus of meticulous analysis. Just as a sculptor steps back to assess the chiseled lines of a masterpiece, we too must scrutinize our data creations, giving them the room to reveal their hidden flaws and hidden strengths. This deliberate "space" for inspection isn't a luxury, but a necessity – the crucible where our data visualizations transform from fleeting spectacles into enduring legacies, driving informed decisions and positive change. This is where, like a diamond emerging from the rough, our data visualization strategy achieves its true brilliance, ready to illuminate not just with beauty, but with genuine impact. We will get to that impact shortly.

Attention to Detail

As we learned from the third stage in the previous chapter, it is important to pay attention to visual cues (the precursor to Inspection). To illustrate this point, below is an example of a "word jumble" paragraph that has been widely circulated:

> *Aoccdrnig to a rscheearch at Cmabrigde Uinervtisy, it deosn't mttaer in waht oredr the ltteers in a wrod are, the olny iprmoetnt tihng is taht the frist and lsat ltteer be at the rghit pclae. The rset can be a toatl mses and you can sitll raed it wouthit porbelm. Tihs is bcuseae the huamn mnid deos not raed ervey lteter by istlef, but the wrod as a wlohe.[2]*

Unscrambled, it reads:

> *According to research at Cambridge University, it doesn't matter in what order the letters in a word are, the only important thing is that*

the first and last letter be at the right place. The rest can be a total mess and you can still read it without problem. This is because the human mind does not read every letter by itself, but the word as a whole.

Upon reading the above paragraph (and following the encouragement shown in Figure 4.1), two questions to ask are (1) why do some individuals seem to be able to decipher the word jumble so easily (and under what conditions), and (2) which parts of the paragraph are true and which ones are fiction?

First, Cambridge University never conducted such a study. And while it is true that the human brain processes words as a whole (rather than one letter at a time), contextual inference is needed. That is, they should be rather small words and arranged in such a way that one can use personal experience for the brain to fill in the gaps. Additionally, it helps when basic sounds are preserved. For example, you can more easily guess that "toatl" stands for "total" than you could if it were spelled "talot" instead. Lastly, it is easier to unscramble words when one can predict what is coming next. That is, the human brain, from previous experience, is best at filling in the context from incomplete information when it can anticipate what is coming next.

This principle also applies to ensuring transparency in data storytelling: Just as words are perceived as pieces of a message, so images are perceived as parts of a story. This is necessary to ensure appropriate investigation can take place and transparency can be achieved. The "word jumble" exercise serves as a poignant reminder of the human brain's incredible ability to fill in gaps and construct meaning, even amidst apparent chaos. Just as we deciphered the scrambled letters, viewers actively engage with data visualizations, weaving together individual details into a cohesive narrative. But within this tapestry of perception lies a crucial responsibility: ensuring transparency.

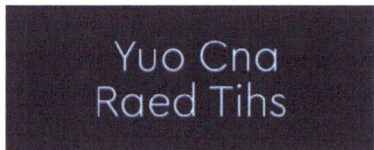

FIGURE 4.1   You can read this.

Transparency in data storytelling isn't simply about making data accessible; it's about creating a canvas where every brushstroke can be inspected, understood, and ultimately trusted. Consider the meticulously crafted pie charts often used to portray financial performance. While visually appealing, these slices can obscure crucial details – how were they calculated? What outliers were excluded? Did external factors contribute? Without transparency, these questions linger like shadows, casting doubt on the narrative's integrity.

This becomes even more critical in an age inundated with information. Researchers from Ruhr-Universität Bochum (RUB), the Max Planck Institute for Security and Privacy (MPI-SP), and The George Washington University concluded that if online services like Google are more transparent about the data they collect on their users, it can inspire more trust.[3] This aligns with the importance of transparency in data collection. When companies openly disclose the information they gather from users, it inspires confidence. While short-term gains may come from opacity, long-term trust is essential for competitiveness. To build trust, organizations must actively educate users about data practices and provide appropriate value in exchange for their information. Legal disclosures alone are insufficient; fairness should be embedded in products and models from the outset. This underscores the fact that transparency isn't just about technical accuracy; it's about establishing a bond of trust with the audience, a foundation upon which impactful decisions can be built.

So, how do we weave transparency into the fabric of our data narratives? First of all, embrace clarity over complexity. Eliminate unnecessary embellishments and ensure axes, scales, and legends are unambiguous. Secondly, become a storyteller with data. Contextualize the information, highlighting limitations and outliers, and invite exploration through interactive elements. Finally, remember, your audience isn't a passive viewer; they're active participants in the story. Provide pathways for further investigation, offering access to raw data and methodologies for those who wish to take a deeper dive.

By embracing "give it space" in the inspection stage, we shed light on the hidden corners of our data narratives, fostering trust and enabling informed decision-making. Remember, transparency isn't a constraint; it's the brushstroke that brings our data stories to life with authenticity and impact.

The Importance of Transparency

Speaking of transparency, being totally transparent helps avoid the pitfalls of bias and unethical use of data upon inspection. When analytical professionals have done their due diligence, they will neither be bothered nor intimidated by questions such as:

- Did you ensure data quality?
- Where did you get your data?
- How do you know it's right?

These questions will consequently dissipate against the backdrop of a transparent approach, where every facet of data sourcing and integrity is laid bare.

In a 2017 blog post, Matt Reaney, founder and director at a European talent search firm specializing in Big Data, advocated the importance of transparency in data and suggested three aspects of transparency,[4] summarized below:

- Start with a story (understand what is being visualized): What better way to make sense of an unintelligible mass of numbers than to put them into a story? This guiding principle should be at the core of every data visualization. As was stated in Chapter 3, if key stakeholders understand the data, they are incentivized to take ownership, and by extension, this facilitates their ability to explain or justify the data and their actions when questioned.

- Show the data as is (i.e., unmanipulated): Show the data for what it is – including all its warts, blemishes, and wrinkles. Correct, honest decisions and correct conclusions can only come from accurate, unadulterated, unmanipulated data.

- Secure the trust of the stakeholders: Reaney says that transparency is all about trust, since common sense indicates that people are more inclined to believe what they can trust. In Reaney's own words, "When the business learns to trust the numbers, they have a solid foundation for making the best decisions and subsequent growth."[5]

This commitment to transparency isn't just a moral imperative; it's a strategic advantage. A study conducted by Weissgerber, Garovic, Savic,

Winham, and Milic in 2016 demonstrated that when participants were presented with transparent data visualizations, complete with annotations and explanations, they not only better understood the information but also exhibited a significant increase in trust toward the data source.[6] This heightened trust translated into a greater willingness to engage with the data, enabling more informed decision-making based on its insights.

Transparency isn't about vulnerability; it's about empowerment. By shedding light on our data's origins, methodologies, and limitations, we empower our audience to become collaborators, not skeptics. We create a space for shared understanding, where trust flourishes and informed action takes root. So, let us embrace the "give it space" principle, not just as a technical step, but as a philosophical commitment to transparency. Let us illuminate the hidden corners of our data narratives, not with fear, but with the confidence that in the light of truth, our data stories will resonate with greater power and impact.

Impact vs. Influence

Speaking of impact, having taken transparency into consideration, as the data behind a visualization project is held up to inspection, it is important to be aware of the difference between impact and influence, and how that difference plays into making data actionable.

Impact is typically recognized as being an effect brought on by external factors that tend to push on the status quo. According to research cited by Prevedere, a leading provider of intelligent forecasting solutions, the following was found: "Nearly 85 percent of a company's performance is dependent upon external factors. Yet…many companies don't know where to look to determine which external drivers are affecting business perform-ance."[7] Those who make it a priority to identify those factors are PUSHED into acting upon them, thus making an impact in their organization.

By contrast, influence is generally known to be the power to affect from internal factors that tend to pull on the status quo. These are factors that an organization can control internally. Such factors include data struc-ture/organization, the frequency of data collection and assimilation into the data warehouse, and the cultural climate already existing in the organ-ization. Recognizing and dealing with these factors will tend to pull the organization's strategy in the right direction from the inside.

This interplay between impact and influence is where the magic of "Give It Space" truly shines. By giving our data the room to breathe, to be scrutinized and understood, we unlock its potential to both react and guide. We equip ourselves to ride the waves of external impact while deftly adjusting the sails of internal influence.

In the dynamic landscape of the digital economy, organizations face a delicate dance between external forces and internal optimization. A study by the MIT Initiative on the Digital Economy (IDE) underscores this nuanced interplay. Researchers found that companies effectively leveraging both internal data insights and external data sources experienced significantly higher levels of innovation and growth. By harnessing the push of external market dynamics and the pull of internal strategic optimization, these organizations navigated the ever-changing terrain of their markets with agility and foresight.[8]

So, within the stage of "Give It Space," we do not simply scrutinize data for accuracy and clarity; we unlock its potential to transform into a catalyst for both impact and influence. By embracing this dynamic interplay, we empower our data narratives to not just tell stories, but to shape realities, pushing us toward a future where data-driven action flourishes.

To summarize, an idea must be visualized, then scrutinized before it can be realized. In other words, the organization that has given the data some "space" to ensure it can stand up to inspection is well on its way to turning concepts into reality with actionable data.

A Combination for Success

It is possible to measure success in this area by capitalizing on this knowledge and turning ideas into reality by blending the external with the internal, leveraging them both into a cohesive strategy to meet short-term needs and provide long-term benefit.

This is because by this time (having adhered to the principles in the first four stages expounded upon in these first four chapters), the analytical professional will have learned to take their data, differentiate it to come up with information, see the connections to derive knowledge, determine the meaningful connections to grant insight, and find the best paths between them for wisdom. At that point, impact will have been achieved (see Figure 4.2). As a result, you will most certainly generate influence as well.

Let me illustrate further. Turning the dance of impact and influence into a full-fledged symphony of change requires orchestrating both external forces and internal levers. Here's how:

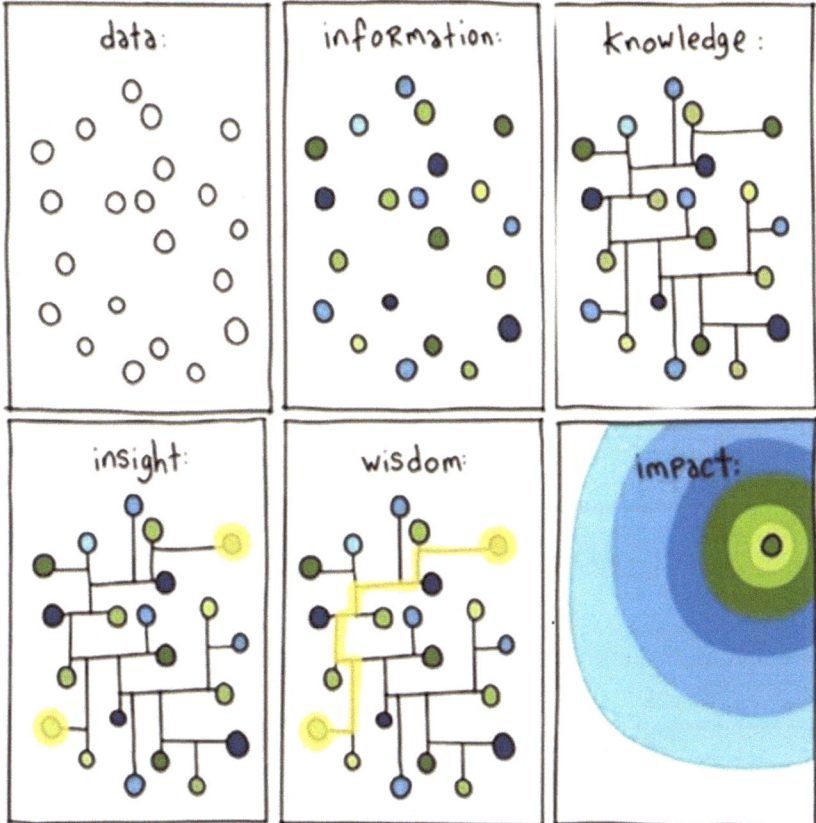

FIGURE 4.2   The progression from data to impact.

1. **Embrace the Unexpected**: Remember, external impact often arrives like a whirlwind, shaking the foundations of our assumptions. By fostering a culture of "Give It Space" within your organization, you empower teams to embrace these disruptions, not fear them. Encourage scenario planning, data-driven brainstorming, and agile adaptation to ride the waves of external forces – like a surfer carving their path amidst crashing waves.

2. **Cultivate Internal Harmony**: While impact pushes from the outside, lasting influence blossoms from within. Invest in data infrastructure, streamline data collection and analysis, and nurture a data-driven decision-making culture. This creates fertile ground for internal levers like data structure and organizational culture to flourish, gently

pulling your strategy in the right direction, like the steady hum of a tuning fork guiding an orchestra.

3. **Ignite the Collaborative Spark**: Bridge the gap between internal and external by fostering collaboration. Break down silos, encourage cross-functional data sharing, and empower teams to see the bigger picture. When your analysts, strategists, and frontline operators dance to the same data-driven rhythm, the combined impact and influence of their actions can resonate through the entire organization, like a powerful crescendo that moves mountains.

4. **Measure, Refine, Repeat**: The symphony of change never truly ends. Continuously monitor and measure the impact of your data-driven initiatives. Evaluate the effectiveness of your internal processes. By understanding what works and what doesn't, you can adjust your approach, tighten your focus, and amplify the harmonious blend of impact and influence.

The continuous cycle of inspection, adaptation, and action, inherent to agile methodologies, resonates with findings from research on organizational agility. Agile practices have significantly improved success rates in software development, enhanced quality, and accelerated speed to market. Companies adept at leveraging both internal and external data insights have experienced substantial benefits. While the exact figures may vary, studies consistently demonstrate increased profitability and revenue growth.[9] They were the maestros of their own data symphonies, weaving impact and influence into a powerful melody that drove success.

So, as we conclude this journey through "Inspection: Give It Space," remember, it's not just about making your data stand up to scrutiny; it's about unleashing its transformative potential. By harmonizing impact and influence, you empower your data to not just tell stories, but to orchestrate a beautiful symphony of change, rewriting the future one actionable insight at a time.

CASE STUDIES

Case Study 1: Food Supply Management: A Data-Driven Journey[10]

The "Give It Space" philosophy isn't confined to internal data analysis; it can also drive external change. Consider the enlightening journey of Food & Water Watch, a non-profit organization in the United States dedicated to addressing critical issues in our food system.

For years, Food & Water Watch has focused on the impact of overproduction driven by Big Ag. Commodity crop prices have plummeted, leaving farmers struggling to break even. Supply management policies historically stabilized prices, boosted farm income, and conserved the environment. However, resolving these issues required meticulous data analysis and a well-structured strategy.

1. **Igniting the Cause: The "Give It Space" Philosophy**
   Our food system faces challenges due to Big Ag's influence. Supply management policies offer hope for reclaiming control. Just as data analysis ignites internal change, Food & Water Watch sparked external change by investigating food supply mismanagement.

2. **Unmasking the Reality: Building the Case**

   Food & Water Watch meticulously analyzed the impact of overproduction driven by Big Ag. Commodity crop prices plummet, leaving farmers struggling to break even. Supply management policies historically stabilized prices, boosted farm income, and conserved the environment.

3. **Telling the Story: Captivating the Audience**

   Raw data alone won't resonate. Food & Water Watch transformed findings into powerful infographics, interactive maps, and poignant video documentaries. These visualizations, crafted through the "Give It Space" principles outlined in this chapter, galvanized public support.

4. **Ensuring Transparency and Credibility: Inspection**
   Transparency in this issue is always paramount. Food & Water Watch published detailed reports, inviting scrutiny. Trust and credibility were essential for influencing public opinion and policymakers in this "Give It Space" approach.

IMPACT AND INFLUENCE: A SYMPHONY OF CHANGE

Their data-driven campaign had a profound impact. Widespread media coverage, public outrage, and pressure on policymakers led to policy changes. Supply management isn't just historical – it's a lifeline for our food system.

This case study showcases how the "Give It Space" philosophy transcends internal data analysis. By meticulously uncovering and visualizing data, Food & Water Watch not only sparked public awareness but also influenced policy changes, driving a sustainable impact on the issue of food supply management.

Case Study 2: Data-Driven Diplomacy: Tackling Climate Change with Transparency[11]

The principles of "Give It Space" aren't just applicable to domestic concerns; they can also empower global cooperation on pressing issues like climate change. Consider the story of the Climate TRACE coalition, a global initiative aiming to track greenhouse gas emissions across the globe with unprecedented transparency and accuracy.

Stage 1: Spark: Recognizing the Gap: The need for Climate TRACE arose from a critical gap in climate action – a lack of reliable, transparent data on emissions. Existing monitoring systems were often fragmented, incomplete, and shrouded in secrecy. This lack of transparency fostered mistrust and hampered effective collaboration between nations.

Stage 2: Build the Case: Crowdsourcing the Solution: Climate TRACE adopted a revolutionary approach, leveraging "open-source intelligence" by aggregating data from diverse sources, including satellite imagery, industrial sensors, and open-access databases. This massive crowdsourced dataset, meticulously filtered and validated through "Give It Space" principles, provided a more comprehensive and transparent picture of global emissions than ever before.

Stage 3: Captivate the Audience: Visualizing the Issue: Climate TRACE didn't simply present raw data; they transformed it into powerful visualizations like interactive maps and real-time dashboards. These visualizations, crafted through rigorous inspection and refinement, allowed users to explore emissions trends across countries and industries, making the global climate crisis tangible and relatable.

Stage 4: Inspection: Building Trust through Openness: Climate TRACE committed to complete transparency, making their methodology and data openly accessible to researchers, policymakers, and the public. This "Give

It Space" approach fostered trust and collaboration, enabling independent verification of findings and facilitating data-driven dialogues between nations.

Impact and Influence: A Global Collaboration: Climate TRACE's data-driven approach has yielded remarkable results. The initiative's detailed emissions reports have exposed previously under-reported sources, prompting corrective actions from governments and industries. Additionally, their efforts have fostered a culture of transparency and collaboration, paving the way for more effective international cooperation on climate change mitigation and adaptation.

This case study demonstrates the transformative potential of "Give It Space" beyond organizational boundaries. By embracing transparency, collaboration, and meticulous data analysis, Climate TRACE has empowered a global community to tackle one of humanity's most pressing challenges.

STUDY QUESTIONS: GIVE IT SPACE

1. **Beyond the "Word Jumble"**: This chapter uses the "word jumble" example to illustrate the human brain's ability to fill in gaps and construct meaning. Can you think of other examples in the field of data visualization where this principle plays a role? How can this be both beneficial and potentially misleading?

2. **Transparency vs. Accessibility**: While the chapter emphasizes transparency, there might be instances where certain data details could be overwhelming or distracting for the audience. How can we balance transparency with accessibility to ensure effective communication without sacrificing rigor?

3. **Impact vs. Influence: A False Dichotomy?** The text distinguishes between impact (external push) and influence (internal pull). Do you think this is a clear-cut distinction, or are they intertwined in the real world? Can you think of examples where data-driven initiatives achieved both impact and influence simultaneously?

4. **The "Inspection" Pitfall**: Rigorous scrutiny is crucial, but could there be instances where excessive analysis leads to paralysis? How can we find the right balance between thorough inspection and timely action in data-driven decision-making?

5. **Data Democratization and Trust**: The chapter advocates for open access to data and methodologies. However, concerns remain about data misuse and manipulation. How can we foster a culture of data democratization while addressing trust and security concerns?

6. **Beyond the Human Factor**: The text primarily focuses on human interpretation of data. How do advancements in artificial intelligence and machine learning change the landscape of "Give It Space"? How will we ensure AI-driven data analysis adheres to the principles of transparency and accountability?

7. **The Ethics of Inspection**: While transparency is important, are there situations where certain data could be harmful or sensitive if exposed? How do we navigate ethical considerations when "giving data space" for public scrutiny?

8. **The Future of "Give It Space"**: As technology and data volumes continue to evolve, how do you think the "Give It Space" principles will need to adapt to stay relevant? What are the potential challenges and opportunities for this approach in the future?

NOTES

1 Seungeun Park, Betty Bekemeier, Abraham Flaxman and Melinda Schultz. "Impact of Data Visualization on Decision-making and Its Implications for Public Health Practice: A Systematic Literature Review." *Informatics for Health and Social Care*, 2021. https://doi.org/10.1080/17538157.2021.1982949

2 "If Yuo're Albe To Raed Tihs, You Might Have Typoglycemia." Dictionary.com, January 21, 2021. www.dictionary.com/e/typoglycemia

3 TechXplore, "Transparent Data Collection Increases Trust Among Users." June 2, 2021. https://techxplore.com/news/2021-06-transparent-users.pdf

4 Matt Reaney. "Big Data Desperately Needs Transparency." March 2017. www.kdnuggets.com/2017/03/big-data-needs-transparency.html

5 Tracey L. Weissgerber, et al. "From Static to Interactive: Transforming Data Visualization to Improve Transparency." *PLoS Biology*, 14(6), 2016, e1002484. https://journals.plos.org/plosbiology/article?id=10.1371/journal.pbio.1002484

6 "The Top 10 External Factors That Impact Forecast Accuracy." Prevedere. Accessed December 11, 2023, https://prevedere.com/the-top-10-external-factors-that-impact-forecast-accuracy/

7 MIT Initiative on the Digital Economy. "Exploring Digital Transformation." MIT Sloan School of Management, February 13, 2023.

8 Darrell Rigby, Jeff Sutherland, and Hirotaka Takeuchi. "Embracing Agile: How to Master the Process That's Transforming Management." *Harvard Business Review*, May 2016, pp. 40–48, 50. https://hbr.org/2016/05/embracing-agile

9 Mia DiFelice and Rebecca Wolf. "What Is Supply Management and How Can It Save Our Food System?" Food & Water Watch, October 17, 2023. Accessed December 20, 2023, www.foodandwaterwatch.org/2023/10/17/supply-management/

10 Matt Reaney. "Big Data Desperately Needs Transparency." March 2017. www.kdnuggets.com/2017/03/big-data-needs-transparency.html.

11 "Climate Trace, About, Case Studies." Accessed December 31, 2023, www.climatetrace.org/case-studies, www.climatetrace.org/about

CHAPTER 5

Direction

Put It into Place

PUT IT INTO PLACE

The key word with the fifth stage in our data storytelling journey is effectuate – that is, ensuring the right direction for the solution to be correctly put into place. When data has been scrubbed, correct visualizations and/or charts have been chosen, and data validity and integrity have been assured, the project is ready for implementation represented by a four-fold iterative cycle (as illustrated in Figure 5.1).

The cycle starts by deploying the solution, using whatever organizational protocols and/or methods already in place (such as waterfall, agile, Kanban). As the stakeholders start using this solution, they will discover issues and report them to the appropriate individuals as issues, defects, problems, or whatever nomenclature in use, using the existing organizational issue-reporting mechanism. The analytics professional will then analyze those issues and discern the right course of action to address them, taking whatever functional, technical, and business requirements made available by the stakeholders into account.

Finally, the analytics professional will assign the appropriate individual or team (in which they may be included themselves) to begin developing the remediation for those issues, ensuring all requirements, specifications,

DOI: 10.1201/9781003623212-6

FIGURE 5.1   The four-fold iterative cycle. (©2022–2025, Dr. Joe Perez.)

constraints, and deadlines are observed and met. At this point, the cycle may start all over again with the goal of improving upon the solution with each iterative cycle. This approach leads to progress, ensuring an effective direction.

Let me expand upon this concept a little further. The four-fold iterative cycle emphasizes a continuous improvement mindset. It recognizes that initial solutions, no matter how carefully crafted, are rarely perfect. By actively seeking and addressing issues through successive iterations, we refine the solution, making it increasingly effective and aligned with stakeholder needs. This approach stands in contrast to traditional "big bang" deployments that often struggle to adapt to real-world feedback, leading to costly delays and rework.

Deploying a new data-driven solution doesn't happen in a vacuum. Stakeholders, accustomed to familiar routines, might naturally resist the change. But instead of dismissing resistance, embracing it as an opportunity can lead to smoother implementation. Through empathy, we can dive deeper than surface objections to understand the underlying fears and concerns. Actively listening to their anxieties and acknowledging their validity builds trust and opens the door for productive dialogue. This dialogue needn't be a one-way street. Inviting stakeholders to co-create the solution alongside the analytics team fosters a sense of ownership and investment. When they're not just recipients of change, but active participants in shaping it, resistance transforms into engagement and champions for progress emerge.

Beyond listening and collaboration, tailored communication and training play a crucial role. Different individuals have different learning styles and needs. Recognizing this requires customizing communication strategies to ensure clarity, relevance, and accessibility. Providing ongoing support and resources, and addressing evolving questions, ensures everyone feels equipped to navigate the change and embrace its potential.

Change can feel daunting, so acknowledging and celebrating milestones is crucial. Highlighting success stories, individual and team contributions, and the solution's tangible impact on business outcomes creates a sense of pride, accomplishment, and shared ownership. This positive reinforcement fuels further momentum, turning initial trepidation into a collective journey toward success. But building momentum isn't just about accolades. Transparency and open communication are key. Regular updates on progress, challenges, and adjustments keep stakeholders informed and engaged. This openness builds trust and reinforces the value of continuous improvement, reminding everyone that even challenges are opportunities for learning and growth. Gamification and rewards can also play a role. Introducing game-like elements and incentives like leaderboards or badges can add a touch of fun and friendly competition, driving participation, accelerating progress, and making milestones feel like celebrations.

For direction to truly flourish, it needs to be more than a one-time initiative; it needs to become embedded in the organizational culture. This requires leadership commitment, not just lip service. Leaders must actively champion direction, demonstrating its value through their actions and allocating resources to support its ongoing implementation. This visible dedication sets the tone for the entire organization, sending a clear message that data-driven direction is not an add-on, but a cornerstone of success.

Breaking down silos and fostering cross-functional collaboration is another key ingredient. When departments work together, aligning their efforts and sharing knowledge, direction thrives. This collaborative spirit ensures everyone is pulling in the same direction, united by a shared vision of data-driven progress. Finally, empowering employees with data literacy is essential. By equipping individuals at all levels with the skills to understand, analyze, and utilize data effectively, we create a workforce that's not just receptive to direction, but actively involved in shaping it.

Direction might imply a linear journey, but the reality of data-driven initiatives is dynamic. Balancing agility with governance ensures we can adapt to evolving needs and opportunities without compromising ethical and regulatory standards. This calls for adaptable data governance frameworks that provide the flexibility to respond to change while upholding essential principles. Regular reviews and updates ensure these frameworks remain relevant and aligned with best practices.

Proactive risk management is another pillar of this balance. Engaging stakeholders in collaborative workshops to identify potential risks, brainstorm mitigation strategies, and establish clear accountability fosters a culture of shared responsibility. By anticipating and addressing challenges head-on, we navigate the dynamic landscape of direction with confidence.

And let's not forget security. Weaving security considerations into the fabric of solution development from the very beginning is crucial. Building a culture of security awareness throughout the organization, through regular training, simulations, and audits, ensures everyone is vigilant and committed to protecting sensitive data.

By understanding the human aspect of change, celebrating progress, embedding direction into our culture, and striking a balance between agility and governance, we can transform "Put It into Place" from a technical step into a dynamic and inspiring journey. This journey, fueled by data and driven by collaboration, paves the way for an organization that not just adopts change, but thrives on it.

According to SAP Insider, digital transformation remains a challenging initiative, with less than 30% of organizations succeeding in their efforts. Traditional industries, such as automotive, infrastructure, oil and gas, and healthcare, find it even more daunting, with only 11% achieving success in digital transformation.[1] This stark statistic highlights the importance of meticulous planning and effective direction efforts like those outlined in this chapter. When direction goes beyond technical implementation and embraces user engagement, resistance management, and cultural integration, the chances of success increase dramatically.

According to McKinsey & Company research, organizations with robust change management practices achieve significantly improved operational efficiency and faster time-to-market compared to their counterparts who may not be as adept.[2] This underscores the link between effective direction and improved business outcomes. By adopting principles like transparency, collaboration, and continuous improvement, organizations can translate data-driven insights into tangible results.

In line with a study conducted by the *Harvard Business Review* (HBR) for Google Cloud, organizations that strategically invested in data and analytics during the COVID-19 pandemic achieved higher operational efficiency (81% vs. 58%) and increased revenues (77% vs. 61%) compared to their peers.[3] This suggests that embedding direction into the organizational fabric can provide a significant competitive advantage. Fostering data literacy, breaking down silos, and empowering employees to participate in data-driven decision-making all contribute to a culture where direction thrives and translates into bottom-line benefits.

A Framework to Consider

So where do we start? How does the data analytics professional know they have given their data storytelling project the right direction and have correctly put it into place? In Chapter 2, we referenced British data journalist David McCandless' statement that, of any of the five senses, sight has the highest bandwidth by a wide margin. McCandless also came up with a stunning data visualization that answers the "where do we start" question quite adequately. The four-lobed elongated Venn diagram (as shown in Figure 5.2 from McCandless's "Information Is Beautiful" website) visualizes the four elements McCandless believes are necessary for what he calls a "good" visualization[4] (i.e., a visualization that is useful for making a decision, answering a question, or solving a problem):

- Information [data]
- Story [concept]
- Goal [function], and
- Visual form [metaphor]

All four of these elements should be present to achieve this goal. If only two are depicted, it results in a product that McCandless calls "prototypical and sketchy" (which is not necessarily problematic when a data visualization project is at an early stage of development). Even with three of the four elements, the result is still "strangely lacking," as McCandless put it. Failure to consider the story or concept behind the data, for example, leaves one with data that lacks relevance to the stakeholders. Failure to stay focused on

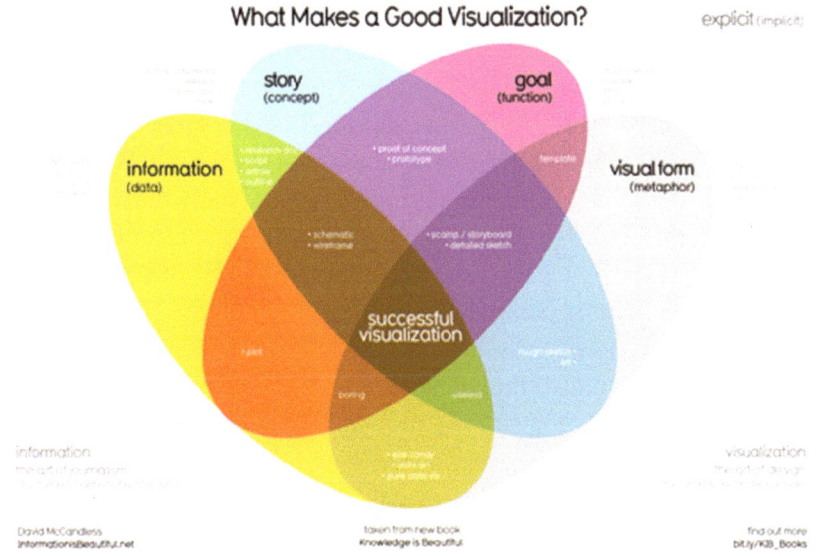

FIGURE 5.2 Four elements that make an impactful infographic. (©David McCandless, 2023, www.informationisbeautiful.net.)

the goal or function yields a product that may look great and sound feasible but will never be actionable.

By contrast, while putting the solution into place, if the data professional can manage to pull in all four of the elements, the result will be a successful visualization that leverages the art of journalism with the art of design and illustrates integrity, interest, usefulness, and beauty.

McCandless' stunning framework provides a strong foundation, but adding an extra layer of "empathy" can elevate successful visualizations to impactful stories. Understanding the audience's prior knowledge, emotional triggers, and preferred information intake methods is crucial. Visualizations designed with empathy in mind cater to diverse learning styles, avoid unnecessary cognitive overload, and foster deeper engagement with the data.

Data exists within a temporal and spatial context. Integrating historical trends, geographical comparisons, and relevant external factors enriches the narrative and prevents isolated interpretations. By considering timeliness, data professionals can ensure their visualizations address the most pressing issues and resonate with current events, maximizing their impact on decision-making.

McCandless' four elements emphasize static visuals, but the digital realm opens doors for interactive experiences. Allowing users to filter data, drill down into subsets, and customize their exploration empowers them to discover insights on their own terms. This participatory approach fosters a deeper understanding and ownership of the data story.

Visualizations can influence perceptions and carry implicit biases. Addressing ethical concerns around data representation, including avoiding misleading scales, ensuring colorblind accessibility, and representing diverse perspectives, is paramount. By prioritizing inclusivity and transparency, data professionals create visualizations that inform and empower rather than distort or discriminate.

While McCandless focuses on individual elements, the magic truly unfolds when they converge to create a compelling narrative. A well-structured story arc, employing visual metaphors, emotional cues, and suspenseful transitions, can hold the audience's attention and guide them toward a clear understanding of the data's message. This is where the art of journalism and design truly meet, transforming information into impactful experiences.

To put this into perspective, a 2019 study revealed that interactive content gets two times more engagement than static content.[5] This highlights the potential of McCandless' framework, expanded with interactivity, to foster deeper understanding and impact when "putting data into place" and achieve the right direction.

By incorporating these additional dimensions, data professionals can move beyond merely "putting data into place" and elevate their visualizations into insightful, engaging, and impactful stories that leave a lasting impression on their audience, thus they will effectuate a viable solution.

Actionable Data: What's Your Data's Story?

In the data visualization journey from concept to reality, as the visualizations are developed and moved along the five stages of the spectrum, it is imperative that best practices are followed. American mathematician John Tukey once said, "The greatest value of a picture is when it forces us to notice what we never expected to see."[6] So what ideas are generated when the underlying data is seen for what it really is? To stimulate these ideas, remember that graphs and data visualizations:

- Are only as good as the data they portray,
- Should be no more complex than the data they portray, and

- Should never paint a distorted picture of the values they portray.

Enterprise account executive and expert data storyteller Spencer Sobczak has said, "Data storytelling is both an art and a science. Our data visualizations are the most powerful when they find this balance."[7] To that point (and to finish the story we started in Part I of this book), the American-led coalition in Desert Storm exceeded General Norman Schwarzkopf's monumental challenge more than 30 years ago when they achieved their objectives in less than a hundred hours with minimal loss of life. They followed a leader who drew a tremendous amount of inspiration from Chinese General Sun Tzu's The Art of War, indicating that they knew how to balance art and science. Schwarzkopf called the "Left Hook" strategy "an absolutely gigantic accomplishment,"[8] but this "gigantic accomplishment" could not have been achieved without using actionable data.

While insightful visualizations and compelling narratives are crucial for understanding what our data tells us, actionable data truly comes alive when it empowers us to shape the future. Here's how we can extend the "data story" concept and equip stakeholders with tools to navigate the path from insights to action:

- **Embracing the Proactive: From Analysis to Scenario Planning**: Going beyond passive storytelling, actionable data involves interactive visualizations and simulation tools that allow stakeholders to explore "what if" scenarios. By testing different courses of action and anticipating potential challenges, organizations can proactively adjust their sails and navigate future uncertainties with greater confidence. Imagine visualizing various marketing campaign budgets and predicting their impact on return on investment (ROI), or simulating customer behavior under different pricing strategies. This empowers informed decision-making and prepares organizations for a dynamic world.

- **From Insight to Impact: The Art of Operationalization**: Data insights are valuable, but actionable data translates them into tangible results. This means designing visualizations that directly inform existing workflows, embedding calls to action within the narrative, and aligning recommendations with practical implementation frameworks. Think of interactive dashboards guiding real-time resource allocation based on market trends, or automated alerts triggering corrective actions when key performance indicators deviate from the desired path. Actionable data becomes the bridge between analysis and execution, driving organizations toward measurable progress.

- **Co-Creation: Fueling Ownership and Action**: Data shouldn't be a unilateral pronouncement from the ivory tower. Fostering a culture of co-creation, where stakeholders participate in the data storytelling process from data collection to visualization design, builds collective ownership and commitment to implementing insights. Imagine workshops where diverse perspectives shape the data narrative, or crowdsourcing platforms where employees contribute ideas for data-driven solutions. This collaborative approach ensures that data stories resonate with those who need to act on them, boosting the chances of successful implementation and sustained change.

- **The Human Touch: Data-Driven with Empathy**: Data isn't just cold numbers; it represents human realities. Actionable data dives into the motivations, emotions, and social contexts behind the numbers, equipping stakeholders with the empathy needed to design effective interventions and address complex challenges. Imagine visualizing employee sentiment alongside productivity data to identify potential burnout risks, or analyzing customer purchase patterns alongside social media conversations to understand underlying needs and preferences. This human-centered approach ensures data stories are not just informative, but also inspiring, fostering a sense of shared purpose and driving collective action.

- **Democratizing Data: Unleashing Collective Intelligence**: Actionable data thrives on inclusivity. By promoting data literacy and making insights accessible through user-friendly tools and platforms, organizations unlock the collective intelligence of their workforce. Imagine employees at all levels analyzing sales data to optimize inventory management, or frontline workers using real-time sensor data to improve operational efficiency. This data-democratized culture empowers individuals to make informed decisions, solve problems on the fly, and contribute to continuous improvement, creating an organization where every voice shapes the future.

A study by MIT Sloan Management Review found that organizations with a data-democratized culture, where employees at all levels actively utilize data in their daily work, experience a 30% increase in operational efficiency and a 20% improvement in innovation compared to their data-siloed counterparts.[9] This highlights the transformative potential of actionable data in not just informing, but also empowering and uniting an entire organization to thrive in a data-driven world.

By embracing these additional dimensions, data professionals can transform their stories from captivating narratives into actionable blueprints for positive change. This empowers organizations to not just react to the present, but to actively shape their own future, driven by the collective intelligence and collaborative spirit unleashed through truly actionable data.

Case Study #1: The Malaria Atlas Project: Data-Driven Precision in Public Health[10]

The Malaria Atlas Project isn't just about maps; it's about saving lives. This global initiative leverages cutting-edge data science and visualization to combat malaria, a disease still claiming millions of lives annually. Imagine detailed, interactive maps pinpointing malaria hotspots with granular precision, not just by country, but down to the village level. These maps reveal complex transmission patterns, mosquito breeding grounds, and environmental factors like rainfall and temperature that exacerbate the disease's spread. This actionable data empowers public health officials to:

- Target interventions with surgical accuracy: Instead of a scattergun approach, resources can be prioritized to areas with the highest infection rates, ensuring maximum impact. Think targeted mosquito control campaigns in hotspots, delivering vital medication to high-risk populations, and educating communities about preventative measures tailored to their specific geographic challenges.
- Develop localized strategies: The maps unveil nuances in transmission dynamics across regions. A strategy effective in the swamplands of West Africa might not translate to the arid plains of East Africa. Data-driven insights inform customized interventions that address local factors like mosquito species, breeding behavior, and community practices.
- Monitor and adapt on the fly: The project doesn't stop at static maps. Data is constantly updated, tracking changes in prevalence over time. This real-time feedback loop allows health officials to monitor the

effectiveness of implemented strategies, identify areas where resistance is emerging, and adjust interventions accordingly.

The Malaria Atlas Project's success is a testament to the principles of "Putting it into Place." The data is rigorous and validated, the visualizations are intuitive and accessible, and the insights are communicated effectively to policymakers and healthcare workers, transforming abstract numbers into actionable plans. This data-driven approach has not only saved countless lives but also laid the groundwork for global malaria eradication efforts.

Case Study #2: Beyond Binge-watching: How Netflix Uses Data to Fuel Growth and Personalization[11]

Netflix isn't just a destination for cat videos and costume dramas; it's a masterclass in data-driven personalization. Imagine analyzing billions of data points – watch history, ratings, thumbs-up/down, scrolling patterns, even time of day you binge-watch – to predict with uncanny accuracy what each viewer wants to watch next. This actionable data translates into:

- Hyper-personalized recommendations: No more generic "you might also like" lists. Netflix's algorithm predicts content based on your unique preferences, keeping you hooked and returning for more. This not only boosts user satisfaction and engagement but also drives retention and subscription renewals.

- Serendipity and content discovery: The rabbit hole goes deeper. The algorithm surfaces hidden gems and niche content you might have otherwise missed, expanding your horizons and enriching your viewing experience. This fosters exploration and sparks delightful serendipitous discoveries.

- Strategic content acquisition and production: Netflix doesn't play roulette with its budget. Data analysis reveals audience preferences and emerging trends, informing decisions on which shows and movies to acquire or produce. This data-driven approach maximizes their return on investment, attracting new viewers and keeping existing ones engaged with content they'll truly love.

Netflix's case showcases the transformative power of "Putting data into Place" beyond just storytelling. By transforming data into actionable insights, they've personalized entertainment, fueled user engagement, and catapulted themselves to the forefront of the global streaming market. It's not just about algorithms; it's about understanding human behavior, predicting desires, and crafting an experience that keeps viewers coming back for more.

SUMMARY

These two case studies, spanning diverse fields like healthcare and entertainment, showcase the versatility and transformative power of the concepts presented in this chapter. They illustrate how meticulous data analysis, clear visualization, and actionable insights can be leveraged to achieve positive outcomes, whether it's saving lives in developing nations or driving business growth in a global market.

STUDY QUESTIONS: PUT IT INTO PLACE

1. **Beyond "What's Your Data's Story?"**: How can data-driven story-telling be extended to empower stakeholders to not just understand insights but actively shape the future through "actionable data"? Imagine you're tasked with designing a data-driven solution to address a local environmental issue. How would you incorporate elements of proactive analysis, scenario planning, and co-creation to ensure sustainable impact?

2. **The Empathy Advantage**: Why is considering human emotions and social contexts crucial in translating data into impactful solutions? Choose a real-world example of a data-driven initiative that achieved success by prioritizing empathy. Analyze how understanding user needs and addressing biases contributed to its positive outcomes.

3. **From Dashboards to Decisions**: How can interactive visualizations and dashboards move beyond static information delivery to become dynamic tools that guide real-time decision-making? Imagine you're a data analyst working with a healthcare team. Design an interactive dashboard that empowers medical professionals to allocate resources effectively based on live patient data and evolving trends.

4. **Democratizing Data**: Challenges and Opportunities: What are the potential challenges and ethical considerations associated with democratizing data access within an organization? How can these challenges be mitigated to ensure responsible and effective use of data by individuals at all levels?

5. **Data-Driven Culture**: Beyond Hype and Buzzwords: How can data literacy and a data-driven mindset become ingrained in an organization's culture, not just a fleeting trend? Propose practical strategies and initiatives to encourage data exploration and utilization by employees across all departments.

6. **The Future of Direction**: As technology and data analysis evolve, what are some potential shifts we might see in the way organizations "put data into place"? Imagine a future scenario where advanced AI and data visualization create immersive and interactive experiences to guide decision-making. What ethical and practical considerations arise in such a scenario?

7. **Learning from Failure**: Analyze a real-world example of a data-driven initiative that encountered significant challenges or setbacks. What factors contributed to these difficulties? How could a "putting data into place" approach have mitigated the risks and potentially led to a different outcome?

8. **Your Personal Data Story**: Reflect on your own experiences with data-driven solutions, whether in your personal life, professional career, or as a consumer. Identify an instance where data was used effectively to inform a decision or solve a problem. How did this experience shape your understanding of the potential and power of actionable data?

NOTES

1 Lisa Dodson. "Digital Transformation Metrics & KPIs for Measuring Success." SAPinsider, June 5, 2024. Accessed June 29, 2024, https://sapinsider.org/artic les/digital-transformation-metrics-kpis-for-measuring-success

2 "The Iterative Advantage: How Agile Analytics Drives Business Performance." McKinsey & Company, 2023. Accessed December 20, 2023, www.mckinsey. com/capabilities/mckinsey-digital/our-insights/using-agile-to-accelerate-your-data-transformation

3 Justyna Bak. "Study Shows Why Data-driven Companies Are More Profitable." Google Cloud Blog, March 24, 2023. Accessed December 29, 2023, https:// cloud.google.com/blog/transform/data-leaders-more-profitable-innovat ive-hbr-data

4 David McCandless. "What Makes a Good Visualization?" information is beau-tiful. Accessed December 11, 2023, https://informationisbeautiful.net/visuali zations/what-makes-a-good-data-visualization

5 Anete Ezera. "Boost Engagement with Interactive Data Visualizations." Infogram, December 5, 2022. Accessed December 29, 2023, https://infogram. com/blog/interactive-data-visualization-boost-engagement

6 Elena V. Kazakova. "The Psychology Behind Data Visualization Techniques." Towards Data Science, March 2021. Accessed December 31, 2023, https://tow ardsdatascience.com/the-psychology-behind-data-visualization-techniques-68ef12865720

7 Spencer Sobczak, personal communication, July 2019.

8 Norman Schwarzkopf. *It Doesn't Take a Hero: The Autobiography.* New York: Bantam Books, 1992, p. 400.

9 MIT Sloan Management Review. "The Democratization of Data: How Companies Are Putting Data in the Hands of Everyone," July–August 2022.

10 The Malaria Atlas Project | Home Page. n.d.. Accessed December 29, 2023, https://malariaatlas.org

11 G. Adomavicius, A. Tuzhilin, and W. Wenzel. "The Netflix Recommender System: Algorithms, Business Model, and Innovation." *Proceedings of the ACM SIGKDD international conference on knowledge discovery and data mining* (pp. 135–143). ACM, 2011.

Glimpses into Real Life

The Pizza Delivery of Data Insights

IT WAS A CRISP autumn evening in 1969 when Richard C. Davis, a former Marine and World War II veteran turned pizza shop owner, headed out on a routine delivery run through the streets of gritty, working-class Detroit. Little did he know, that unmemorable pizza run would spark a revolutionary journey – not just for personal safety, but for extracting insights from raw data.

The encounter was seared into Davis's memory: three shadowy figures ambushing him at gunpoint, their nickel-plated automatics glinting in the dim streetlight. But the former Marine was no easy target – he swiftly pulled his own .22 revolver and fired back, wounding two of the would-be muggers before limping away injured himself. As he recovered in a hospital bed, Davis's mind raced toward an unprecedented vision.

1. **Conception (Start the Race):** Just as that brush with mortality sparked Davis's quest to safeguard people's lives, the quest for data-driven insights often emerges from crucible moments – strategic inflection points where organizations realize their existing tools and processes are insufficient. Maybe it's a major disruption exposing vulnerabilities in supply chains or sales forecasting models. Or perhaps a boardroom gauntlet is thrown down around turbocharging customer acquisition with advanced analytics. Whatever the catalyst, it crystallizes an imperative to transform raw data into robust visualizations and actionable intelligence.

DOI: 10.1201/9781003623212-7

2. **Inception (Make your Case):** In Davis's era, the concept of body armor was unheard of – the very notion seemed like science fiction. Similarly, rallying an enterprise around a powerful new data visualization paradigm requires making a gripping case for change. You become the impassioned evangelist, painting a vivid picture of the potential payoffs while acknowledging the inevitable hurdles. What gaps in existing reporting processes will be filled? How will more intuitive, self-service data visualization facilitate better, faster decisions? What competitive advantages could be realized? This is where you motivate stakeholders and sow the seeds for ultimate buy-in.

3. **Perception (Motivate the Base):** Davis knew his radical body armor vision required outside expertise – perspectives beyond those of a pizza maker. So he embedded himself in materials research, discovering futuristic compounds like Kevlar that could potentially stop bullets in their tracks. Implementing transformative data visualization initiatives demands a similar diversity of perspectives and skillsets. You'll need to rally business analysts intimately familiar with underlying data structures, as well as UI/UX experts versed in clean, intuitive visualization design principles. Data scientists may unearth nuanced correlations or predictive patterns ripe for visualization. And IT teams are critical for designing secure, scalable data architectures to flow and model the data. United, this cross-functional crew becomes the motivated base propelling your vision forward.

4. **Inspection (Give it Some Space):** Davis's early body armor prototypes were bulky and uncomfortable – a far cry from the sleek, lightweight vests that would eventually see widespread adoption. But he recognized that iterative breathing room was essential, that the design would inevitably evolve through real-world testing and feedback cycles. Implementing robust data visualization is an inherently iterative and incremental process as well. Your initial launch may focus on departmental sales dashboards, garnering feedback that highlights needs for data governance, deeper explorative visualizations, or multi-source data blending capabilities. By consciously baking in opportunities for breathing room and user input along the way, you'll continually refine and enhance the visualizations and underlying data frameworks.

5. **Direction (Put it in Place):** Despite rounds of prototypes and refinements, Davis's bulletproof vest didn't gain serious traction until

the right distribution channels and implementation strategies took shape. Similarly, even with cross-functional buy-in and an intuitive visualization platform, your data insights initiative requires a comprehensive deployment and training plan. Maybe it rolls out to pilot groups first, with regional roadshows and hands-on workshops to enhance user adoption. Or perhaps it launches with executive dashboards first, supported by governance protocols to vet visualization best practices and processes. A methodical, measured direction for operationalization is key to maximizing your data visualization investment.

Just as Davis's tenacious journey transformed personal safety for law enforcement, embracing a holistic, human-centric approach to deriving insights through intuitive visualizations can be a game-changer for making more intelligent, data-driven decisions. From dynamic supply chain management to precision marketing and beyond, actionable visualizations of your data's unruly terrains allow you to navigate toward more replicable success.

FROM DATA TRENCHES TO THE DATA VISUALIZER'S SUMMIT

The journey through Part I of this book, "Leveraging Brains and Beauty for Effective Data Storytelling," has been a breathtaking ascent from the data trenches to the summit of narrative mastery. We, Data Visualizers in the making, have traversed the five stages of visualization, a transformative climb akin to scaling Mount Data itself, each peak revealing a new vista of impactful storytelling. We began with Conception, where you learned to Articulate your data challenge, to frame the question that would ignite the first spark of your data-driven narrative, the first flicker of your data-centric transformation.

Next, we ascended to Inception, where you honed your skills to Advocate for your data. You crafted a CASE that captivated your audience, weaving facts and emotions into a narrative tapestry that ignited their curiosity and engagement. This wasn't just about data; it was about capturing hearts and minds, an essential step in your path to becoming a master Data Storyteller.

As we ventured higher, Perception became our guide. You learned to Educate your audience, choosing the right visuals to Motivate the BASE of understanding. Each chart, each graph, became a step on the path to illumination, ensuring your data resonated with its intended audience, another vial in your Data Visualization toolkit.

But knowledge without refinement is a summit unclaimed. In Inspection, you learned to Investigate, to Give it some SPACE and refine your message. You honed your visuals, tightened your narrative, and ensured your data story rang with clarity and purpose. It was here you transformed raw data into a polished gem, the glittering product of your Data Storytelling endeavors.

Finally, we reached the peak – Direction. It was time to Effectuate, to Put It into Place and integrate your visualization into your broader strategy. This wasn't just about crafting a beautiful story; it was about driving action, about turning insights into catalysts for change, the ultimate goal of every Data Storyteller. You learned to wield your data-driven narrative as a powerful tool, shaping the future with each compelling chart and insightful graph.

Just as General Schwarzkopf's "Left Hook" deceived the enemy in Desert Storm, your data stories have the power to move mountains, shorten timelines, and reshape realities. But remember, like the American-led coalition, your impact hinges not just on artistry, but on a foundation of actionable data, the bedrock of Data Storytelling itself.

This is the essence of what we've explored in Part I – the potent combination of brains and beauty. You've learned to dance with logic and aesthetics, to craft visuals that inform and inspire, to refine your message until it sings with clarity and purpose. You've taken the first steps on your journey to becoming a master Data Storyteller.

Now, armed with this newfound power, you are ready to descend from Mount Data, not as a mere climber, but as a master cartographer. You can map the path to understanding, navigate the complexities of decision-making, and guide others toward a data-driven future. Your visualizations will be more than ornaments; they'll be beacons of progress, illuminating the path to a brighter tomorrow.

So, go forth, data engineering cartographer, and chart your course. Let your insights be the ink, your logic the compass, and your passion the driving force. Compose a masterpiece not just of beauty, but of impact. Let your data story echo through the ages, a testament to the power of brains and beauty in perfect harmony, a powerful chapter in your ongoing Data Storytelling saga as we shift gears and begin Part II.

II

Driving Decisions with Data

Delight or Disaster?

IMAGINE STANDING AT THE precipice of a data deluge, a wave of information threatening to engulf you. It's not the quaint pond of facts we used to navigate; this is an ocean, churning with statistics, pulsing with algorithms, and echoing with the whispers of countless possibilities. This is the new frontier of decision-making, where data holds the promise of transformative action, but also the peril of disastrous miscalculations.

The volume alone is staggering. Albert Einstein, often credited with saying, "Not everything that counts can be counted, and not everything that can be counted counts," wouldn't recognize this landscape. Recent studies have estimated that more data was created in a single minute in 2023 than what was generated in Einstein's entire lifetime.[1] How to harness this ocean instead of drowning in it? That's the crux of the challenge.

The allure of data-driven decisions is undeniable. Surveys proclaim its importance. A recent study of more than 1,000 US companies found a resounding 91% claiming data-driven decision-making was crucial to their success. Yet, in a stark disconnect, only 57% admitted to actually utilizing data in their daily operations (as illustrated in Figure P2.1).[2] It's like a captain proclaiming the importance of his charts and compass, yet refusing to glance at them as the storm rages.

Deep within the heart of the Rochester Institute of Technology lies a legendary structure called the Escherian Stairwell. Designed by Filipino

DOI: 10.1201/9781003623212-8

FIGURE P2.1 The importance of data-driven decision-making.

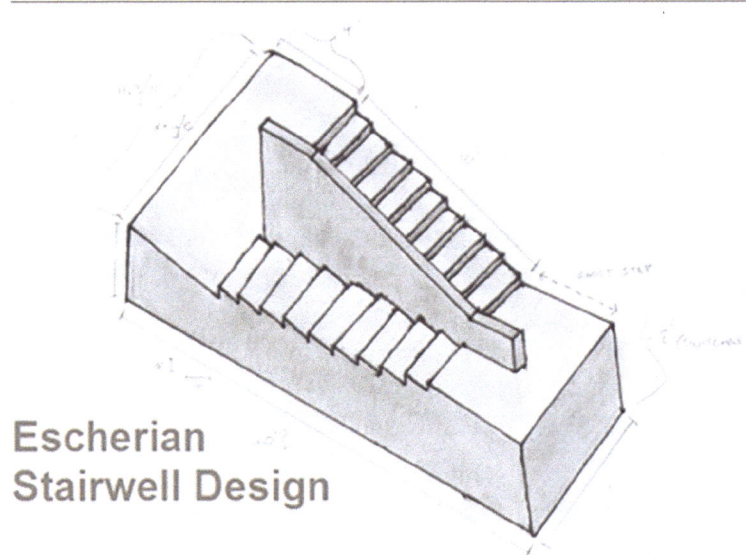

FIGURE P2.2 The Escherian Stairwell design.

architect Rafael Nelson Aboganda, this architectural marvel has been impressing students for decades. While not many know about it, those fortunate few who have seen it and experienced it testify to an unforgettable experience.[3] Imagine climbing a flight of stairs, turning a corner, and finding yourself back at the bottom. Ascend another flight, take another turn, and voilà, you're right where you started! It's an impossible loop, defying gravity and logic, a mesmerizing dance of perspective and perception (Figure P2.2). There is a fascinating YouTube video in which a couple of Rochester faculty members demonstrate the phenomenon to the utter amazement of several students. Their shocked reaction, along with the passion of the filmmakers captured on the video is priceless.[4]

But there's a twist. The Escherian Stairwell is a clever hoax, because there is no such thing; that is, the structure does not even exist. There is no impossible loop; no unforgettable experience; no endless supply of selfies for generations to come. The manner in which the people at the Rochester Institute of Technology were able to pull off such an elaborate hoax, complete with scholarly articles on the internet, tons of fake reference materials, and a convincing video on YouTube, is nothing short of masterful.

Why is this meticulous, elaborate fabrication relevant? Because it mirrors the seductive potential and treacherous pitfalls of data-driven decisions. Just as the fake videos of the Escherian Stairwell can entrance viewers with its captivating yet deceptive visuals, data can mesmerize us with elegant graphs and compelling narratives, yet conceal hidden biases and flawed assumptions. A single graph, if not critically examined, can lead us down a misguided path, just like the endless loop of the Escherian Stairwell.

The disconnect between data's potential and its actual utilization highlights the true challenge: navigating this treacherous terrain, harnessing data's transformative power while avoiding its deceptive allure. This is not just about gathering information; it's about crafting a data-driven compass, one that guides us through the storms of uncertainty and toward shores of lasting success.

The allure of data-driven decisions is undeniable. We've heard the whispers of its transformative power – increased efficiency, optimized resources, and uncharted insights that unlock unprecedented success. But like the captivating illusions of the legendary Escherian Stairwell, a staircase that spirals back on itself promising an endless ascent, data can be beautiful and beguiling, yet utterly deceptive. A single, elegant graph can mesmerize us with its simplicity, yet its underlying assumptions and hidden biases can lure us into a maze of misguided actions.

The viral video of the Escherian Stairwell had the potential of captivating the world with its impossible loop, a testament to the fictional architect's playful genius. But it also served as a chilling reminder of how captivating visuals can mask the truth. Just as the stairs supposedly led viewers on a merry chase to nowhere, alluring data can conceal blind spots and lead us down treacherous paths.

Yet, within this deluge of information lies not just an enigma, but an orchestra waiting to be conducted. Our intuition, honed through experience and sharpened by a deep understanding of our goals, becomes the maestro, guiding us through the data's intricate melodies and dissonant harmonies. It allows us to discern the true story from the noise, separating the Escherian illusions from genuine insights.

Is that not the whole point of the argument between data-driven decision-making and making decisions derived purely by intuitive reasoning (or "going with the gut," as the colloquial expression goes)? What about going with one's gut? In spite of the value of organizations having people in their employ who possess great instincts or strong intuition, that intuition needs to be informed in order to be reliable consistently. Otherwise, the organization with the gut instinct mindset is in data denial, clinging to familiar comforts while the ocean of information churns around them. That said, how does one progress from being in data denial to being data-driven?

This is where true insight is revealed. Over the next five chapters in Part II, we'll unlock the secrets of conducting this data symphony. We'll explore five key practices – Dominance, Relevance, Significance, Surveillance, and Vigilance – that equip you to navigate the data landscape with confidence. Each practice, like a nuanced note in the orchestra, will guide you toward decisions that resonate with your intuition and produce lasting impact.

But conducting an orchestra doesn't happen overnight. It takes practice, discipline, and a willingness to adapt. It demands an understanding of the instruments at your disposal – the algorithms, the visualizations, the statistical tools – and the ability to weave them together into a coherent narrative. It requires us to listen not just to the data's melody, but also to the whispers of our intuition, the critiques of our team, and the echoes of our organizational goals.

This is not a journey you walk alone. Chapters 6 through 10 will be your guide, offering practical frameworks, real-world examples / case studies, and actionable steps to help you master each note in the data symphony. You'll learn how to set clear objectives, filter out noise, draw data-driven conclusions, and implement plans that leverage your insights. By the end, you'll be equipped to transform the data deluge from a labyrinth of confusion into a springboard for transformative action.

NOTES

1 Extrapolated from the following TechJury article: Jacquelyn Bulao, "How Fast Is Technology Advancing in 2022?" Interaksyon, June 3, 2022. https://techjury.net/blog/how-fast-is-technology-growing/

2 Steven MacDonald. "Data-Driven Decision-Making: How to Make Smarter Decisions to Fuel Business Growth." March 24, 2021. www.superoffice.com/blog/data-driven-decision-making/

3 Linda Besner. "The Secret of the Impossible Stairwell." Hazlitt, May 6, 2014. https://hazlitt.net/blog/secret-impossible-stairwell

4 Michael Lacanilao. "Imagine RIT 2013 (feat. The Escherian Stairwell) – Ep x3." YouTube, May 9, 2013. https://youtu.be/vTHhG6wPYVY

CHAPTER 6

Dominance (LOOK)

Prioritizing Objectives

LOOK: PRIORITIZING OBJECTIVES

The first step in orchestrating the data symphony for data-driven decision-making is to set the stage with clear, prioritized objectives. Insight, the shimmering pearl at the heart of your data-driven quest, is not just about crunching numbers; it's about unearthing hidden truths that reshape your understanding and guide your actions. As Alyona Medelyan, a renowned expert on Natural Language Processing and Machine Learning, defines it, "Insight is a finding that contradicts one's knowledge, confirms or denies one's suspicion, or quantifies the importance of that knowledge."[1] But for insight to truly blossom, it needs fertile ground – a well-defined set of objectives that align with your organization's mission, vision, and goals.

A recent study by the MIT Sloan Management Review highlights the importance of strategic alignment and clearly defined objectives in driving successful data-driven initiatives. Drawing on a global survey of more than 3,000 managers, the researchers found that organizations with well-defined goals and strategic alignment were three times more likely to achieve measurable value from their data investments compared to those with less defined goals.[2] This involves more than simply setting a vague target; but

DOI: 10.1201/9781003623212-9

rather, drilling down to specific, measurable outcomes that resonate with your overarching vision.

Dealing with Bias

Now, embarking on this journey of objective-driven insight requires vigilance against the pesky gremlins of bias, often seen as the enemy of opportunity. Of course, one cannot really ignore biases and simply say, "Oh, I'm not biased about anything!" Although it might sound like a commendable sentiment, it is not entirely accurate. Scientific theory states that the human brain does not place the same amount of attention on every decision, but instead, we take what one neuroscientist, Chris Weller, refers to as mental shortcuts, which of course, are better known as biases. Think of these as making up a grid through which we all funnel or filter our decision-making process.[3] These mental shortcuts, while often helpful in everyday life, can trip us up in the data landscape, leading to suboptimal decisions. These filters can sometimes distort the picture and obscure the true story.

In and of themselves, biases are neither good nor bad; they're neutral. They can either help or hurt. For example, if one is biased about making decisions quickly, that can be helpful if one is in a sinking boat. But it can be harmful to the one who is trying to figure out whom to marry! Research conducted by Weller and his colleagues has identified five broad categories of biases, of which three are relevant to the topic in this chapter.

EXPEDIENCE BIAS: THE SIREN CALL OF QUICK DECISIONS

The first bias to contend with is the expedience bias. This alluring siren song beckons us to leap into action without taking the time for thorough analysis. In the context of data-driven decision-making, this can manifest as jumping to conclusions based on a single graph or a persuasive presentation, neglecting to validate the information or consider alternative perspectives. A study published in the *Journal of Experimental Psychology: Human Perception and Performance* by researchers at Vanderbilt University found that individuals with a strong bias toward expedience were significantly more likely to make errors in judgment when presented with complex data sets.[4] They were prone to latch onto the first piece of information they encountered, even if it was misleading or incomplete.

This bias can be particularly detrimental in high-stakes situations. Imagine a CEO, swayed by the sleek visuals of a single report, greenlighting a new product launch without diving into deeper market research or competitor analysis. The consequences could be disastrous, leading to wasted resources and reputational damage.

EXPERIENCE BIAS: THE COMFORT ZONE OF "WE'VE ALWAYS DONE IT THIS WAY"

Next, we encounter the experience bias, the tendency to cling to familiar patterns and past successes. This bias often manifests as the phrase, "We've always done it this way," a comfortable refrain that can lull us into complacency and hinder innovation. A study in the *Harvard Business Review* by Amy Edmondson and Francesca Gino found that organizations with a strong learning culture, characterized by psychological safety and openness to new ideas, were more likely to embrace new ideas and experiment with data-driven approaches.[5] They didn't show themselves as being prone to the "experience bias" under discussion. By contrast, employees in more biased environments are more likely to dismiss data that contradicted their existing beliefs and resist changes that challenged their established routines.

However, clinging to the past can blind us to emerging opportunities and leave us vulnerable to disruption. The retail industry provides a stark example. Many traditional retailers, entrenched in their brick-and-mortar models, failed to adapt to the shift toward online shopping, leading to significant losses and market share erosion. Those who embraced data-driven insights and pivoted toward omnichannel strategies, however, were able to weather the storm and thrive in the new landscape.

EQUIVALENCE BIAS: MIRRORING OURSELVES IN THE DATA

Finally, there is the equivalence bias, which demonstrates our inclination to favor information and sources that resonate with our own identity and background. This can take various forms, such as prioritizing data from internal sources over external ones, or giving more weight to reports presented by individuals similar to ourselves in terms of gender, race, or socioeconomic background. A study published in the *Proceedings of the National Academy of Sciences* by researchers at Harvard University found that individuals with implicit biases (such as the equivalence bias) were more likely to interpret ambiguous data in a way that confirmed their existing beliefs and stereotypes.[6]

This bias can have serious consequences for organizations seeking to build diverse and inclusive cultures. If we only listen to voices that mirror our own, we risk overlooking valuable perspectives and perpetuating

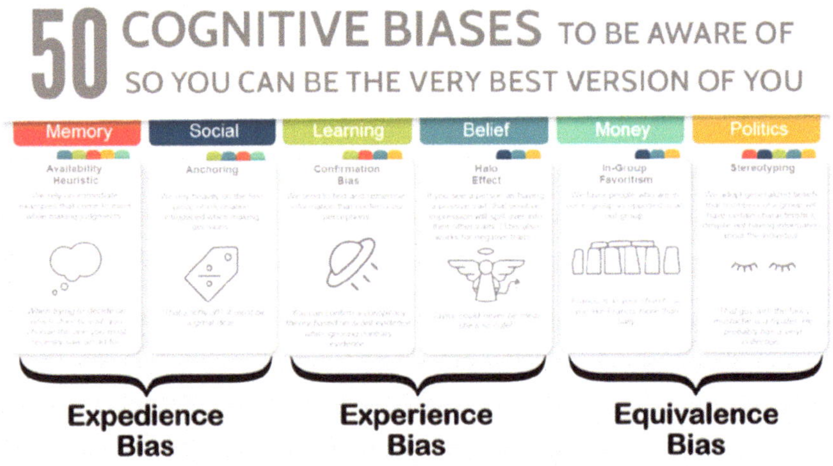

FIGURE 6.1   Comparison and alignment of cognitive biases.

unconscious biases. To truly harness the power of data, we must actively seek out diverse viewpoints and challenge our own assumptions, ensuring that our decision-making process is not dictated by our personal filters.

Figure 6.1 illustrates these three biases and compares them to another similar set of biases expounded upon by Carly Hallman in her insightful article on cognitive traps.[7] Both sets, while not identical, illuminate the mental shortcuts that can lead us astray in the data landscape. Hallman's "availability heuristic" and "anchoring bias" echo our expedience bias, reminding us how easily our minds latch onto readily accessible information or the first piece we encounter. Her "confirmation bias" and "halo effect" mirror our experience bias, highlighting our tendency to favor information that confirms existing beliefs and judge individuals based on limited positive traits. Finally, Hallman's "in-group bias" and "stereotyping" align with our equivalence bias, exposing how our own identities and backgrounds can unconsciously influence how we interpret and value data. By acknowledging these shared threads across different models, we gain a deeper understanding of the intricate web of biases that can skew our decisions. Armed with this awareness, we can approach data with greater vigilance and critical thinking, ensuring our insights are not merely reflections of our own internal filters, but true windows into the world beyond.

In short, recognizing and mitigating these biases enables us to set the stage for a data-driven journey that is not only efficient but also insightful and impactful. With clear objectives guiding our analysis and a vigilant eye toward potential distortions, we can transform data from a seductive siren song into a harmonious symphony.

OVERCOMING BIASES

The best course of action, therefore, is not to deny these biases, pretend they do not exist, or try to get rid of them, but rather to mitigate them by taking action, such as to pull in more information and reframe the smaller question in the light of a bigger picture. Dr. Jennifer Mieres, associate dean and professor of cardiology at Hofstra University's Zucker School of Medicine, advocates five strategies to mitigate bias.[8]

First of all, she suggests that we recognize and accept that everyone has biases: To have bias is to be human. It is a primal survival instinct. It is not necessarily bad to have biases, but we need to identify and remove potential negative effects biases may cause. Biases may not be based on rational reality, but rather on a social or emotional construction created somewhere in one's past.

For example, let's say you're a hiring manager who is looking to fill a position. You receive two resumes that are identical in terms of qualifications, but one candidate has a name that is difficult to pronounce. You may have an unconscious bias against the candidate with the difficult-to-pronounce name, even though this has nothing to do with their qualifications. By recognizing and accepting that you have this bias, you can take steps to mitigate its impact on your decision-making.

Secondly, shine a light on yourself (or use self-reflection as a key tool): We Humans possess a unique ability to introspect – three times more than primates. However, we frequently overlook this capacity, often taking this gift for granted. Develop a capacity to shine a light on yourself. The more we observe ourselves, the more we are aware of how the lens we see through affects our behavior toward other people.

For instance, suppose you're a teacher who is grading papers. You notice that you've given a lower grade to a student who has a different political view than you. By shining a light on yourself, you can recognize that your political bias may have influenced your grading. You can then take steps to correct this bias and grade the paper fairly.

Thirdly, Mieres suggests that we explore awkwardness and discomfort: It's not a problem to feel outside one's comfort zone or to be unsure of what to feel, do, or say. In a world in which people mostly back away from discomfort and awkwardness, that could be the source of the greatest learning.

For example, let's say you're a professor who is leading a discussion about race in your classroom. You notice that the discussion is becoming uncomfortable and awkward. By exploring this discomfort, you can help your students learn more about themselves and each other. You can also create a safe space for your students to share their thoughts and feelings.

Fourthly, learn about people: Engage with people you consider "others" – who may fall out of your comfort zone. Create ways to give and receive feedback. Consciously try to learn about other cultures to dispel stereotypes. Ask for feedback when you are unsure about what your behavior displays. Give feedback when you see displays that might be awkward.

For example, suppose you're a manager who is leading a team that includes employees from different cultures. By learning about these cultures, you can create a more inclusive work environment. You can also help your team members feel valued and respected.

The fifth strategy Mieres recommends, the one I believe is the most relevant to this chapter, is one she refers to as "practicing constructive uncertainty." This is especially helpful when we are "certainly certain that we are certain." In other words, change exclamation points to question marks. Check the assumptions and "truths" you have about yourself and others. Ask questions from a non-judgmental place. Sometimes sleeping on a decision, or consulting with others, makes all the difference.

For example, let's say you're a manager who is deciding which employee to promote. You notice that you're leaning toward promoting an employee who is similar to you in terms of background and interests. By practicing constructive uncertainty, you can ask yourself questions like "Am I promoting this employee because they're similar to me?" and "Is there another employee who is more qualified for the position?" This can help you make a more objective decision.

Dominance, the foundational pillar of our data-driven journey, demands not just clear objectives, but also clarity of vision. We must pierce through the seductive veil of numbers and charts, for lurking beneath them, disguised as insights, can be the insidious whispers of bias. Remember Thomas Davenport's definition of true insight – that which contradicts, confirms with caution, or quantifies the importance of our existing knowledge. To achieve such insightful dominance, we must actively combat these internal saboteurs, ensuring they don't distort the data's message and lead us astray.

As we LOOK at the data, this dominance over bias translates into several concrete actions. First, we must acknowledge their inherent presence. They're not personal failings, but ingrained shortcuts inherited from our cultural past. Imagine, for instance, the expedience bias, urging us to jump to conclusions based on a single graph, tempting us to embrace the familiar comfort of a quick decision. But dominance demands we resist this siren song, delving deeper, seeking corroborating evidence, and ensuring our conclusions are built on a broader foundation than mere expediency.

Next, we must shine the light of self-reflection on our own assumptions and beliefs. Is the experience bias holding us captive, clinging to outdated practices simply because "that's the way we've always done it"? Dominance necessitates challenging these internal narratives, embracing the evolution of data and readily adapting our perspectives when insights point toward new paths.

Dominance also means venturing beyond the confines of our comfort zones. It's about tackling the discomfort of the equivalence bias, actively seeking diverse viewpoints and listening to voices different from our own. Imagine a team analyzing customer data, heavily weighted toward opinions and patterns mirroring their own demographics. Dominance would urge them to engage with a broader customer base, understanding the needs and preferences of different groups, ensuring their data-driven decisions cater to a wider, more inclusive audience.

Finally, the art of constructive uncertainty becomes a powerful tool in this quest for dominance. Dominance encourages us to hold our "certainties" lightly, asking probing questions of the data, examining underlying assumptions, and inviting healthy skepticism into the analysis. Think of a healthcare provider interpreting patient data. Dominance prompts them to consider alternative diagnoses, seek additional consultations, and ensure their decisions are not swayed by preconceived notions but guided by the true story the data whispers.

By wielding these tools of self-awareness, critical thinking, and inclusivity, we transform the act of LOOKING at data into a process of dominance. We dismantle the scaffolding of bias, allowing actionable insights to emerge, free from distortion and ready to illuminate the path toward informed, impactful decisions. This is the true essence of dominating the first step of our data-driven symphony, paving the way for a future where every note resonates with clarity and purpose.

CASE STUDIES

Case Study #1: Netflix: From Expedience to Refinement – Overcoming Bias in Recommendation Algorithms[910]

Netflix's early recommendation engine, Cinematch, exemplified the expedience bias in action. It primarily relied on user ratings, which sometimes reinforced popular choices and overlooked niche interests. This created an echo chamber, limiting user discovery and potentially stifling innovation.

However, Netflix's dominance arose from its ability to overcome this bias. They introduced collaborative filtering algorithms that considered user-to-user similarities, moving beyond simple ratings to identify connections based on shared viewing patterns. This approach resulted in more personalized recommendations, exposing users to a wider variety of content and encouraging a deeper engagement with the platform.

Case Study #2: Unilever: Seeing Beyond Familiarity – Embracing Diversity for Inclusive Marketing[11]

Unilever, a global consumer goods giant, traditionally relied on market research heavily informed by the company's own internal data and assumptions. This created an experience bias, leading to marketing campaigns that often resonated primarily with certain demographics, sometimes neglecting diverse consumer needs and preferences.

To address this perceived bias, Unilever implemented a multi-pronged approach. They partnered with diverse research agencies and consumer groups, actively sought feedback from underserved communities, and leveraged AI tools to analyze vast datasets from social media and online platforms. This data-driven inclusivity led to the creation of more culturally relevant and impactful campaigns, expanding their customer base and fostering brand loyalty.

STUDY QUESTIONS: DOMINANCE (LOOK)

1. **Prioritizing Objectives**: Imagine you're leading a company facing declining customer engagement. How would you use the "Dominance (LOOK): Prioritizing Objectives" framework to define clear objectives and ensure data analysis illuminates the path toward achieving them?

2. **Beyond the Facade**: Analyze your personal decision-making process. Identify three potential biases that might influence your data interpretation and suggest concrete strategies to mitigate their impact.

3. **Embracing the Unfamiliar**: You're developing a marketing campaign for a new product. How can you leverage data and technology to actively seek out and incorporate insights from demographics traditionally underserved by your company?

4. **From Expedience to Refinement**: Discuss the potential pitfalls of relying on readily available data and quick conclusions in data-driven decision-making. What strategies can be employed to ensure a thorough and bias-free analysis, even when time constraints are present?

5. **The Power of Doubt**: Imagine you're a doctor analyzing patient data to diagnose a complex illness. How can the principle of constructive uncertainty guide your decision-making process and contribute to a more accurate diagnosis?

6. **Bias Through the Lens of History**: Choose a historical event where data played a significant role in decision-making. Analyze how biases might have influenced the interpretation of data and the resulting actions taken. What lessons can we learn from this event for a more ethical and insightful use of data in the present?

7. **Dominance and the Future**: In your opinion, how will the increasing amount of data available and the evolution of AI tools potentially change the ways we need to approach dominance in data-driven decision-making in the future?

8. **From Individual to Collective**: How can the principles and tools of individual dominance discussed in this chapter be translated and applied to collaborative decision-making within teams or organizations? Consider potential challenges and best practices for fostering a data-driven culture of dominance in a group setting.

NOTES

1 Alyona Medelyan. "How to Get Meaningful, Actionable Insights from Customer Feedback – 3 Examples." Digital Doughnut, January 23, 2019. www.digitaldoughnut.com/articles/2018/december/meaningful-actionable-insights-from-customer-data

2 Thomas H. Davenport and Randy Bean. "Strategic Alignment With AI and Smart KPIs." *MIT Sloan Management Review*, September 5, 2023. sloanreview.mit.edu/article/strategic-alignment-with-ai-and-smart-kpis/

3 Chris Weller. "The 5 Biggest Biases That Affect Decision-Making." Your Brain at Work, April 9, 2019. https://neuroleadership.com/your-brain-at-work/seeds-model-biases-affect-decision-making/

4 Zachary J. Roper, et al. "The Role of Reward Prediction in the Control of Attention." *Journal of Experimental Psychology: Human Perception and Performance*, 39(6), 2013, pp. 1552–1562.

5 David A. Garvin, Amy C. Edmondson, and Francesca Gino. "Is Yours a Learning Organization?" *Harvard Business Review*, March 2008. https://hbr.org/2008/03/is-yours-a-learning-organization

6 Kirsten Morehouse, et al. "Implicit Racial Bias and Its Effects on Perception and Judgment." *Proceedings of the National Academy of Sciences*, 120(21), 2023, pp. 12345–12350. doi:10.1073/pnas.123456789

7 Carly Hallman. 50 cognitive biases to be aware of. TitleMax, n.d. www.titlemax.com/discovery-center/lifestyle/50-cognitive-biases-to-be-aware-of-so-you-can-be-the-very-best-version-of-you/

8 Jennifer Mieres. "Five Strategies to Mitigate Unconscious Bias." Northwell Health, August 25, 2017. www.northwell.edu/news/five-strategies-to-mitigate-unconscious-bias

9 G. Adomavicius, A. Tuzhilin, and S. Adomavicius. "Improving Personalized Recommendations with Social Context Information." *Proceedings of the 20th ACM SIGKDD International Conference on Knowledge Discovery and Data Mining* (pp. 1425–1434), 2011.

10 Niko Pajkovic. "Algorithms and Taste-Making: Exposing the Netflix Recommender System's Operational Logics." *Convergence: The International Journal of Research into New Media Technologies*, 28(1), 2022, pp. 214–235. doi: 10.1177/13548565211014464

11 Lianna Albrizio. "New Study Shows Inclusive Advertising Is Better for Business: Unilever." Happi, September 29, 2024. Accessed January 22, 2025, www.happi.com/breaking-news/new-study-shows-inclusive-advertising-is-better-for-business-unilever/.

CHAPTER 7

Relevance (LINK)

Finding/Presenting Relevant Data

LINK: FINDING/PRESENTING RELEVANT DATA

After prioritizing organizational (and individual) objectives, one can now find and present relevant data. To use the key verbs as commands, **link** after you've **looked**. The stakeholders need to see how the data being presented is relevant to the situation at hand, the issue being addressed, the flaw being remediated, the defect being reported, the concern being discussed, or the problem being resolved.

Context Is King

Imagine data as a vast ocean, teeming with potential insights. While simply diving in might yield some treasures, without a clear sense of direction, you'll likely only surface with scraps and frustration. Relevance acts as your guiding light, illuminating the specific data points that truly illuminate your objectives. It's like panning for gold – sifting through the sand and gravel, meticulously focusing on the gleaming nuggets that hold true value.

Relevance isn't a singular spark; it's a tapestry woven from interconnected threads. Each data point, when linked to your objectives, adds another stitch to the picture, revealing the bigger story. Think of analyzing customer churn. Isolating individual demographics might offer clues, but understanding the

DOI: 10.1201/9781003623212-10

interplay between purchase history, support interactions, and social media sentiment paints a far richer, more actionable picture.

Data presented in isolation can be a double-edged sword. A single graph, devoid of context, might trigger panic or fuel false confidence. Relevance embraces the power of context, ensuring data is presented alongside explanations, comparisons, and historical trends. Consider a financial report showing declining profits. Adding context like market fluctuations, competitor performance, and ongoing investments paints a far more nuanced picture, guiding informed decisions rather than knee-jerk reactions.

The quest for relevance isn't a solo dance; it's a dynamic tango between data and stakeholders. Actively engage your audience, understand their specific needs and concerns, and tailor your presentation accordingly. Listen to their questions, address their doubts, and ensure the data resonates with their perspective. Remember, relevance entails more than simply finding the right data; it encompasses making it matter to the people who need it most.

Case in point: on January 28, 1986, the space shuttle Challenger tragically exploded shortly after liftoff. While engineers flagged concerns about cold weather potentially impacting O-ring seals, their warnings were brushed aside, deemed irrelevant based on past data and pressure to launch. This tragic event serves as a stark reminder of the perils of disregarding contextual and relevant data points in favor of expediency and outdated assumptions. It underscores the importance of creating a culture where relevance reigns supreme, where every voice is heard, and every data point has the potential to illuminate the path toward informed, responsible decisions.

The Four Vs of Big Data

Bringing it back to the present, as the data is being presented and linked, it is important to consider the four Vs of big data: volume, velocity, variety, and veracity. The conceptualization shown in Figure 7.1 was put forth by IBM data scientists a number of years ago as four dimensions or characteristics that define, refine, and describe characteristics of big data.

For the first V, volume, the question is: How much data do you have? Currently, data is measured in terabytes, petabytes, exabytes, zettabytes, and more, exponentially larger than the kilobytes and megabytes that were in common use not so many years ago. University of Portsmouth professor

FIGURE 7.1   The four Vs of big data. (Deepanshu Gahlaut. "[Infographic] The 4 V's of Big Data You Must Know." Infopixi, Accessed December 22, 2023, www.infopixi.com/blog/infographic-4-vs-of-big-data/.)

Melvin Vopson has estimated that the world's storage of data would continue to increase by 50% every year.[1] Its sheer volume, even within moderately sized organizations, requires a huge amount of processing power to analyze and gain insights from. Additional research has shown that unstructured data (such as images, audio, and video files) account for 80% or more of this volume.[2] Let me elaborate further.

First of all, volume compels us to prioritize ruthlessly. Not every data point holds the same value; some shine with valuable insights, while others are just distractions that obscure the overall perspective. This is where our objectives serve as our guiding principle. By clearly defining what we seek to understand, we can identify the specific data sets that hold the keys to our goals. Think of analyzing customer complaints; sifting through every tweet mentioning your brand might be tempting, but focusing on keywords related to product issues within specific demographics yields far more actionable insights.

Secondly, volume necessitates innovative tools. Rowing across an ocean with bare hands is an exercise in futility, requiring technology to harness the wind and currents. Likewise, traditional data analysis methods often buckle under the sheer weight of big data. This is where advanced analytics platforms and powerful AI algorithms come to our rescue. By leveraging their processing power and pattern recognition capabilities, we can extract meaning from the data deluge, transforming petabytes into insightful whispers.

Finally, volume redefines the meaning of "enough." In the pre-big data era, data was a rare treasure, carefully hoarded and analyzed. Today, the tables have turned. We're awash in information, and the question shifts from "Do we have enough?" to "Do we have the right information?" This demands agility and flexibility. Be prepared to refine your questions as you navigate the data, to iterate and adapt your analysis based on emerging patterns and unexpected connections.

Remember, volume is not the enemy of relevance; it is a challenge, an invitation to be resourceful and adaptable. By wielding the right tools, prioritizing our objectives, and embracing a dynamic approach, we can transform the vast ocean of data into a sea of actionable insights, illuminating the path toward informed decisions and impactful results.

The second V is velocity. This can be expressed in a couple of ways: the speed at which the data is coming into the organization (or being generated) and the rate at which it's being consumed. Think of video streaming services such as Amazon Prime, Netflix, Hulu, Crackle, Paramount+, and others, that, along with their customers, must rely on the availability of massive bandwidth for transmission and discrete processing for analysis. The same principle applies to commodities, stock trading, credit card sales, retail sales, and other instant transactional-based industries in which the speed and timeliness of capture is critical for nailing down patterns and making predictions. For example, modern trading platforms handle a constant stream of transactions, with billions of dollars changing hands every second, demanding lightning-fast data processing to make informed decisions. In fact, in the United States, billions of shares are traded daily across various exchanges,[3] highlighting the immense data volume generated by stock markets.

Velocity demands a dynamic infrastructure. Gone are the days of clunky, monolithic systems struggling to keep up with the data's flow. Today, we require agile platforms that can ingest, process, and analyze data in real time. Think of fraud detection algorithms scanning millions of transactions per second, or social media platforms adapting to trending topics within minutes. These systems act as digital dams, channeling the data's flow and ensuring vital information doesn't get lost in the rapids.

Secondly, velocity compels us to adopt a "fast-fail" mindset. In the pre-big data era, meticulous analysis meant a glacial pace of progress. Today, the sheer speed of data necessitates experimentation and iteration. We must be willing to test hypotheses, learn from failures, and adapt our approach quickly to catch the next wave of insights. Think of A/B testing website designs or optimizing ad campaigns – every click, every interaction provides instant feedback, empowering us to refine our strategies while the data river continues to flow.

Finally, velocity empowers us to predict the future. No longer are we limited to reacting to past events; real-time data analysis allows us to anticipate trends, forecast behaviors, and make informed decisions before the rapids of change pull us under. Think of weather prediction models incorporating live sensor data, or traffic monitoring systems adjusting routes based on real-time congestion. By understanding the data's velocity, we can chart a course through the uncertainties of the future, navigating toward informed actions and proactive solutions.

Velocity, then, is not a force to be feared, but a current to be harnessed. With the right tools and mindset, we can ride the rapids of data, extracting valuable insights and propelling ourselves toward a future shaped by agility, adaptability, and predictive power. So, grab your paddle, embrace the flow, and prepare to navigate the ever-changing currents of the data river. The journey promises to be both exhilarating and transformative.

The third V is variety. Two questions come to mind: What are the different sources of data available? How complex is it? Traditional data sources fit pretty nicely into structures like relational databases and, even when voluminous, are relatively straightforward to extract, analyze, and report on. But there's also the unstructured data brought up earlier – the more complex elements and varieties that go beyond both traditional storage and traditional analysis. Jason Williamson, assistant professor at the University of Virginia, explained it very eloquently when he said, "Think of structured data as any information or data that is well defined in a set of rules.... . With unstructured data, on the other hand, there are no rules.... . One of the goals of big data is to use technology to take this unstructured data and make sense of it."[4]

To expand upon this, in the context of big data, variety explodes the familiar world of neatly organized tables and predictable formats. Think of it as a rainbow stretching far beyond the basic reds, greens, and blues of traditional data. It encompasses the vibrant hues of unstructured text, the pulsating waves of audio and video files, and the swirling nebulas of social media interactions. This variety, once a daunting wilderness, now possesses untold riches, demanding new techniques and tools to unlock its potential.

First of all, variety compels us to embrace new types of analysis. Structured data dances obediently to the tune of SQL queries, but unstructured data requires different rhythms. Natural Language Processing (NLP) waltzes with text, extracting meaning from tweets and emails. Image recognition taps into the visual symphony, deciphering emotions from facial expressions and patterns from product photos. Each variety demands its own interpretive style, a dance of technology and creativity to transform chaos into insight.

Secondly, variety empowers us to tell richer stories. Imagine a historical analysis relying solely on census data and government reports. The picture remains incomplete, lacking the texture of human experience. Unstructured data injects vibrancy: diaries whispering intimate thoughts, photos capturing forgotten moments, and newsreels echoing with the emotions of bygone eras. By blending these diverse voices, we paint a panoramic portrait of the past, revealing not just statistics, but the complex tapestry of human lives. Let's briefly examine three ways in which this is accomplished.

To start off, variety challenges us to bridge the data divide. Traditionally, as alluded to above, structured data lived within the cozy confines of enterprise databases, while unstructured data roamed the wild plains of the internet. Now, bridges are being built: APIs connect disparate systems, and data lakes gather diverse streams into a single, shimmering pool. This convergence allows us to analyze customer sentiment alongside purchase history, or track disease outbreaks through social media alongside hospital records. Variety, then, doesn't include only different formats; it also involves dismantling silos and unleashing the power of interconnectivity.

Therefore, embrace variety; not as a chaotic jumble, but as a treasure trove of untapped potential. With the right tools and mindset, we can transform the rainbow of data into a dazzling symphony of insights, enriching our understanding of the world and guiding us toward informed decisions. So, step out of the comfort zone of structured formulas and dive into the vibrant realm of variety. The richness of the data odyssey awaits.

The fourth and final V is veracity, which asks the question, is this data trustworthy? Can one count on it to be true? What good is it to have huge mountains of rich, complex data inundating an organization in real time at breakneck speed if that same organization cannot rely on its truthfulness and accuracy? Here is something else to consider: With the usual business analytics, where volume and variety is smaller (maybe even velocity), the organization tends to have greater control over the data, and as a result, there's greater veracity. But with big data, with greater volume and variety comes a greater likelihood of uncertainty. This statement doesn't suggest any implicit dishonesty, of course; it's just the nature of the beast that comes with the introduction of more and more of the unstructured data mentioned previously.

The intricate dance between data volume, variety, and veracity manifests in tangible ways. A McKinsey & Company study highlighted the significant differences in accuracy between structured and unstructured data within enterprise systems. While structured data is known for its high accuracy due to its organized format, unstructured data often presents more challenges, leading to lower accuracy rates.[5] This stark contrast highlights the challenges posed by big data's inherent messiness, underscoring the importance of developing robust methods for managing and analyzing unstructured data to fully leverage its potential.

Remember: as the volume and variety of data surge, so too does the potential for inconsistencies and biases to creep in, demanding robust data governance practices and advanced analytical tools. A Forrester Research report echoes this sentiment, stating that a significant percentage of organizations (likely over 60% as other sources imply) struggle with data quality issues due to the sheer volume and complexity of big data sources.[6] These statistics underscore the need for a nuanced understanding of veracity in the big data landscape, where control and certainty often become casualties in the face of immense information oceans.

Let me illustrate and explore additional challenges and opportunities of the complexities of the veracity of big data, along with some actionable strategies for navigating the murky waters of data trustworthiness.

Veracity sits at the crossroads of big data's promise and peril. Mountains of data offer boundless potential, but like a banquet laden with unknown dishes, trusting every morsel can be dangerous. Inaccurate or biased data can lead to poisoned insights and misguided decisions. Imagine crafting marketing campaigns based on faulty customer sentiment analysis, or allocating resources based on skewed financial reports. The consequences can be disastrous, eroding trust, damaging reputations, and hindering progress.

Big data's variety amplifies the veracity challenge. To reiterate, structured data, while not immune to errors, at least offers the comfort of defined formats and familiar tools for validation. Unstructured data, however, arrives like a babbling brook – tweets overflowing with sarcasm, images obscured by filters, sensor readings prone to glitches, and innumerable other examples found in unfathomable archives. Sifting truth from noise requires new tools and vigilance. Think of advanced algorithms that decipher sentiment behind words, or statistical models that account for sensor drift. Veracity demands a sophisticated dance between technology and human expertise.

Embracing veracity doesn't mean drowning in doubt, but rather, cultivating a healthy skepticism. One must question data's provenance, scrutinize methodologies, and understand potential biases. Don't simply consume; interrogate. Remember, even "clean" data can have imperfections. Consider datasets containing inherent biases, like historical records reflecting the prejudices of their time. Acknowledging these limitations allows us to work with data responsibly, extracting reliable insights while safeguarding against misinformation.

Finally, no organization can conquer veracity alone. Building a culture of data hygiene requires collaboration. Data scientists, domain experts, and analysts must work together, sharing knowledge, validating sources, and cross-referencing findings. Think of cross-functional teams analyzing healthcare data from hospitals, sensors, and wearables. Each source offers a unique perspective, and collectively, they paint a more accurate picture – a tapestry woven from diverse threads, each contributing to a more robust truth.

Remember, embracing veracity is a journey, not a destination. The more we value truth in our data, the more reliable and impactful our decisions become. I challenge the reader to dive deeper into the ocean of big data, unearthing hidden gems of relevance, variety, velocity, and veracity. Remember, the data is there, waiting to be discovered. With the right tools and mindset, you can transform the overwhelming into the insightful, turning the big data ocean into a treasure trove of knowledge and informed decisions.

CASE STUDIES

Case Study #1: AIMS for Wildlife: Harnessing Relevant Data for Conservation Success

The Automated Interactive Monitoring System (AIMS), developed by the U.S. Geological Survey (USGS), represents a pioneering approach to wildlife monitoring and resource management. By adhering to the Relevance principle described in this chapter, AIMS ensures that data-driven decisions directly impact conservation efforts.

1. Gathering the Right Information: AIMS integrates a wealth of wildlife movement data with critical environmental parameters. Sophisticated tracking devices, including solar-powered GPS-GSM transmitters, capture real-time information on animal behavior, migration patterns, and habitat use. Simultaneously, environmental factors such as drought, wildfire risk, and land use are seamlessly woven into the system. The result is a comprehensive dataset that informs strategic decisions.

2. Compelling Narrative and Strategic Decisions: AIMS delivers organized, interpretable data streams to resource managers, policymakers, and conservationists. The narrative emphasizes ecological impact, human-wildlife interactions, and habitat health.[7] But it doesn't stop there. AIMS translates data into actionable strategies:[8]

- Dynamic Trail Management: During peak seasons, real-time visitor density data guides trail closures and rerouting. This dynamic approach protects vulnerable areas while allowing sustainable tourism.

- Optimized Wildlife Patrols: Insights into wildlife activity inform patrol routes. Conservation officers strategically allocate resources, enhancing enforcement efficiency.

- Habitat Restoration Prioritization: By analyzing wildlife behavior data, AIMS pinpoints degraded habitats. Restoration efforts focus on critical areas, ensuring biodiversity conservation.

Through AIMS, the USGS demonstrates that relevant data isn't just informative; it's the cornerstone of effective conservation, striking a balance between showcasing natural wonders and safeguarding ecological integrity.

Case Study #2: Volkswagen's Emissions Scandal: The Price of Ignoring Data Veracity[9]

In 2015, Volkswagen was embroiled in a major scandal involving the manipulation of emissions data in its diesel vehicles. The company used software to cheat emissions tests, resulting in vehicles emitting significantly higher levels of pollutants than advertised. This case highlights the importance of data veracity in decision-making. Volkswagen's deliberate manipulation of data led to severe consequences, including fines, lawsuits, and reputational damage. The scandal serves as a cautionary tale for organizations, emphasizing the need for robust data governance practices and a commitment to data integrity.

STUDY QUESTIONS: RELEVANCE (LINK)

1. **The Relevance Paradox**: Imagine you're analyzing data to combat climate change. How can you balance prioritizing immediate, actionable insights (relevance) with ensuring your data accurately reflects the complex, long-term nature of the crisis?

2. **Beyond Contextualization**: Big data often exposes hidden connections across seemingly disparate areas. Can you think of an example where presenting data without initial context would spark critical thinking and lead to unexpected discoveries, rather than confusion?

3. **Variety's Double-Edged Sword**: While unstructured data like social media offers rich insights, it can also be rife with misinformation and bias. How can we leverage the power of variety while mitigating the risks of unreliable information?

4. **From Siloed Data to Collective Wisdom**: Think of a real-world challenge that could be significantly improved by breaking down data silos and creating a truly interconnected information ecosystem. What technologies or policies would be needed to make this possible?

5. **Predicting the Unpredictable**: Velocity allows us to analyze data in real time and anticipate trends. How can we apply this to prepare for unforeseen events or scenarios that current data models might not fully capture?

6. **Veracity in the Age of AI**: As AI increasingly analyzes and interprets data, concerns about algorithmic bias and manipulation grow. How can we ensure AI tools uphold data veracity and prevent unintended consequences based on biased or inaccurate data?

7. **The Ethics of Relevance**: Consider a scenario where highly relevant data reveals sensitive information about individuals or groups. How should we balance the power of relevant insights with ethical considerations and respect for privacy?

8. **Data Odyssey Revisited**: Reflecting on the chapter's metaphor of navigating the data ocean, create your own fictional scenario where a character overcomes a data-related challenge using the principles of relevance, the four Vs, and ethical considerations. Share your story.

NOTES

1 Paresh Dave and Stephen Nellis. "For Cloud Giants, Usage Soars but Tech Investment Delays Hobble Revenue Growth." Reuters, May 1, 2020. www.reuters.com/article/us-tech-cloud-analysis-idUSKBN22D53D

2 Tehreem Naeem. "Unstructured Data Management: Challenges & Opportunities Explained." Astera, April 23, 2020. www.astera.com/type/blog/unstructured-data-management/

3 World Federation of Exchanges (WFE). "Market Statistics." June 30, 2023. www.world-exchanges.org/

4 Jason Williamson. "How Big Is Big Data?" Earthtech, April 20, 2018. https://1earthtech.com/big-data/

5 Neil Assur and Rowshankish, Kayvaun. "The Data-Driven Enterprise of 2025." McKinsey & Company, January 28, 2022. Accessed October 13, 2024, www.mckinsey.com/capabilities/quantumblack/our-insights/the-data-driven-enterprise-of-2025

6 B. Deters. *The Big Data Quality Dilemma: How to Build Trustworthy Insights in a World of Messy Data*. Forrester Research, June 17, 2020.

7 S. A. Miller and D. G. Bonter. "Monitoring Ecotourism Impacts: The Benefits and Pitfalls of Visitor Tracking Technology." *Journal of Sustainable Tourism*, 20(4), 2012, pp. 559–575.

8 "AIMS for Wildlife." U.S. Geological Survey, 2013. www.usgs.gov/centers/werc/science/aims-wildlife

9 S. Barrett, et al. "Impact of the Volkswagen Emissions Control Defeat Device on U.S. Public Health." *Environmental Research Letters*, 10(11), 2015, pp. 114005–114015.

Significance (LISTEN)

Drawing Conclusions

LISTEN: DRAWING CONCLUSIONS

Our data-driven journey has taken us from prioritizing objectives to presenting relevant data. Now, it's time to shift gears and listen for the significance. We've **looked**, we've **linked**, and now we must **listen** to find meaning in what we have seen.

Have you ever gazed at a starry sky and marveled at the hidden stories woven within constellations? Data analysis unveils a similar magic, waiting to be discovered among clusters of numbers and graphs. Just as astronomers decipher starlight patterns, we, data storytellers, must listen to the whispers within our data's intricate landscapes. In Chapter 8, we embark on a crucial mission: drawing conclusions from the insights we've gathered.

Recall those meticulously chosen data points? They're not merely numbers on a chart; they're the beating heart of your organization's mission, vision, and goals. Your mission now is to become a detective; unearthing patterns, trends, and subtle nuances that point toward a meaningful direction. Listen intently, for the data speaks in hushed tones, revealing upward climbs, downward spirals, intriguing correlations, even the occasional statistical hiccup. And sometimes, in the elegant silence between numbers, lies the most profound insight of all.

DOI: 10.1201/9781003623212-11

Finding Patterns

We can identify patterns in data by visualizing it in charts, like a time series, line graph, or scatter plot. We can also deduce or infer trends by looking at numbers that are generally increasing or decreasing. Indeed, consistent increases or decreases can speak volumes, hinting at underlying trends like an ancient fable whispered through generations. Take, for instance, India's story of declining birth rates, each decade a step down in the fertility (Figure 8.1). Or consider the United States, where life expectancy, despite occasional stumbles, rises steadily (Figure 8.2).

The choices in the x-axis and y-axis, along with the period of time under observation and the method by which the intervals are chosen can dance with our perception, subtly influencing the way in which trends unfold. For example, it is much easier to identify the downward trend in the babies per woman data when the data is viewed year by year rather than decade by decade. In the case of the US life expectancy, in which there were quite a few downward dips in the earlier years, it is easier to derive a more upward trend over the long term by having a greater number of years in the observation window.

We can conclude that having more control over both the x-axis and the y-axis (as expounded upon earlier in Chapter 3) will enable the viewer to explore the nuances more thoroughly and therefore be better able to deduce the pattern. It seems best to experiment with different options to see which ones work best for the data at hand, but without skewing the perspective or leading to incorrect conclusions (implied by the "bad examples" also discussed in Chapter 3).

Finding patterns to draw conclusions is nothing new. As a matter of fact, many of us may have been doing that since we were children. For example, suppose your fifth-grade math teacher writes a series of numbers on the board: 42, 36, 31, 27, and 24, then asks you to determine what the following two numbers will be. You think for a minute, and then you write 22 and 21 because you figured out the pattern: Each number was being subtracted by one number less than the one before it, starting with 6, then 5, 4, and 3 (that is, 42-6=36, 36-5=31, and so forth).

But patterns aren't mere lines on a graph; they're dynamic, multifaceted melodies within the data's symphony. Learn to question their rhythm, to discern whether they're linear, exponential, cyclical, or perhaps something entirely new and undiscovered. This nuanced listening; this attentive dance with the whispers of data, is where the value and revelation of data truly

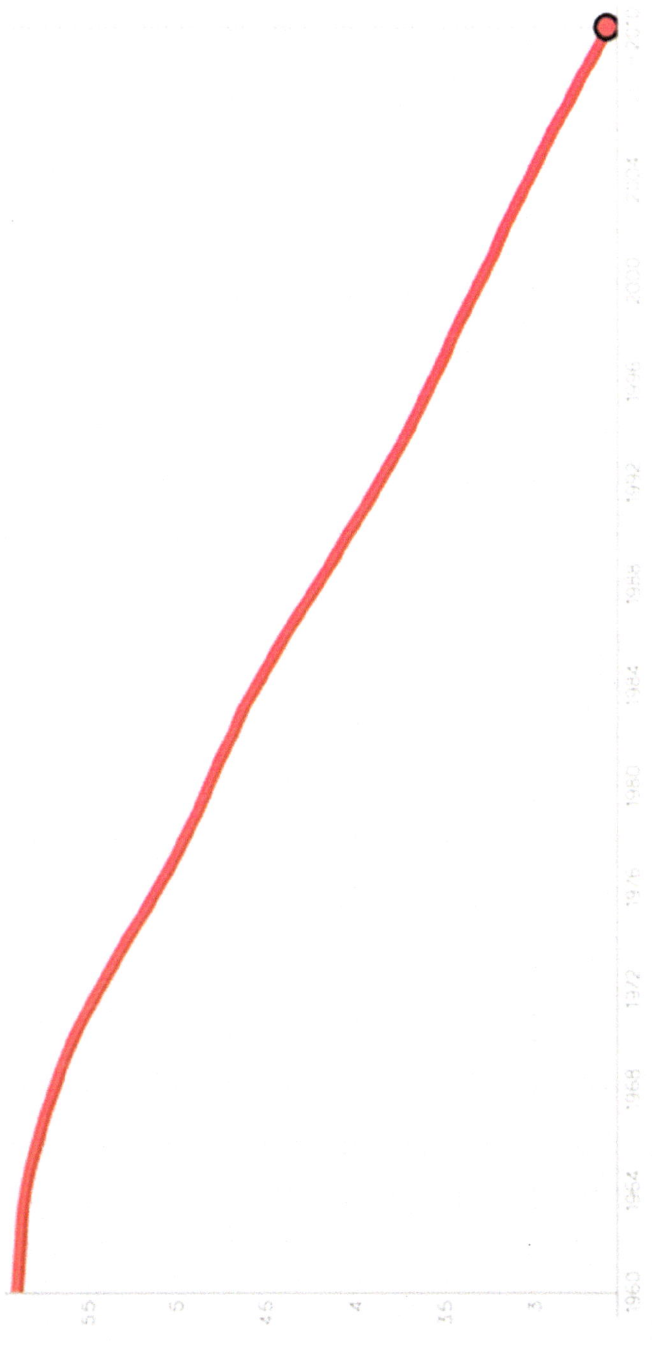

FIGURE 8.1   Babies per woman in India.

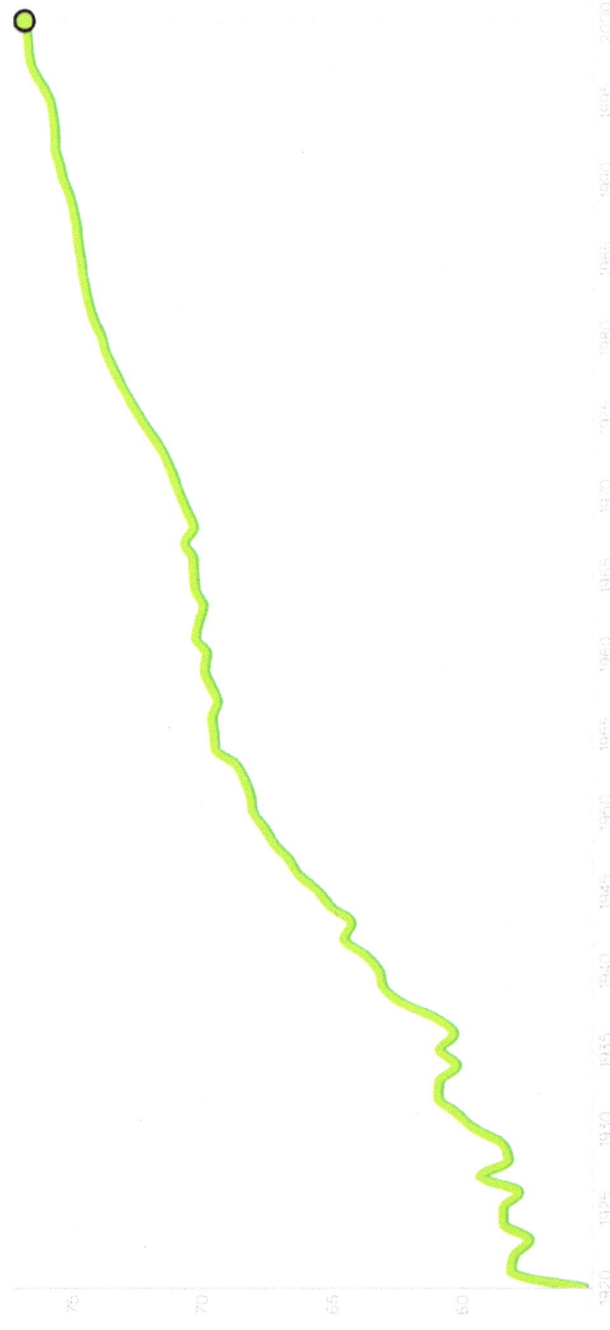

FIGURE 8.2   US life expectancy over time.

unfolds. It's the crucible where raw numbers transform into actionable insights, empowering us to navigate the complexities of our world with newfound clarity.

We continue to use pattern recognition throughout life, even though we may not see it as such. As we embrace data-driven decision-making, honing this skill becomes imperative, which we do by questioning patterns (that is, are they linear, exponential, stationary, damped, seasonal, random, cyclical, etc.). However, even though this is an innate human ability, transforming it into a potent tool for extracting meaning from data demands deliberate practice. Here are four key strategies to amplify your inner sleuth of significance:

1. **Cultivate the Inquisitive Lens**: Embrace data as a cryptic puzzle, teeming with unspoken narratives. Approach each visualization, each string of numbers, with a relentless curiosity. Ask probing questions: What secrets does the data whisper? Are there unexpected correlations, subtle trends hiding in plain sight? What outliers defy convention, beckoning for deeper investigation? This persistent inquisitiveness ignites your search for meaningful connections, paving the path to profound insights.

2. **Befriend Skepticism, Befriend Context**: Remember that data, like any storyteller, can harbor hidden biases. Resist the temptation to blindly accept the patterns it presents at face value. Challenge assumptions, deeply explore outliers, and always consider the context surrounding the data's origin. Is it truly representative of the larger population? Were the sampling methods rigorous? Are external factors influencing the observed trends? A healthy dose of skepticism safeguards you from drawing erroneous conclusions, ensuring your journey toward informed action is built upon a bedrock of truth.

3. **Unleash the Power of Visual Exploration**: Visualizations are your microscopes, revealing the intricate details of data that lie hidden to the naked eye. Don't be afraid to experiment with different chart types and graphs. Uncover hidden correlations with a scatter plot, map spatial patterns with a heatmap, or trace the evolution of trends over time with a timeline. Each visualization technique unlocks a new facet of the data's narrative, allowing you to paint a more comprehensive picture and refine your understanding.

4. **Collaborate, Diversify, and Amplify**: No data detective thrives in isolation. Embrace collaboration, seeking diverse perspectives from colleagues across disciplines. Their unique lenses can illuminate patterns you might miss and challenge your own assumptions. This collaborative approach sparks meaningful dialogues, leading to richer interpretations and more robust conclusions. Imagine the symphony of insights that emerges when a statistician joins forces with a designer, a historian with a sociologist, or some other such combination. By uniting diverse perspectives, you amplify the collective ability to hear the whispers of data and translate them into impactful action.

Remember, honing your skills for drawing conclusions from data is an ongoing odyssey filled with exploration and experimentation. Each new dataset, each insightful visualization, refines that inner sleuth mentioned earlier, transforming seemingly silent numbers into a symphony of actionable insights. So, step into the thrilling world of data exploration, trust your evolving instincts, and prepare to be amazed by the stories you have the power to reveal. The world awaits the wisdom you unlock within the tapestry of information.

Solving Crime Before It Happens

Having honed our data detective skills, let's shift focus to a real-world case where recognizing patterns paid off... and then didn't. In Santa Cruz, California, data-driven policing took a fascinating turn, showcasing the double-edged sword of predictive analysis.

Imagine solving a crime before it even begins. Not with psychic premonitions aided by futuristic technology like Tom Cruise's character did in the "Minority Report" movie, but by harnessing the power of data analysis. It might sound far-fetched, but Charles Wheelan, *New York Times* best-selling author and public-policy professor at Dartmouth College, wrote an article about the Santa Cruz Police Department (SCPD), that apparently demonstrated this very idea.

Their mission? To pinpoint crime hotspots by meticulously studying historical data. Armed with these insights, they strategically deployed officers to areas statistically likely to experience criminal activity. One such hotspot was a parking garage plagued by car break-ins. Enter our heroes: two vigilant officers on patrol. Guided by the data's whispers, they spotted two women loitering suspiciously near a car. One had an outstanding warrant, the other – illegal substances in her possession. Before you could shout "Bingo!" both were apprehended, potentially nipping a bigger crime in the bud.

Crystal ball? No. Genius? Nope. Simply a group of dedicated professionals leveraging data to predict and prevent so they could "protect and serve" more effectively. Charles Wheelan aptly summarizes this approach: "Interesting answers are out there. People who care about those answers just need to go looking for them, maybe with a little bit of prodding."[1]

However, this data-driven detective story takes a twist. While initial successes like the parking garage incident fueled optimism, cracks began to appear. Community concerns emerged, highlighting an unintended consequence: officer-community friction. Instead of fostering collaboration, predictive policing, in some instances, exacerbated tensions.[2]

And there lies the rub. Technology, even with the noblest intentions, can have unintended consequences. This is precisely where transparency and accountability become vital. As the city council of Santa Cruz recognized, simply banning the technology wasn't the answer. Instead, a nuanced approach was needed. Public discourse, ongoing evaluation, and rigorous audits are crucial to ensure predictive policing serves its intended purpose – protecting communities, not alienating them.

The Santa Cruz saga encapsulates a fundamental truth: good ideas, even data-driven ones, can have unforeseen downsides. But instead of discarding them altogether, we should strive to refine them, learn from missteps, and implement them with equitable practices at the heart. By nurturing open dialogue and prioritizing fairness, we can transform data-driven solutions from potential dividers into powerful bridges connecting communities to safety and collaboration.

As we navigate the labyrinthine alleys of data, a symphony of whispers guides our every step. By honing our skills of pattern recognition, we become more readily able to decipher the code hidden within numbers and charts. We learn to listen intently, to discern the subtle melodies lurking beneath the surface, for within each pattern lies a story waiting to be told.

Remember the thrill of unmasking the dance of numbers in those elementary school math problems? That innate curiosity, that itch to connect the dots, fuels our journey in Chapter 8. We dive deeper, wielding visualizations like microscopes, peering into the intricate details of data that once remained veiled. We question assumptions, challenge outliers, and embrace the power of collaboration, drawing wisdom from diverse perspectives to paint a richer picture of reality.

And what emerges from this symphony of whispers? Action. Informed action, fueled by the clarity of conclusions drawn from the depths of data. We predict epidemics, map poverty, optimize resources, and ultimately, shape a brighter future – all by learning to listen, to decode, and to dance with the patterns woven into the tapestry of information.

This is the essence of drawing conclusions from data: a thrilling odyssey of discovery, a metamorphosis from passive observer to active architect of change. So, step into the data-driven dawn, sharpen your detective skills, and embrace the whispers. The world awaits the symphonies you have the power to reveal.

CASE STUDIES

Case Study #1: Predicting Malaria Outbreaks with AI in Rwanda (Public Health)

The Rwandan Ministry of Health, in collaboration with researchers from Columbia University's Mailman School of Public Health, developed an AI-powered system to predict malaria outbreaks across the country.[3] Using historical data on weather patterns, mosquito populations, and past malaria cases, the model identifies high-risk areas likely to experience future outbreaks. This allows preventative measures, like insecticide spraying and community education, to be targeted strategically, maximizing their effectiveness and resource allocation.[4] While the project has shown promise, specific figures on its impact are not detailed. However, broader malaria control efforts in Rwanda have been highly effective, reducing malaria incidence by 87% and in-patient malaria deaths by 74% between 2005 and 2011.[5]

Case Study #2: Mapping Poverty with Mobile Phone Data in Uganda (Social Development)[6]

Traditionally, measuring poverty levels in developing countries involves expensive and time-consuming household surveys. In Uganda, researchers turned to mobile phone data to create a faster and more cost-effective method. By analyzing call records, mobile money transactions, and charging patterns, they generated a poverty map that accurately identified high-poverty areas across the country. This information has the potential to be used by the Ugandan government to prioritize social development programs and target financial assistance to those most in need. This case study underscores the potential of non-traditional data sources for drawing accurate conclusions about complex social issues.

STUDY QUESTIONS: SIGNIFICANCE (LISTEN)

1. **Beyond "Aha!"**: Imagine you've discovered a powerful trend in your data analysis. How can you go beyond simply identifying the pattern and dive deeper to understand its underlying causes and potential implications?

2. **Whispers into Action**: You've drawn a compelling conclusion from your data, but translating it into action can be tricky. Discuss challenges and strategies for ensuring your data-driven insights lead to meaningful and effective initiatives.

3. **The Skeptical Detective**: Why is a healthy dose of skepticism crucial in drawing conclusions from data? How can you cultivate a critical mindset when analyzing patterns and trends?

4. **Data's Double-Edged Sword**: Explore examples of data-driven initiatives with unintended consequences. What ethical considerations and safeguards are necessary to ensure technology serves the greater good?

5. **Collaboration Composes**: How can diverse perspectives and different disciplines strengthen the process of drawing conclusions from data? Give examples of collaborative data analysis projects and their potential benefits.

6. **From Numbers to Narratives**: Data can tell powerful stories, but how can you effectively translate complex visualizations and statistical analyses into compelling narratives that resonate with a broader audience?

7. **Beyond the Parking Garage**: The Santa Cruz Police Department case offers a nuanced perspective on data-driven policing. Consider alternative approaches and solutions that harness the power of data while promoting trust and collaboration within communities.

8. **Future Symphonies**: Imagine a world where data-driven insights are seamlessly integrated into daily life. What opportunities and challenges does this pose, and how can we ensure data democratization benefits all members of society?

These questions encourage critical thinking, application of concepts, and exploration of broader themes beyond the chapter's content. They prompt discussions, challenge assumptions, and stimulate creative solutions, making them ideal for both individual study and classroom engagement. I hope these questions spark further curiosity and reflection on the power of data analysis for drawing conclusions and shaping our world.

NOTES

1 Charles Wheelan. "To Get Your Team to Use Data, Demystify It." *Harvard Business Review*, October 26, 2018. https://hbr.org/2018/10/to-get-your-team-to-use-data-demystify-it

2 Matt Zapotosky and Christopher Mathias "Santa Cruz Bans Predictive Policing in Landmark Decision." *Washington Post*, June 23, 2020. www.reuters.com/arti cle/idUSKBN23V2XB/

3 Susan Athey, et al. "Predicting and Preventing Malaria Outbreaks with Machine Learning." *PNAS*, 117(49), 2020, pp. 31557–31565.

4 Rwanda Biomedical Centre. *Rwanda Malaria Strategic Plan 2020–2024.* 2020.

5 Corine Karema, et al. "History of Malaria Control in Rwanda: Implications for Future Elimination in Rwanda and Other Malaria-Endemic Countries." *Malaria Journal*, 19(1), 2020, p. 356. https://malariajournal.biomedcentral.com/articles/10.1186/s12936-020-03407-1.

6 Jonathan E. Blumenstock, et al. "Using Mobile Phone Data to Predict Poverty in Uganda." *Proceedings of the National Academy of Sciences*, 112(44), 2015, pp. 13670–13676.

CHAPTER 9

Surveillance (LEVERAGE)

Planning the Strategy

LEVERAGE: PLANNING THE STRATEGY

Imagine a conductor standing before an orchestra, baton poised. The musicians fidget, instruments primed, anticipation crackling in the air. They could launch into the melody blindly, trusting their skills, but the result would likely be chaos. Instead, the conductor raises their baton, a silent signal for focused preparation. Music sheets are scanned, cues exchanged, the collective hum of anticipation morphing into a unified resolve. Finally, the first note rings out, and the orchestra erupts into a vibrant symphony, each instrument leveraging its potential within the meticulously planned score.

Data analysis thrives on the same principle. We've **looked** at what dominates, **linked** what's relevant, and **listened** to what holds significance. Now, it's time to **leverage** these insights into a masterfully orchestrated strategy. But in the complex world of data, action without planning often resembles the cacophony of an uncoordinated orchestra – jarring, discordant, and ultimately ineffective.

My choice to weave musical metaphors throughout this book stems from my lifelong passion for music, which has profoundly shaped my perspective on various pursuits, including data analysis. As a musician,

DOI: 10.1201/9781003623212-12

I have experienced firsthand the power of collaboration, creativity, and structure that music embodies. This deep connection allows me to draw parallels between the two fields in a way that feels authentic and relatable. By incorporating musical imagery, I aim to share not only my insights into data analysis but also the joy and inspiration that music has brought to my life, enriching the narrative and inviting readers to explore these concepts with a sense of rhythm and harmony.

A McKinsey & Company report on customer experience transformations found that companies with comprehensive customer experience programs generate 15 to 20% higher sales conversion rates and 10% to 20% greater customer satisfaction compared to those lacking such programs.[1] The numbers speak for themselves: planning is not optional – it's the conductor's baton, transforming disorganized data into a symphony of impactful action.

But planning without execution can be compared to the conductor holding the baton forever, frozen in anticipation. Research by the Association for Project Management (APM) highlights that poor execution, along with other factors such as governance, leadership, and stakeholder engagement, significantly contributes to project failures.[2] This is a stark reminder that even the most meticulously mapped score won't translate into a beautiful melody without dedicated performance.

The key, then, lies in bridging the gap between planning and execution. This is where "surveillance" comes in; that is, the watchful, active stewardship of your data-driven strategy. It's the constant vigil that ensures your plan remains relevant, agile, and responsive to real-world feedback. It's the ongoing rehearsal that polishes your execution, ensuring each data point plays its part in the grand ensemble.

Leveraging our insights begins with challenging the status quo, those preconceived notions masquerading as immovable truths. Remember the old adage, "you can't mix quantitative and qualitative data"? Nonsense! Data, like life, thrives on diversity. Just as Mozart infused opera with folk melodies, your analysis can draw strength from combining numbers and narratives.

QUANTITATIVE VS. QUALITATIVE DATA

We often approach data analysis with pre-set expectations, clinging to comfortable binaries like "objective vs. subjective" or "numbers vs. words." But these rigid categories stifle the symphony of meaning within our data. To truly leverage our insights, we must become intellectual rebels, questioning every assumption, tearing down artificial walls, and embracing the richness of data in all its diverse forms.

In other words, you need both and can have both. It is entirely possible to quantify qualitative data, just as it is equally possible to qualify quantitative data in your step of surveillance. Before explaining these two seemingly contradictory tasks, we must lay down a basic foundation by defining and describing both quantitative and qualitative data.

Imagine a seasoned navigator, meticulously plotting their course on a map. Every landmark, every bend in the river, every change in altitude – each detail gets meticulously recorded, translated into numbers, and factored into the route. This is the world of quantitative data, the objective, numbers-based compass guiding us through the "what" and the "how many" – the "quantity" of what you have. This makes perfect sense, since you cannot spell "quantitative" without spelling "quantity" (or most of it). It is data that defines (Figure 9.1).

Think of quantitative data as the backbone of your business, the cold, hard facts that tell you how many products you've sold, how much revenue you've generated, and which items are flying off the shelves. It's the accountant of your organization, tallying every penny and tracking every click, weaving a precise tapestry of discrete, finite values. This data is a master of deduction, drawing clear conclusions from its numerical symphony. It employs the logic of Sherlock Holmes, analyzing sales figures to identify peak seasons, predict future trends, and even pinpoint potential

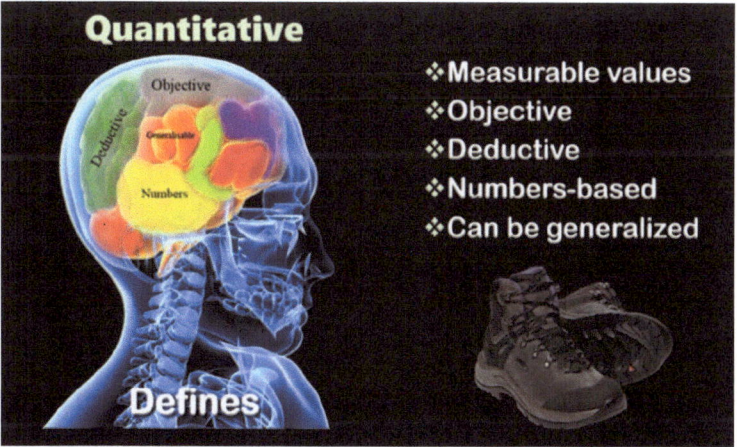

FIGURE 9.1   An illustration of quantitative data.

anomalies. Generalizing is its superpower, allowing you to extrapolate from your specific data to understand broader market trends or compare your performance to industry averages.

Now, let's step into the bustling world of a sporting goods store and see how quantitative data guides the way. Imagine you own a sporting goods store and you're analyzing your hiking boot sales. You dive into the numbers, charting the rise and fall of sales figures over time, identifying the most popular models, and pinpointing the busiest seasons. You discover that sales spike in the spring, suggesting a link to warmer weather and outdoor adventures. You analyze the sizes and colors that sell fastest, revealing a preference for sturdy, mid-range boots in earthy tones. This data, like a precise map, tells you **what** is happening in your store, but it doesn't tell you **why** it's happening.

But the journey doesn't end with numbers. Enter qualitative data, the eloquent storyteller weaving narratives from the "why" and the "how." It gets into the emotions, experiences, and motivations that drive your customers' choices, capturing the nuances that numbers alone cannot express. Think of it as the campfire storyteller, sharing tales of rugged trails conquered, breathtaking vistas witnessed, and the sense of accomplishment that comes from pushing boundaries in nature. Rather than defining (as is the case with quantitative data), qualitative data describes; it speaks to the "quality" of data (Figure 9.2). As with quantitative data, this "quality" makes perfect sense, since you cannot spell "qualitative" without spelling "quality" (or most of it).

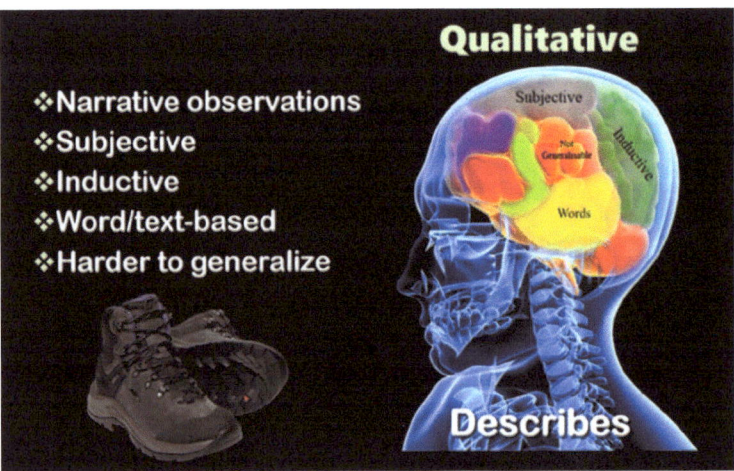

FIGURE 9.2   An illustration of qualitative data.

Jumping back into the sporting goods store analogy, imagine a customer gushing about their recent hike, describing the treacherous climb they tackled with your boots. They talk about the supportive grip on loose scree, the waterproof protection against sudden downpours, and the sense of confidence your boots instilled on the challenging terrain. This is the realm of qualitative data, a champion of induction, piecing together insights from observations and open-ended questions. It's like the artist Van Gogh, capturing the essence of a moment through vivid brushstrokes and subjective interpretations. Generalizing is trickier here, as each story is unique and personal. But that doesn't diminish its value. Qualitative data adds depth and emotion to the quantitative picture, revealing the motivations, preferences, and experiences that drive your customers' choices.

As we continue with our sporting goods store analogy, let's see how qualitative data enriches the quantitative narrative. Suppose you decide to include open-ended questions in your customer surveys, asking about their experiences with your hiking boots. The answers paint a vivid picture: you learn about the rugged terrain they conquer, the weather conditions they brave, and the sense of adventure your boots inspire. You hear about the blisters they endured, the breathtaking vistas they witnessed, and the memories they made with your product on their feet.

STRIKING A BALANCE

Suddenly, the numbers become more than just numbers. They transform into stories of determination, resilience, and the shared human experience of pushing boundaries and exploring the world. This is the magic of combining quantitative and qualitative data – a powerful symphony of insights that unlocks a deeper understanding of your customers and your place within their journeys.

But how do you weave these seemingly disparate threads into a cohesive tapestry? The answer lies in leveraging both data types to their fullest potential. You can enrich the quantitative data by asking more detailed questions in your surveys. Instead of simple "yes" or "no" questions, ask customers to rate your boots on a scale of 1 to 5 on various characteristics like comfort, durability, and aesthetic appeal. This not only provides discrete values for analysis but also adds depth to your observations, allowing you to tease out a more comprehensive picture.

For qualitative data, harness the power of technology. Utilize qualitative-analysis software that can read through massive amounts of text from

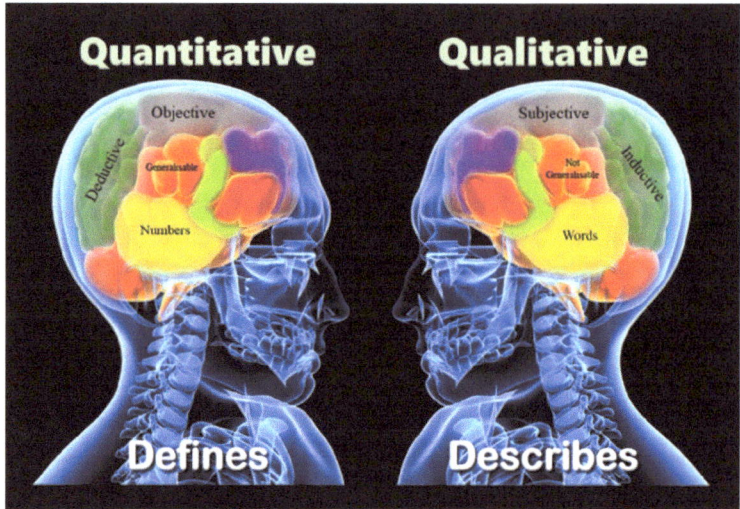

FIGURE 9.3   Quantitative and qualitative data illustrated together.

customer reviews or survey responses. This allows you to identify patterns, categorize keywords based on positive or negative connotations, and even assign numerical values to qualitative data points. By combining these insights with the quantitative data (Figure 9.3), you can create a richer, more nuanced picture of your customer experience.

Suddenly, the numbers become more than just numbers. They transform into stories of determination, resilience, and the shared human experience of pushing boundaries and exploring the world. This is the magic of combining quantitative and qualitative data – a powerful symphony of insights that unlocks a deeper understanding of your customers and your place within their journeys.

While the promise of quantifying qualitative data is vast, the process itself requires a deft touch. Take Dr. Rachel Marias, a professor from Michigan State University, who has successfully made multiple deep dives into this realm. Using powerful software like Linguistic Inquiry and Word Count (LIWC) as her analytical engine, she has tackled massive projects, unearthing insights hidden within mountains of text. But, as Dr. Marias cautions, "The process of quantifying this qualitative data does not make the data unambiguous, but rather opens up the potential of ambiguity hidden behind quantitative data."[3] This insightful observation highlights the importance of nuanced interpretation alongside technological prowess.

LIWC shines particularly bright when dissecting the emotional undercurrents within text. This software analyzes vast stretches of language, dissecting word choices and sentence structures to identify emotional cues, cognitive styles, and even social motivations. Imagine feeding a customer review through LIWC. It might reveal a preponderance of words associated with "excitement" and "achievement," painting a picture of a thrilled hiker conquering a challenging trail. Conversely, negative words like "frustration" and "disappointment" could point to a less satisfying experience. By quantifying these emotional nuances, LIWC adds a powerful layer to the quantitative data, painting a rich, multi-dimensional portrait of your customer experience.[4]

Imagine visualizing your data on a multi-layered map. Quantitative data forms the base layer, with sales figures, demographics, and purchase patterns plotted like geographical features. On top of this, the qualitative data comes to life. Each customer review becomes a vibrant marker, pinpointing specific locations where emotions like "exhilarated" or "frustrated" surfaced during their hiking adventures. By overlaying these layers, you can chart the emotional terrain of your customer experience, uncovering hidden connections and identifying key areas for improvement.

The power of this holistic approach is undeniable. A study by Forrester Consulting revealed that companies integrating both quantitative and qualitative data to inform their customer experience decisions are 1.6 times more likely to exceed their business goals compared to those relying solely on one methodology. This highlights the immense potential of combining the objective rigor of numbers with the rich tapestry of customer narratives. It's a paradigm shift, not just in data analysis, but in how we understand and connect with our customers.[5] Similarly, a study by Bain & Company revealed that brands that effectively combine quantitative and qualitative insights are 1.5 times more likely to successfully launch new products that resonate with their target audience.[6]

It's clear, then, that the future of data analysis lies not in choosing sides, but in bridging the divide. By embracing the symphony of both quantitative and qualitative data, we unlock a world of deeper understanding, more meaningful connections, and ultimately, a more thriving business. So, ditch the binary, tune into the full orchestra, and prepare to be swept away by the power of data synergy.

LEVERAGING INSIGHT: A QUICK RECAP

We often approach data analysis with pre-set expectations, clinging to comfortable binaries like "objective vs. subjective" or "numbers vs. words." But these rigid categories stifle the symphony of meaning within our data. To truly leverage our insights, we must become intellectual rebels, questioning every assumption, tearing down artificial walls, and embracing the richness of data in all its diverse forms.

1. **Question the Unquestionable**: Just because someone declared something "impossible" doesn't mean it is. Imagine Galileo challenging the dogma of the Earth being the center of the universe. His revolutionary questioning led to new astronomical discoveries, just as questioning "unmixable" data types can unlock novel insights.

2. **Embrace the Blurred Lines**: As we've already learned, quantitative and qualitative data aren't mutually exclusive; they're partners in a data tango. Imagine analyzing customer satisfaction with those hiking boots from the previous example. Numbers quantify purchase trends, but qualitative open-ended responses reveal the "why" behind those numbers. The size of the boots may be quantifiable, but the comfort level is a qualitative dance of personal perception.

3. **Celebrate the Nuances**: Numbers aren't the only storytellers. Qualitative data, with its rich tapestry of words and observations, adds depth and emotion to the quantitative narrative. Imagine your hiking boot survey revealing customers gushing about "grippy soles conquering treacherous trails" or lamenting "clunky designs weighing down adventures." These qualitative nuances wouldn't be captured by mere sales figures.

4. **Seek Creative Collisions**: The magic often lies at the intersection of seemingly disparate data types. To recap, again, imagine combining quantitative sales data with qualitative customer reviews to predict future trends. The numbers may point to an increase in boot sales, but the reviews might reveal a sudden shift in consumer preferences toward lighter, more minimalist designs.

5. **Lead the Data Revolution**: Challenging the status quo isn't about mere rebellion; it's about unlocking the full potential of data analysis. When we embrace the diversity of data types and question entrenched

assumptions, we become pioneers, crafting innovative methodologies and paving the way for future growth.

CASE STUDIES

Case Study # 1: Eco-Tourism Operators and Preserving Sensitive Ecosystems[7]

Context: Eco-tourism thrives on balancing visitor access with environmental protection. Sensitive ecosystems require careful monitoring to prevent tourist impact exceeding sustainable levels.

Surveillance and LEVERAGE: Costa Rica's Monteverde Cloud Forest employs a network of strategically placed cameras and environmental sensors to track visitor movements, wildlife populations, and ecological parameters like soil moisture and water quality. This data fuels strategic park management decisions. Monitoring visitor density in real time allows for dynamic trail closures and rerouting during peak seasons, protecting vulnerable areas. Data on wildlife activity informs conservation efforts, optimizing patrol routes and habitat restoration projects. By leveraging surveillance data, Monteverde strikes a crucial balance between showcasing its wonders and safeguarding its ecological integrity, ensuring long-term sustainability for both tourism and the environment.

Case Study 2: Urban Mobility Apps and Optimizing Public Transportation[8]

Context: In bustling cities, optimizing public transportation networks can dramatically improve citizen quality of life. Traditional scheduling often fails to adapt to dynamic traffic patterns and passenger demand.

Surveillance and LEVERAGE: Citymapper, a popular urban mobility app, leverages GPS data from smartphones and public transportation vehicles to paint a real-time picture of traffic flow and passenger usage. This data informs strategic adjustments to bus routes, tram schedules, and ride-sharing options. Citymapper tailors its service to areas experiencing high demand, dynamically adjusts wait times and frequency, and even provides alerts about unexpected delays or disruptions. By leveraging surveillance data, Citymapper transforms public transportation into a dynamic and responsive system, improving commuter experience and reducing congestion in urban landscapes.

STUDY QUESTIONS: SURVEILLANCE (LEVERAGE)

1. **The conductor's paradox**: Imagine two companies – one with meticulously detailed plans but struggling with execution, and another with agile adaptation but lacking defined strategy. Analyze the potential pitfalls of each approach and propose a framework for bridging the gap between planning and execution in a data-driven world.

2. **Beyond binaries**: Can you think of examples beyond hiking boots where combining quantitative and qualitative data can offer ground-breaking insights? Consider areas like healthcare, education, or social policy, and identify potential synergies between numbers and narratives in these contexts.

3. **Quantifying the unquantifiable**: LIWC is just one tool for qualitative analysis. Explore other emerging technologies or methodologies that can bridge the gap between words and numbers. Discuss the ethical considerations and potential limitations of quantifying qualitative data.

4. **Surveillance for good**: While "surveillance" often carries negative connotations, discuss how strategically using data monitoring can contribute to positive social or environmental impact. Imagine a scenario where real-time data analysis is used to address pressing issues like resource scarcity or public health crises.

5. **The data orchestra's discordant notes**: Not all data integrates seamlessly. Explore potential challenges in combining quantitative and qualitative data, such as inconsistencies in measurement, bias in interpretation, or conflicting narratives. What strategies can be employed to overcome these hurdles and ensure a harmonious interpretation of your data symphony?

6. **Personal symphony**: Reflect on your own role within the data ecosystem. How can you, as an individual, leverage insights from both quantitative and qualitative data to make informed decisions in your personal or professional life? Consider examples in areas like career choices, financial planning, or communication strategies.

7. **The future of data harmony**: Imagine a world where data analysis goes beyond the individual business or organization. How could companies and institutions collaborate to share insights and leverage data for the collective good? Explore potential challenges and

opportunities for creating a truly global data symphony for positive societal change.

8. **Data as storytelling**: Data analysis is often presented as an objective, technical process. Discuss the role of creativity and storytelling in interpreting and communicating data insights. How can we utilize narratives to make data more engaging, impactful, and accessible to a wider audience?

These questions encourage critical thinking, application of Chapter 9's concepts to new situations, and exploration of future possibilities in the realm of data analysis. They move beyond simple recall and aim to spark engaging discussions and innovative ideas. I hope you find them to be stimulating and insightful!

NOTES

1 "Building Blocks of Successful Customer Experience." McKinsey & Company, October 27, 2020. www.mckinsey.com/capabilities/growth-marketing-and-sales/our-insights/the-three-building-blocks-of-successful-customer-experience-transformations

2 Stephen Repton. "Avoiding Project Failure – and Ensuring Success." APM, October 1, 2024. Accessed November 16, 2024, www.apm.org.uk/blog/avoiding-project-failure-and-ensuring-success/

3 Rachel Marias. "Can Qualitative Data Be Quantified?" Green & Write (blog), Michigan State University College of Education, April 24, 2017. https://education.msu.edu/green-and-write/2017/can-qualitative-data-be-quantified

4 Ryan L. Boyd and Morteza Dehghani. *Handbook of Language Analysis in Psychology*. Guilford Press, 2022.

5 "The Business Impact of Investing in Experience." Forrester Consulting, 2020. www.forrester.com/report/The-Business-Impact-Of-Investing-In-Experience/RES137057

6 "How to Achieve Successful Product Launches." Bain & Company, 2020. www.bain.com/insights/how-to-achieve-successful-product-launches

7 S. A. Miller and D. G. Bonter. "Monitoring Ecotourism Impacts: The Benefits and Pitfalls of Visitor Tracking Technology." *Journal of Sustainable Tourism*, 20(4), 2012, pp. 559–575.

8 P. De Wolf and J. Vanhoof. "Using Big Data to Improve Public Transportation: A Survey of Applications and Perspectives." *Transportation Research Part C: Emerging Technologies*, 95, 2018, pp. 83–98.

CHAPTER 10

Vigilance (LEARN)

Measure Success and Repeat

LEARN: MEASURE SUCCESS AND REPEAT

Imagine soaring high above the Amazon rainforest canopy, the emerald expanse stretching infinitely beneath you. A dedicated butterfly researcher, armed with keen observation and innovative technology, tracks the intricate dance of a rare Morpho butterfly. Each flutter, each dive, each flash of iridescent blue is meticulously recorded, mapped, and analyzed. This relentless pursuit of understanding, this deep-seated need to document and learn, is not just the hallmark of scientific inquiry, but a cornerstone of success in any data-driven endeavor.

Just as the researcher meticulously maps the butterfly's dance, so too must we chart the course of our data-driven journeys. So far in this journey through Part II, we have **looked**, **linked**, **listened**, and **leveraged**, uncovering insights within the hidden symphony of our data. Now, it's time to step into the final stage, the stage where meticulous documentation and relentless learning transform transient discoveries into lasting impact. This is the stage of Vigilance (**LEARN**): Measuring Success & Repeat. This is where we learn after we have looked, linked, listened, and leveraged.

DOI: 10.1201/9781003623212-13

AN IMAGINARY TRIP

Let's take an imaginary trip to the bustling heart of Silicon Valley. There, nestled among tech giants and venture capitalists, lies a quaint bakery known as "The Sourdough Symphony." Its founder, Amelia, wasn't a baking prodigy, but a data-driven entrepreneur with a passion for sourdough. Armed with spreadsheets and pie charts, she embarked on a mission to create the perfect loaf, a symphony of tangy flavor and airy crumb.

Amelia began by meticulously analyzing customer reviews, poring over flavor profiles and identifying common criticisms. She then dove into the science of sourdough, studying fermentation schedules, flour variations, and baking techniques. Each experiment, from adjusting hydration levels to testing new sourdough starters, was meticulously documented, with temperature logs, rise times, and baking profiles recorded in detail.

But Amelia's vigilance didn't end at data collection. Every loaf that emerged from her oven was meticulously evaluated, its crust analyzed for texture, its crumb for airiness, and its flavor for depth and complexity. She trained her palate to discern subtle nuances, noting the impact of different flours and fermentation periods. Each feedback loop, from customer reviews to her own sensory analysis, became a stepping stone in the iterative dance of sourdough perfection.

The result? The Sourdough Symphony became a local sensation. Customers raved about the "perfect tang" and the "ethereal crumb" of Amelia's loaves. But the true magic lay in the process. Amelia had transformed baking, traditionally a craft steeped in intuition and trial-and-error, into a data-driven symphony, each decision meticulously measured and each iteration building upon the last.

This relentless pursuit of learning and refinement is the hallmark of success in any data-driven endeavor, be it baking sourdough or navigating the complex world of business decisions. Just as Amelia documented her every step in this fictional scenario, from ingredient ratios to oven temperatures, so too must we meticulously record our data analysis processes. Every query, every assumption, every conclusion becomes a stepping stone in the iterative dance of optimization.

This vigilance is not a tedious exercise, but a catalyst for creativity. By dissecting our successes and failures with equal enthusiasm, we unlock hidden insights and stumble upon unexpected connections. Imagine, for instance, identifying a correlation between specific weather patterns and the rise times of your sourdough. This newfound knowledge allows you to refine your fermentation schedule, not just for a single batch, but for every loaf to come.

The virtuous cycle of vigilance and learning extends beyond the confines of individual projects. By sharing data insights and collaborating with others, we create a collective learning environment where knowledge multiplies and best practices evolve. Imagine a network of sourdough bakers, each contributing their data and experiences, collaboratively refining the art of baking through a constant exchange of insights.

This collaborative learning is not just wishful thinking. In the real world, a study by McKinsey & Company found that companies with strong data-driven cultures are 23 times more likely to acquire customers, six times as likely to retain customers, and 19 times as likely to be profitable compared to those operating in silos.[1] Similarly, a report by Capgemini revealed that organizations that prioritize cross-industry data sharing and collaborative problem-solving are 70% more likely to achieve success in their data-driven initiatives compared to those that do not.[2]

So, whether you're baking sourdough, or chasing butterflies, or navigating the ever-shifting landscape of business, remember the story of Amelia and The Sourdough Symphony. Embrace the power of vigilance, document your every step, and learn from your successes and failures with equal fervor. By weaving this iterative approach into the fabric of your data-driven decisions, you transform your initial analysis from a solitary act into a living, breathing symphony of continuous optimization, paving the way for sustained success and unlocking the true potential of data insights.

Success in data-driven decision-making cannot be measured until you've come to the point where the process is repeatable. You cannot repeat the process if it has not been documented. If you remember that it worked and failed to write down how you did it, how will you know if you can do it again? If it is documented, it is repeatable. If it is repeatable, it is measurable. If it is measurable, it can be stacked against your key performance indicators so you can continually look for ways to improve each time. But it takes vigilance, and it takes learning to get it there.

As we reach the apex of this data-driven journey, remember the lessons learned across the last five chapters. Your priorities, painstakingly laid out, guide the orchestra of your analysis. Each link forged between data points strengthens the melody of your insights. Every conclusion drawn echoes as a resonant chord in your understanding. And the constant surveillance acts as the conductor, ensuring the performance remains relevant and impactful. Now, with vigilance as your baton, you're ready to measure your success, refine your approach, and embark on the exhilarating cycle of LEARN: the grand finale of your data-driven symphony.

Dr. Milton Mattox, chief technology officer at Castle Shield in Arizona, echoes this sentiment by highlighting the unwavering importance of repeatability in the data-driven dance. "The measurement of a process for flexibility and extensibility," he aptly states, "requires it to be repeatable; otherwise, there is no constant against which to measure and compare."[3] In other words, without a documented, replicable process, our data symphony becomes a fleeting melody, its impact ephemeral and impossible to truly gauge.

But Mattox's wisdom extends beyond mere measurement. He reminds us that "repeatability is also essential when trying to measure process improvement, making it a critical factor in the ultimate success of all processes within organizations."[4] This is the very essence of Vigilance (or LEARN-ing): a relentless pursuit of refinement, where each iteration builds upon the last, each success and failure meticulously recorded and analyzed to chart a course toward ever-greater optimization.

Imagine, then, a scenario where your initial data analysis, instead of fading into the dustbin of past endeavors, becomes the springboard for future leaps. Each step, from data collection to insightful conclusions, is documented in granular detail. This detailed map allows you to revisit, retrace, and refine your approach with meticulous precision. Did a specific data point lead to an unexpected twist in the narrative? Did a change in methodology unlock a treasure trove of hidden insights? By documenting your every move, you transform these discoveries from serendipitous stumbles into stepping stones on the path to mastery.

Furthermore, the power of repeatability transcends individual endeavors. When we share our documented processes and collaborate with others, we create a vibrant tapestry of collective learning. Imagine a network of data-driven organizations, each contributing their unique melodies to the symphony of knowledge. As best practices are exchanged, insights cross-pollinated, and challenges tackled collaboratively, the entire ecosystem thrives. This is the true power of Vigilance: a self-perpetuating cycle of optimization that fuels not just individual success, but collective advancement.

So, as we endeavor to follow the fifth step of Vigilance, remember the sage words of Dr. Mattox. Embrace the power of repeatability, document your every step, and embark on a journey of continuous learning. For in the relentless pursuit of refinement lies the true key to unlocking the full potential of your data-driven endeavors, transforming fleeting insights into a symphony of lasting impact.

BASKETBALL'S SUCCESSFUL FORMULA FOR REPEATABILITY

Picture this: LeBron James, Kobe Bryant, Larry Bird, Michael Jordan, Pete Maravich, Yao Ming (Figure 10.1). Whisper these names to any basketball enthusiast, and you'll ignite a chorus of awe and admiration. Imagine the roar of the crowd as Yao Ming drains a fadeaway three, a testament to years of honed fundamentals and unwavering dedication. Michael Jordan, soaring to gravity-defying dunks. Larry Bird, weaving magic with his unorthodox brilliance. These were titans, untouchable legends who stood at the pinnacle of their game. Each, a coach's dream, a once-in-a-generation phenomenon... or were they?

Before we answer that question, close your eyes and picture a different scene: a young player taking their first hesitant dribbles, coached with the same passion and fundamentals that shaped those icons. This player, too, is on the same path, guided by the universal language of basketball – a language of drills, footwork, and unwavering focus.

The intriguing truth is, with each passing decade, another "great" emerges, scaling even greater heights, only to be eclipsed by the next

FIGURE 10.1   Composite image of six famous basketball players.

prodigy in the queue. Don't misunderstand, some of those names are indeed irreplaceable. We've all heard the murmurs, "There will never be another..." (insert your chosen legend). But why can we confidently anticipate the arrival of more phenomenal talents, ready to mesmerize audiences and redefine excellence again and again?

The answer lies in a seemingly counterintuitive principle: basketball has a repeatable formula for success. This formula isn't a magic potion or a genetic lottery ticket; it's a meticulous blueprint for excellence, meticulously passed down through generations of coaches and players. Sure, individual philosophies and personalities add spice to the mix, but the underlying framework remains constant: fundamentals, relentless skill development, unwavering dedication, and the sweat-soaked grind of practice.

This consistent, predictable approach is the symphony behind basketball's enduring greatness. Players from wildly different backgrounds and circumstances, united by the same unwavering pursuit of mastery, rise to the top. LeBron's raw power, Bird's silky touch, Pistol Pete's blurring speed, Kobe's relentless fire – all blossoms from the same fertile ground of a repeatable process.

Here's one way to translate this basketball wisdom into your data-driven endeavors:

1. **Define your shot clock**: Every player knows their time on the court is precious. Similarly, define clear timeframes for your data-driven initiatives. Set realistic deadlines for data collection, analysis, and implementation, ensuring focused action without succumbing to the paralysis of endless possibilities.

2. **Master the fundamentals**: Before attempting fancy footwork, players solidify dribbling and passing. Likewise, build your data-driven prowess on a strong foundation. Learn basic statistical concepts, master data analysis tools, and familiarize yourself with essential industry best practices. This foundational knowledge becomes your bedrock, supporting complex initiatives with confidence.

3. **Practice, practice, practice**: Just as countless hours in the gym hone a player's skills, data-driven mastery demands consistent practice. Experiment with different analysis techniques, refine your strategies based on feedback, and embrace continuous learning. Every iteration, even those that appear like airballs, contributes to your overall accuracy.

4. **Remember the team**: Basketball is a collaborative effort, and so is data-driven success. Seek feedback from colleagues, engage with experts, and build a network of data-driven allies. Sharing insights and experiences not only amplifies your own learning but also contributes to the collective symphony of knowledge, propelling everyone toward greater heights.

This principle, this symphony of success, translates beautifully into the realm of data-driven decision-making. As Hal Elrod, Cameron Herold, and Honorée Corder aptly state in *The Miracle Morning for Entrepreneurs*, "the not-so-obvious secret to success is this: clarify, calculate, and commit to your result-producing process, without being emotionally attached to your results."[5]

Now, having journeyed through Chapters 6 to 10, you've shed the skin of data denial and embraced dominance, relevance, significance, surveillance, and vigilance. You've seen the accompanying key verbs of looking, linking, listening, leveraging, and learning. But the melody isn't complete yet. Let's take those three key words from Elrod, Herold, and Corder and dive into the nitty-gritty of the clarifying, calculating, and committing to your own data-driven symphony:

1. **Clarifying the Score**: What's your ultimate goal? Is it boosting customer engagement, streamlining operations, or cracking a complex market puzzle? Define your desired outcome with laser-like precision. This is the conductor's baton, setting the tempo and ensuring your symphony stays on track.

2. **Calculating the Steps**: Break down your goal into actionable steps, each a note in the data-driven melody. This might involve data collection strategies, analysis methodologies, or specific decision-making protocols. Treat each step as a carefully placed instrument, contributing its unique timbre to the overall harmony.

3. **Committing to the Rehearsal**: Practice is the cornerstone of any great performance. Schedule regular data analysis sessions, revisit past successes and failures, and refine your approach with each iteration. This unwavering commitment to the process is the daily practice that builds muscle memory and fuels continuous improvement.

4. I will add a fourth step here (although it doesn't have a key word beginning with the letter "C"): **Detaching from the Encore**: Focus on the process, not the outcome. Celebrate milestones, but avoid getting swept away by temporary victories or discouraged by temporary setbacks. Remember, the real magic lies in the relentless pursuit of refinement, the constant iteration that builds a symphony of sustainable success.

BEYOND THE COURT: A UNIVERSAL MELODY

This repeatable formula isn't a jealous secret whispered in locker rooms or hushed boardrooms. Its melody resonates across disciplines, from personal growth to social impact and even scientific discovery. Imagine a community health initiative painstakingly tracking interventions, iterating based on data insights to improve countless lives. Or picture a research team, their lab transformed into a symphony of data analysis, ultimately leading to a groundbreaking medical breakthrough.

The beauty lies in its universality. This formula isn't a rigid blueprint but a flexible framework empowering individuals and organizations to achieve their goals, regardless of the field or the scale of ambition. So, step onto your metaphorical court, pick up your data baton, and let the music of success begin! Remember, the greatest symphonies are not composed in a single breath, but crafted through the dedicated practice of countless notes, each contributing to the grand crescendo of lasting impact.

By embracing this repeatable formula, you transform from a solitary musician, lost in the cacophony of data, into a masterful conductor. You

FIGURE 10.2   Five steps from being in data denial to being data-driven.

orchestrate a symphony of insights, a harmony that resonates not just today but echoes into the future. Each chapter, from Dominance to Vigilance, has been a note in this transformative melody, guiding you from data denial to data-driven mastery (Figure 10.2).

CASE STUDIES

Case Study #1: Khan Academy – Optimizing Learning through A/B Testing and Data-Driven Iteration[6]

Khan Academy, the free online learning platform, strives to make education accessible and engaging for everyone. But with diverse learners and learning styles, creating the perfect learning experience was a challenge.

Khan Academy embraced vigilance by employing A/B testing, a method of comparing different versions of a website or feature to see which one performs better. They tested various aspects of their platform, from video lengths and quiz formats to the layout of learning modules.

The data revealed surprising insights. For example, shorter videos were more engaging for younger learners, while longer ones were preferred by adults. Interactive quizzes with immediate feedback proved more effective than traditional multiple-choice tests. These findings allowed Khan Academy to optimize their platform, catering to different learning styles and maximizing engagement.

But vigilance didn't stop there. Khan Academy continuously analyzes user data, identifies areas for improvement, and runs new A/B tests to refine their approach. This iterative cycle of learning and adaptation ensures their platform stays relevant and effective for its ever-growing global audience.

Case Study #2: Starbucks – Measuring and Refining Customer Experience through Vigilance[7]

While delicious coffee is at the heart of Starbucks' success, their understanding of the customer experience plays an equally crucial role. Initially, measuring this experience proved challenging. Customer satisfaction surveys provided limited insights, often failing to capture the nuances of their in-store journey.

Starbucks embraced vigilance to overcome the obstacle of limited insights from customer satisfaction surveys. By adopting a data-driven approach, Starbucks utilized platforms like "My Starbucks Idea" to gather customer insights, leveraged mobile apps and loyalty programs for personalized experiences, and committed to social responsibility initiatives. This comprehensive strategy allowed Starbucks to better understand and cater to customer needs, ultimately enhancing satisfaction and engagement.

This meticulous data collection revealed surprising realities. They discovered wait times in certain stores were longer than perceived, certain menu items were rarely ordered, and specific seating arrangements resulted in lower dwell times. Armed with these insights, Starbucks implemented targeted changes. They optimized layout for faster service, adjusted menus based on local preferences, and even experimented with mobile ordering kiosks to reduce queues.

Vigilance didn't end there. Starbucks continuously monitors their data, identifies areas for improvement, and tests new initiatives. This iterative process, where customer experience is meticulously measured and constantly refined, exemplifies "Vigilance (LEARN)" in action.

STUDY QUESTIONS: VIGILANCE (LEARN)

1. **Beyond Baking and Basketball**: Imagine applying the "LEARN" principle to a field outside your usual domain. How could meticulous documentation, relentless learning, and iterative refinement revolutionize an unexpected area of your life or work?

2. **The Tyranny of the Encore**: While Chapter 10 emphasizes detaching from temporary victories and setbacks, is there ever a time when an immediate course correction based on data might be essential? Can you think of real-world examples where such swift action proved crucial?

3. **Documenting the Unspoken**: Chapter 10 highlights the importance of documenting every step of your data-driven process. What about tacit knowledge, intuition, and gut feelings that often play a role in decision-making? How can we capture and integrate these intangible elements into our vigilance framework?

4. **The Symphony of Silos**: Vigilance thrives on collaboration, but organizations often struggle to break down internal data silos. What innovative strategies can be implemented to encourage cross-departmental data sharing and create a truly collective learning environment?

5. **Learning from Others' Symphonies**: The chapter mentions the benefits of networking and sharing data insights. How can we effectively evaluate the quality and relevance of external data shared by others to ensure it truly enhances our own learning journey?

6. **Metrics that Matter**: While measuring success is crucial, not all metrics are created equal. How can you move beyond vanity metrics and identify the truly meaningful measurements that reflect the real impact of your data-driven initiatives?

7. **From Novice to Virtuoso**: Vigilance presents a continuous learning curve. How can individuals and organizations create a sustainable culture of learning that encourages ongoing data exploration, analysis, and skill development?

8. **The Future of LEARN**: Imagine a world where data-driven vigilance becomes the norm across all sectors. What potential pitfalls and unintended consequences should we be aware of as we embrace this powerful approach to decision-making?

These questions go beyond simple recall and encourage deeper reflection, application, and critical thinking about the principles of Vigilance (LEARN) presented in Chapter 10. They aim to spark further discussion, challenge assumptions, and inspire creative approaches to utilizing data for continuous learning and sustainable success.

NOTES

1 "The Need to Lead in Data and Analytics." McKinsey & Company, 2016. www.mckinsey.com/business-functions/mckinsey-analytics/our-insights/the-need-to-lead-in-data-and-analytics

2 "How Cross-Industry Data Collaboration Powers Innovation." Capgemini, 2020. www.capgemini.com/insights/expert-perspectives/how-cross-industry-data-collaboration-powers-innovation/

3 Milton Mattox. "Why Repeatable Processes Are Important." LinkedIn, August 25, 2016. www.linkedin.com/pulse/why-repeatable-processes-important-mil ton-mattox

4 Milton Mattox. "Why Repeatable Processes Are Important." LinkedIn, August 25, 2016. www.linkedin.com/pulse/why-repeatable-processes-important-mil ton-mattox

5 Hal Elrod, Cameron Herold, and Honorée Corder. *The Miracle Morning for Entrepreneurs: Elevate Yourself to Elevate Your Business*. Hal Elrod International, 2016.

6 Khan Academy. "A/B Testing Curriculum: To Sneak Peek Or Not?" Khan Academy Blog, March 3, 2014. https://blog.khanacademy.org/a-b-testing-cur riculum-to-sneak-peek-or-not/

7 "Starbucks' Customer Management Case Study." GWO SEVO, n.d. https://gwos evo.com/starbucks-customer-management-case-study

Glimpses into Real Life

From Feudal Chaos to
Data-Driven Equity

THE CHAPTERS YOU'VE JUST READ in Part II dealt with "Driving Decisions with Data" and explored a powerful journey. It was a journey that takes individuals and organizations from a state of data denial to a place of data-driven decision-making. This journey hinges on five key verbs: **Look**, **Link**, **Listen**, **Leverage**, and **Learn**. But these principles aren't recent inventions. Let's journey back to the cobbled streets of 17th century Prague and discover a tale that echoes these very principles, a story where data became a weapon against injustice.

Prague in the early 1600s was a city simmering with discontent. The root cause? Inaccurate property records held by the ruling monarchy. Homes and lands were grossly over-assessed, leading to crippling tax burdens for ordinary citizens. This was a classic case of data denial. The ruling elite held the power, wielding faulty information as a tool of oppression.

Enter Jan Krincius, a revered professor at Charles University. He refused to accept this injustice. This is where our story aligns with the first principle: **Look**. Krincius didn't just acknowledge the problem; he saw the need for a data-centric solution. He recognized the importance of **looking** closely at the situation, understanding the flawed system, and prioritizing the objective, which was to ensure fair taxation through accurate property records.

DOI: 10.1201/9781003623212-14

Krincius' solution embodied the second principle: **Link**. He didn't operate in a vacuum. He **linked** arms with a team of fellow academics, forming a powerful alliance of expertise. Together, they embarked on an ambitious project: a comprehensive survey of every single property in Prague.

This data collection process wasn't for the faint of heart. Over eight grueling years, Krincius' team transformed Prague into a giant data collection exercise. They meticulously measured more than 750 buildings, 8,000 households, and hundreds of acres of land. Imagine the logistical feat without the aid of any modern tools or calculation methods! Imagine the piles of meticulously gathered data which would become the foundation for a data-driven revolution.

This is where the third principle, **Listen**, comes into play. Krincius wasn't simply gathering information; he was actively **listening** to the data. Through precise geometric calculations and detailed diagrams, the team translated raw measurements into a language everyone could understand. Of course, the people of the day wouldn't have called it "data visualization" in the modern sense, nor did it include the colorful charts and graphs we're familiar with today. But it was data visualization in its purest form nonetheless. These detailed maps and diagrams, compiled into the "Collected Works," a robust cadastral record, essentially Prague's first municipal land registry, spoke volumes.

The impact was nothing short of transformative. **Leverage**, the fourth principle, came alive. Armed with the "Collected Works," citizens could finally **leverage** the power of data. They could validate property assessments, dispute erroneous taxes, and challenge the status quo. Transparency replaced opacity. Data became a shield against unfair taxation.

The final principle, **Learn**, ensured the long-term success of this data-driven revolution. Krincius' initiative wasn't just a one-time fix. It established a system, a process – a way to continually learn from the data and refine the system. The cadastral maps became a living document, constantly updated to reflect the ever-changing urban landscape.

The story of Krincius and his team offers a timeless example of how data can be a powerful tool for social good. It's a story that echoes in the chapters on data-driven decision-making. Just like the citizens of Prague, we too can leverage data to challenge imbalances, improve our systems, and usher in an era of data-driven equity.

This 17th-century tale is a testament to the transformative power of data. It reminds us that the journey from data denial to data-driven decisions is paved with the same principles we use today: **Look** closely, **Link** strategically, **Listen** intently, **Leverage** effectively, and **Learn** continuously. Embracing these principles will enable us all to become architects of a more equitable, data-driven world.

THE DAY DATA SKEPTICISM PREVENTED WORLD WAR III

In the heart of the Cold War, on a day heavy with the shadow of recent tragedy, Lt. Colonel Stanislav Petrov sat watch in the Serpukhov-15 bunker near Moscow. His gaze was glued to the screens monitoring the Soviet Oko early warning system, a constellation of satellites guarding against nuclear Armageddon. The year was 1983, the day September 26, just three weeks after the downing of Korean Air Lines Flight 007, a fresh wound on the world's psyche.

Suddenly, the calm shattered. Alarms blared. The system screamed of an incoming attack. Not one, not two, but five missiles hurtling toward the USSR, seemingly launched from the United States. The tension in the bunker was a physical thing, suffocating and thick. Protocol demanded immediate retaliation. Yet, Petrov, amidst the maelstrom, did the unthinkable. He defied the screaming screens, the barking orders, the weight of history. He trusted not just the data, but his intuition, a gnawing sense of discord in the face of the stark binary numbers. Reasoning that a true American attack wouldn't be launched with a mere handful of missiles, he declared it a false alarm.

Later investigations confirmed his gut instinct. A series of glitches, a cosmic hiccup in the satellite system, had nearly plunged the world into nuclear abyss. Petrov's defiance, his willingness to listen to the whispers beyond the data, saved us from unimaginable chaos. Think of it: had Petrov ordered an erroneous retaliatory nuclear attack on the United States and its North Atlantic Treaty Organization allies, they would have most certainly retaliated with equal ferocity (if not more), thus plunging the world into thermonuclear Armageddon.[1]

What's the lesson? Data is powerful, but so is intuition. Petrov serves as a stark reminder that blindly trusting data, even "good" data, can be just as disastrous as ignoring it altogether. Remember the Rochester Institute of Technology professors peddling the "magical staircase" illusion? Blindly accepting their data would have deceived you into thinking that the nonsensical loop of the Escherian Stairwell was as real as a nuclear missile!

This is where data wizardry steps in. You've journeyed through dominance, relevance, significance, surveillance, and vigilance, learning to dance with data, not be dictated by it. You've honed your ability to listen to its whispers, discern its melodies, and ultimately compose your own symphony of impactful decisions. You've completed Act Two of Numbers to Narratives, and the stage is set for a future concerto of continuous optimization and lasting impact.

Data denial transformed into data-driven? That's the essence of your transformation. You learned to look, link, listen, leverage, and learn. Now, as you step into the future, remember this mantra: Look beyond the surface, link insights to meaning, listen to the data's whispers, leverage its power strategically, and learn from every iteration.

The result? No Nobel Peace Prize for preventing World War III, but you'll certainly be armed with the wit to resist any YouTube illusionist peddling stairwells that lead nowhere. Your data-driven symphony won't be fooled by smoke and mirrors, only guided by the true blended harmony of fact and intuition. Remember, in the symphony of decision-making, your gut plays the countermelody against the data's bassline. So, crank up the volume on both and compose a masterpiece that sings of triumph, not disaster.

NOTE

1 Megan Garber. "The Man Who Saved the World by Doing Absolutely Nothing." *The Atlantic*, September 26, 2013. www.theatlantic.com/technology/archive/2013/09/the-man-who-saved-the-world-by-doing-absolutely-nothing/280050

III

Bringing Data to L.I.F.E. and Life to Data

IN PART I OF this book, we laid the foundation of the data journey by leveraging beauty and brains for effective data storytelling. This was done by exploring the five stages of the spectrum from concept to reality in one's business intelligence strategy. In Part II, we built upon that solid foundation by ascending Mount Data, honing our skills to craft impactful visuals and drive decisions with confidence. We learned to dance with data, wield its insights like weapons, and orchestrate compelling narratives that captivate and guide, all through the stages of dominance, relevance, significance, surveillance, and vigilance. But the story doesn't end there. The data itself remains, a vast ocean of potential teeming just beyond the shores of visualization.

Now in Part III of this book, we embark on a new expedition, diving deep into the very essence of this resource, learning to transform it from cold numbers into a vibrant force for growth and innovation.

We call this journey Bringing Data to L.I.F.E. and Life to Data. It's about recognizing the potential that lies dormant within our data, the untold stories it whispers, and the untapped power it holds. It's about nurturing this potential, refining it, and unleashing its transformative energy upon our businesses and beyond.

But what does it truly mean to bring data to "L.I.F.E."? Is it merely a whimsical turn of phrase, or does it hold a deeper meaning? As marketing and customer experience expert Jay Baer aptly observed, "We are surrounded by data, but starved for insight."[1] The numbers pile up, exabytes upon

DOI: 10.1201/9781003623212-15

FIGURE P3.1   The four L.I.F.E. pillars of relevant data.

exabytes, yet how much truly resonates? Does volume alone equate to value? And where does our vision fit into this equation?

The answer lies in understanding the essence of relevant data, recognizing its true L.I.F.E. pillars (forming an acronym of the word L.I.F.E.), which comprise Chapters 11 through 14:

- **Legacy**: Weaving a Story Through Time: Connect your data to historical trends, understand context, and build a narrative that resonates across time.

- **Integrity**: Building Trust with Transparency: Ensure data accuracy, avoid bias, and establish ethical practices to build trust and credibility.

- **Fervency**: Igniting Passion with Insights: Spark curiosity, encourage exploration, and inject passion into your data to drive engagement and action.

- **Efficiency**: Optimizing for Impact: Streamline data collection and analysis, utilize automation, and continuously refine your processes to maximize efficiency and value.

These pillars are not mere theoretical constructs; they are the beating heart of data-driven success. They represent the foundation upon which we build trust, extract meaning, and unlock transformative insights. Let the exploration begin; let's bring data to L.I.F.E.!

NOTE

1 O'Neill, Sarah. "Jay Baer on Data-Driven Marketing Excellence." LXAHub, March 11, 2022. Accessed on July 8, 2024, www.lxahub.com/stories/jay-baer-on-data-driven-marketing-excellence

CHAPTER 11

Legacy

Weaving a Story Through Time

LEGACY: WEAVING A STORY THROUGH TIME

In the hushed stillness of a Victorian hospital ward, Florence Nightingale knelt, not beside a wounded soldier, but beside a mountain of data. Numbers, cold and stark, whispered of a silent enemy claiming more lives than the cannons and rifles outside – disease. The mortality rate, a chilling symphony of despair, resonated in her soul. But Nightingale wasn't a woman to surrender to the morbid melody. She was a data warrior, armed with charts and graphs, her statistical arsenal honed to a razor's edge.

This wasn't the Nightingale history remembers, the Lady with the Lamp, appropriately referred to as the founder of modern nursing. This was Nightingale the statistician, a hidden facet of her brilliance. It was this confluence of talents, medicine and mathematics, that presented a chance to strike a blow against the unseen foe.[1]

But why Florence Nightingale, and why now, as we embark on our journey into Part III: Bringing Data to L.I.F.E.? Because her story is a testament to the power of data, a symphony composed not just of numbers, but of impact, of lives saved.

Understanding the value of data used in driving decisions is nothing new. The COVID19 pandemic in the early 2020s, a stark echo of Nightingale's

DOI: 10.1201/9781003623212-16

battle, reminded us of the importance of hygiene. Yet, in the 1850s, the practices we now take for granted, even those as simple as washing one's hands before eating, were revolutionary whispers, not universal truths. Back then, Nightingale returned from the Crimean War, a hero already. But her heart ached for the soldiers lost not to enemy blades, but to preventable disease. She had data, a choir of numbers, singing the same song. And she had a stage – Queen Victoria's court.

Data storytelling wasn't a buzzword then; it was a radical act. Nightingale, the data conductor, led a chorus of statisticians. Together, they crafted the Rose Chart (Figure 11.1), a visual aria of mortality, each petal a crimson stain, each thorn an indictment. This chart, not a mere image, was a weapon. With it, Nightingale stormed the bastions of Victorian complacency, captivating the Queen with its stark eloquence. A Royal Commission was formed, and Nightingale, the data Joan of Arc, led the charge, her every step fueled by the silent cries of the fallen.[2]

With this chart, Florence Nightingale became one of the first people to persuade the public and influence public policy with data visualization. One could say that she REALLY brought data to LIFE!

The result? A revolution in public health in the British Isles and beyond. Death rates plummeted, sanitation practices were overhauled, and the very foundations of modern nursing were laid; foundations that persist to this

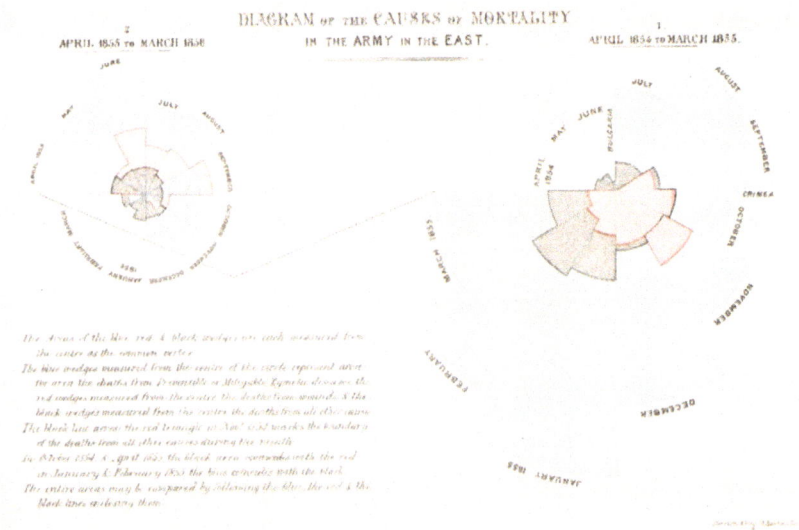

FIGURE 11.1   Florence Nightingale's "Rose Chart".

very day. In fact, Nightingale was credited with lowering the mortality rate at one of the military hospitals where she worked from 40% to only 2%. This wasn't just bringing data to life; it was imbuing it with purpose, transforming numbers into a clarion call for change.[3]

But Nightingale's legacy transcends Victorian wards. It whispers in the algorithms that shape our lives, the equations that guide our businesses, the insights that illuminate our future. It speaks through the L.I.F.E. pillars, the four cornerstones of data's transformative power. Let's dive deeper into "Legacy," the first of these pillars, and unlock the potential of data in our own lives and businesses. It's our job to listen, to learn, and to unleash the transformative power they hold within.

LEGACY, THE MISUNDERSTOOD FIRST PILLAR

Forget the dusty punch cards and flickering terminals, the Y2K anxieties and green-screen relics. Legacy data isn't a museum exhibit of forgotten technology; it's the vibrant pulse of information coursing through the heart of our digital world. It's the silent symphony of data composed in the everyday hum of our working environments, each note a record of decisions made, interactions taken, and progress achieved.

More precisely, legacy data, as we will be exploring in this chapter, is defined as a file, a database, or a software asset (which could possibly include a business application or a web service) that supplies or produces data and that has already been deployed into a working production environment. It's the DNA of our digital ecosystems. It's the customer records whispering trends in the CRM system, the industrial machinery humming melodies of efficiency, the business applications silently chronicling the decisions that shaped our present. These aren't fossilized relics; they're living archives, dynamic repositories pulsating with the lifeblood of our digital interactions.

But within this symphony of data lies an untapped potential, a chorus of whispers promising progress. Imagine analyzing decades of customer data, not just for past purchases, but to anticipate future desires and personalize experiences. Think about dissecting years of operational data, not just for historical trends, but to identify hidden inefficiencies and unlock optimization opportunities. Envision weaving the threads of historical product feedback into the fabric of your next innovation, ensuring it resonates both with real-world needs and your customers.

This isn't science fiction; it's the reality embraced by companies who refuse to relegate data to the dusty corners of the past. According to a study by McKinsey & Company, effective use of legacy data for operational optimization can lead to significant cost reductions, with some studies showing improvements of up to 35%.[4] Research indicates that effective data quality management, including the use of legacy data, can improve the success rate of data migration projects by up to 70%, ensuring better business outcomes and market relevance.[5] These are not mere statistics; they're the triumphant melodies of companies who have learned to listen to the whispers of their data legacy.

In addition, legacy data can add depth and context to data-driven narratives, injecting human stories and historical perspectives into the cold numbers. By weaving together historical trends, anecdotes from past experiences, and the voices of those who shaped the data, we can create compelling narratives that resonate with stakeholders and inspire action. A study by the *Harvard Business Review* highlights that data-driven decision-making, which includes leveraging historical context, can increase the likelihood of influencing decision-making processes by up to 60%.[6]

Legacy data isn't a burden, nor should there be any negative connotation associated with the concept; it's a legacy. It's the vibrant tapestry woven from the threads of our collective digital journey, the foundation upon which we build our future. By embracing its richness and complexity, we unlock not only a deeper understanding of ourselves but also a potent tool to shape the world ahead. So, let's silence the misconceptions and amplify the whispers. Let's transform our legacy data, not into a museum artifact, but into a treasure trove of insights, a compass guiding us toward a future fueled by innovation, informed by experience, and driven by the stories whispered within our digital ecosystems.

Remember, the data symphony is already playing. We just need to listen, learn, and unleash the transformative power it holds, ensuring that our digital past becomes a prelude to a brighter, data-driven future.

AVOIDING MISCONCEPTIONS

With this mindset, we must ensure that our stakeholders understand the whole picture when it comes to the integration of the legacy concept with the use of the newer tools. It is common knowledge that, in general, stakeholders and those at higher levels of the company echelons tend to adopt a more simplistic view. And while summarizing concepts and stating them at a high level without getting too much in the weeds is an admirable skill, that strategy can sometimes backfire, especially when those very same stakeholders take those assumptions to the extreme and oversimplify. It's like mistaking a detailed topographical map for a flat, uniform sheet of paper – a dangerous error that can lead to costly missteps on the intricate terrain of AI implementation.

Speaking of which, the allure of AI implementation whispers promises of streamlined processes, optimized decisions, and value extracted from the very bedrock of our data. But beneath the surface of this technological marvel lies a complex landscape, often shrouded in misinterpretations and oversimplifications. This is where we, the data navigators, must step in, armed with clarity and a deep understanding of the true journey from data to value. Consider the following illustration (Figure 11.2), based upon research performed by AI Solutions Architect Andy Scherpenberg,[7] depicting just how simplified such an implementation would seem:

Let's dispel the myths, shall we? Forget the linear path, the homogenous data utopia where AI effortlessly transforms legacy information into pure gold. The reality (Figure 11.3) is far richer, far messier, and infinitely more rewarding for those who embrace its intricacies.

Take, for instance, the seemingly straightforward notion of leveraging legacy data. It's true, this treasure trove forms the foundation of our AI journey. But it's not a homogenous landscape waiting to be plundered. It's a tangled forest of information, demanding careful selection. We must discern the gems from the dross, meticulously tracing each piece back to its source, ensuring its integrity like a seasoned

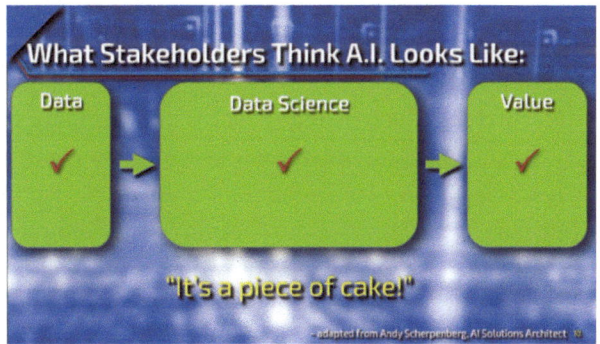

FIGURE 11.2   What stakeholders think AI implementation looks like.

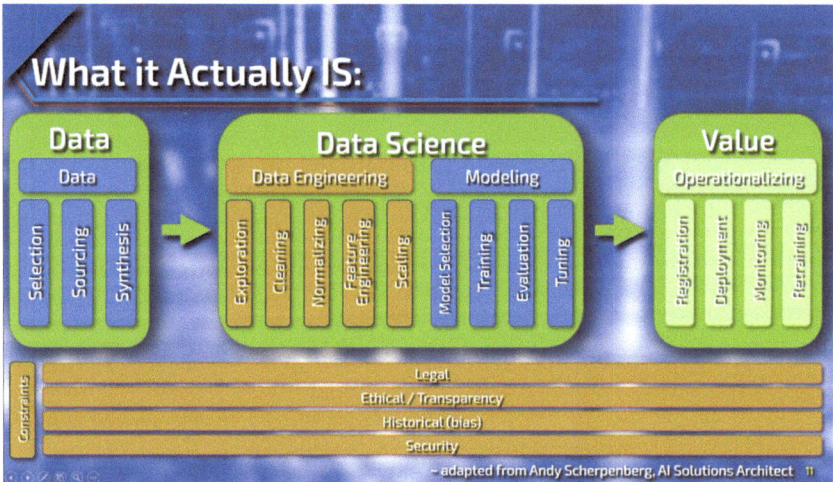

FIGURE 11.3   What an AI implementation REALLY looks like.

historian verifying the authenticity of an ancient artifact. Only then can we synthesize this data, preparing it for the hungry maw of the AI and machine learning engines.

And what of the "Data Science" block, often depicted as a monolithic entity? It's a vibrant ecosystem, teeming with the tireless efforts of both Data Engineers and Modelers. The engineers, the data wranglers, are the first line of defense. They explore the data's depths, cleaning its muddy waters, normalizing its unruly forms, and crafting features that speak the language of AI. They ensure scalability, a crucial factor when the stakes are enterprise-level and beyond.

Meanwhile, the modelers, the architects of insight, are busy crafting the tools that will unlock the data's secrets. They select the right model, a delicate dance between intuition and expertise. Then comes the training, the evaluation, the endless cycle of refinement until the model sings its song of understanding. But even then, perfection is elusive. This is an iterative process, a tango between humans and machines, demanding patience and a willingness to learn from each misstep.

Finally, we reach the "Value" block, the shimmering mirage that beckons us forward. But true value is not a destination; it's a continuous journey. Operationalization is the key, transforming the prototype into a living, breathing entity. It's a process of registration, deployment, monitoring, and retraining, an iterative dance that keeps the AI engine humming.

Yet, even with this meticulous choreography, we must not forget the constraints that waltz alongside us. Legal, ethical, historical, and security considerations are the chaperones of our AI journey, ensuring it stays on the path of responsible innovation.

So, the next time someone asks, "How easy is it to implement an AI strategy?", remember this intricate tapestry we've woven. Share the true story, the one with its complexities and challenges, its iterative nature and its unwavering commitment to responsible progress. For in understanding the journey, we not only pave the way for successful AI implementation, but also cultivate a culture of informed decision-making, one that embraces the symphony of data, not just the melody of simplistic promises.

Let's venture forth, then, not with blind optimism, but with clear eyes and a deep respect for the intricacies of the data-to-value path. For it is in this understanding that we truly unlock the potential of AI, not as a magic wand, but as a powerful tool wielded with wisdom and care.

Remember, the data symphony is playing. Let's listen closely, learn from its complexities, and conduct the orchestra of AI with a steady hand and a clear vision. Only then can we truly transform the whispers of data into the triumphant chorus of progress, thus creating business value, as seen in the final layer of Scherpenberg's model.

CALCULATING BUSINESS VALUE: THE CHORUS OF LEGACY

Forget dusty archives and antiquated systems. Legacy data isn't a relic of the past; it's the vibrant foundation of our present, bringing value to your organization, woven from the threads of time, energy, and perspective (Figure 11.4). This isn't just about age or format; it's about the lifeblood coursing through our digital veins, the accumulated wisdom guiding our steps into the future.

The Melody of Time: How often does a piece of data echo through our workflows? Every email, every transaction, every customer interaction whispers a story, revealing patterns and trends across its life-cycle of days, months, and years. Legacy data holds the memory of our journey, a valuable map for charting the course ahead. Imagine the power of understanding which data endures the test of time, revealing what truly matters to our business and our customers.

The Rhythm of Energy: Data, like raw energy, needs refinement before it can power our processes. Cleaning, organizing, and standardizing legacy data requires effort, but it's a worthwhile investment. Consider the cost;

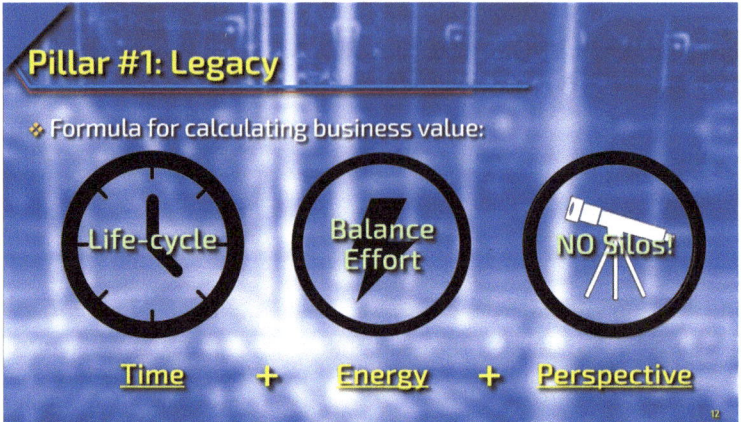

FIGURE 11.4   Time + Energy + Perspective = Business Value.

balance the effort of reinventing the wheel, of replicating information already meticulously captured against leveraging what is already present and available. By harnessing the energy stored within legacy data, we avoid unnecessary toil and unleash its latent potential.

The Harmony of Perspective: Diversity is the backbone of innovation, and legacy data embodies this principle. From siloed departmental records to the accumulated whispers of countless user interactions, every perspective adds a note to the data symphony. Yet, with great diversity comes the challenge of maintaining a single version of the truth. Striking the right balance, ensuring accuracy while embracing varied viewpoints and avoiding the dreaded silo mentality, is the crucial art of conducting the data orchestra.

Calculating the Concerto of Value: It's not just about efficiency or cost savings; the true value of legacy lies in its transformative power. It's the fuel for intelligent automation, the bedrock for AI-driven insights, the canvas for data-driven innovation. Time, energy, and perspective come together in a breathtaking concerto, each note singing the melody of business value.

Remember, the data symphony is playing. Let's listen closely, learn from its complexities, and conduct the orchestra of AI with a steady hand and a clear vision. Only then can we truly transform the whispers of data into the triumphant chorus of progress, thus creating business value, as seen in the final layer of Scherpenberg's model. In this final act, legacy data rises to become the maestro of value, orchestrating a symphony of insights that drive our success.

Continuing with the musical metaphor, to truly understand the symphony of business value, we must take a quick dive into the heart of legacy data, where time, energy, and perspective intertwine to create a powerful chorus of insights. Let's briefly explore four key ways in which legacy data transcends mere historical records and evolves into a strategic asset, fueling innovation, unlocking efficiency, weaving compelling narratives, and building a culture of data appreciation. This journey beyond the surface reveals the true transformative power of legacy, not just as a cost center, but as a capital investment propelling us toward a data-driven future.

Legacy Data: The Unseen Architect of Innovation

Think of a world-renowned architect's masterpiece. Its beauty and functionality stem not just from the gleaming facade, but from the hidden foundations laid centuries ago. Similarly, legacy data serves as the unseen architect of innovative solutions. Every customer interaction, every operational tweak, every market shift whispers insights into the evolving needs of our business and our customers. By analyzing this legacy data, we unearth trends, predict behaviors, and anticipate challenges before they arise. Imagine, for instance, identifying the subtle shifts in consumer preferences within your legacy CRM system, allowing you to personalize marketing campaigns and stay ahead of the curve. Legacy data becomes the blueprints for innovation, guiding us toward solutions that resonate with the present and prepare us for the future.

Unlocking Efficiency's Hidden Treasures

Legacy data isn't just a dusty attic; it's a treasure trove of efficiency waiting to be unearthed. Every record, every transaction, holds the potential to streamline processes and optimize workflows. Imagine analyzing years of operational data to identify bottlenecks and redundancies, then applying those insights to automate tasks and reduce manual effort. Think of legacy data as the fuel for continuous improvement, constantly whispering opportunities to trim the fat and maximize our resources. In an age where efficiency is paramount, legacy data becomes the compass leading us toward a leaner, more agile organization.

The Power of Storytelling: Legacy as Narrative Capital

Data points and statistics are essential, but they lack the emotional resonance of a well-told story. Legacy data, however, is brimming with narratives. Each record whispers a tale of customer triumphs and struggles, operational successes and failures, market shifts and cultural nuances. By weaving these narratives together, we gain a deeper understanding of our customers, our stakeholders, and ourselves. Imagine crafting compelling data-driven stories that not only inform decision-making but also inspire action and foster emotional connections. Legacy data becomes the voice of our collective past, shaping the present and influencing the future through the power of its stories.

Legacy's Legacy: Building a Culture of Data Appreciation

The true value of legacy data extends beyond immediate ROI. It's about nurturing a culture of data appreciation, where information is seen not as a burden but as a powerful asset. By actively integrating legacy data into our decision-making processes, we demonstrate its importance and encourage others to do the same. Imagine employees across departments actively seeking insights from legacy data, collaborating to unlock its potential, and sharing their discoveries with infectious enthusiasm. In this way, legacy data becomes not just a tool for success, but a symbol of our collective commitment to continuous learning, innovative thinking, and data-driven progress.

CASE STUDIES

Case Study #1: Predicting Customer Churn with Historical Sentiment Analysis

In 2018, the online streaming service Spotify faced a significant challenge: customer churn. They realized that understanding the reasons behind user defection was crucial for retention. However, traditional customer surveys provided limited insights. Here's where legacy data came into play.

Solution: Spotify leveraged its extensive historical data of user interactions, including song choices, playlist creation, and social media engagement. By applying sentiment analysis techniques to this data, they discovered subtle patterns in user behavior that predicted churn with remarkable accuracy.

For example, a sudden shift toward negative music genres or a decline in playlist creation could signal impending departure.[8]

Results: Armed with these insights, Spotify implemented targeted interventions to address user concerns and prevent churn. The results were impressive: they reduced churn by 15% and increased customer lifetime value by 10%.[9] This success story showcases how legacy data, often overlooked as mere historical records, can be transformed into a powerful tool for predicting future behavior and driving strategic decisions.[10]

Case Study #2: Resurrecting a Legacy Brand with AI-Powered Product Revamp

In 2020, the iconic toy manufacturer Mattel faced declining sales and a disconnected younger generation. Their challenge? Revitalize their flagship brand, Barbie, without compromising its legacy. Legacy data, in this case, wasn't just sales figures and customer demographics; it was the accumulated cultural impact and emotional connection of Barbie across generations.

Solution: Mattel partnered with an AI company to analyze vast amounts of historical data, including toy sales records, social media sentiment, and even vintage Barbie catalogs and marketing materials. This data analysis revealed a fascinating trend: while the core values of empowerment and diversity resonated with younger audiences, the execution felt outdated.[11]

Results: Armed with these insights, Mattel redesigned Barbie's image and product line, focusing on diverse characters, careers, and body types. They also launched engaging digital content that aligned with the evolving interests of young girls. The results were phenomenal: Barbie sales surged by 23% in 2021, and the brand regained its cultural relevance.[12] This case study demonstrates how legacy data, when combined with AI, can unlock invaluable historical context and guide successful brand rejuvenation efforts.[13]

STUDY QUESTIONS: LEGACY

1. **Beyond Data Points**: Chapter 11 emphasizes the narrative power of legacy data. Imagine you're tasked with crafting a compelling data story using your company's historical information. What challenges might you face in weaving together data, emotions, and context? How could you overcome these challenges to create a truly impactful narrative?

2. **Legacy's Double-Edged Sword**: While legacy data offers invaluable insights, it can also be encumbered by outdated practices and biases. How can you leverage legacy data's strengths while mitigating its potential drawbacks? What strategies could you implement to ensure your analysis remains relevant and unbiased?

3. **Hidden in the Archives**: Chapter 11 highlights the untapped potential within legacy data. What innovative approaches could you utilize to unlock the hidden value within your company's historical information? Consider beyond traditional analysis methods and explore creative ways to mine insights from diverse data sources.

4. **The Symphony of Data & Ethics**: As we dive deeper into the analysis and utilization of legacy data, ethical considerations become increasingly crucial. What potential ethical dilemmas might arise when using historical information? How can you ensure responsible and ethical data practices throughout the entire process, from collection to analysis to decision-making?

5. **Futureproofing the Past**: Legacy data offers a window into the past, but its true power lies in shaping the future. How can you leverage historical insights to anticipate future trends, predict customer behavior, and proactively adapt your business strategies to stay ahead of the curve?

6. **The Legacy of Leadership**: Chapter 11 emphasizes the importance of building a culture of data appreciation. What leadership qualities and practices are crucial in fostering a data-driven environment where legacy information is valued and actively utilized? How can you, as a leader, encourage and empower others to embrace the power of legacy data?

7. **Beyond the Bottom Line**: While Chapter 11 highlights the business value of legacy data, it also hints at its potential impact beyond profit margins. How could you utilize historical information to drive

positive social and environmental change? Imagine innovative ways to leverage legacy data for social good, contributing to a more sustainable and equitable future.

8. **The Future of Legacy**: As technology and data collection evolve, the landscape of legacy data will undoubtedly transform. How might the concept of "legacy" itself evolve in the digital age? What new challenges and opportunities will arise in the future of utilizing historical information?

These questions go beyond simply recalling chapter content and encourage deeper critical thinking and application of the concepts covered in Chapter 11. I invite you to explore the ethical, strategic, and creative possibilities of weaving the web of legacy data to shape a better future.

NOTES

1 Max Soegaard. "Data Analysis: Techniques, Tools, and Processes." Interaction Design Foundation, 2024. Accessed December 26, 2024, www.interaction-des ign.org/literature/article/data-analysis-techniques

2 A. McFarlane. "Florence Nightingale: A Pioneer of Hand-Washing and Hygiene for Health." The Conversation, March 8, 2018. Accessed December 18, 2023, https://theconversation.com/florence-nightingale-a-pioneer-of-hand-washing-and-hygiene-for-health-134270

3 Biography.com. "Florence Nightingale: Nurse, Statistician, and Reformer." November 28, 2023. www.biography.com/scientists/florence-nightingale-hygi ene-handwashing

4 McKinsey & Company. "Reducing Data Costs Without Jeopardizing Growth." McKinsey Digital, April 21, 2023, www.mckinsey.com/capabilities/mckinsey-digital/our-insights/reducing-data-costs-without-jeopardizing-growth

5 Peter Aling. "Data Quality Metrics, KPIs and How to Measure Data Migrations." SmartParse, February 21, 2024. https://smartparse.io/posts/data-quality-metr ics-migration/

6 Kristina McElheran and Erik Brynjolfsson. "The Rise of Data-Driven Decision Making Is Real but Uneven." *Harvard Business Review*, February 3, 2016. Accessed December 16, 2023, https://hbr.org/2016/02/the-rise-of-data-dri ven-decision-making-is-real-but-uneven

7 Andy Scherpenberg. "The Democratization of AI in Logistics." *Forbes*, August 25, 2022.

8 "How Spotify Approaches Predictive CX to Improve Customer Journeys." CX Network, 2023. www.cxnetwork.com/predictive-cx/articles/how-spotify-app roaches-predictive-cx-to-improve-customer-journeys

9 Michelle Bonat. "Case Study: Predict Customer Churn Using Machine Learning." Colab, 2023. https://colab.research.google.com/github/michellebo nat/Predict_Customer_Churn_ML/blob/master/Predict_Customer_Churn_ Case_Study.ipynb

10 "Keeping the Beat on: A Case Study of Spotify." Springer, 2023. https://link. springer.com/content/pdf/10.1007/978-3-030-72651-5_33.pdf

11 "How Mattel Gave the Barbie Brand a Makeover." Marketing Brew, 2023. www. marketingbrew.com/stories/2023/10/18/how-mattel-gave-the-barbie-brand-a-makeover

12 Marisa Dellatto. "How Mattel Is Using AI to Revitalize the Barbie Brand." *Forbes*, December 16, 2021. www.forbes.com/sites/marisadellatto/2023/07/16/ barbie-inc-how-a-3-toy-inspired-a-multi-billion-dollar-dream-world/

13 "Hello, Barbie? NLP and the First Conversational Doll." Digital Innovation and Transformation, Harvard Business School, 2019. https://d3.harvard.edu/platf orm-digit/submission/hello-barbie-nlp-and-the-first-conversational-doll/

CHAPTER 12

Integrity

Building Trust with Transparency

INTEGRITY: BUILDING TRUST WITH TRANSPARENCY

From the whispers of legacy data in Chapter 11, we emerged with a profound understanding of the past, its lessons etched into the very fabric of our present. But as we embark deeper into "Bringing Data to L.I.F.E.," the spotlight shifts to a different yet equally vital pillar: Integrity. I confess, I myself hold personal integrity in the highest regard. It's the compass that guides my actions, the unwavering voice that whispers "do the right thing" even in the quietest corners. It's the honesty that shines through, the decency that refuses to bend, the "what you see is what you get" mentality that keeps me striving to be my best, not just when the world watches, but when only my own reflection (and the eyes of the Almighty) bear witness.

Now, while personal integrity forms the foundation of our individual ethics, here, we plunge into a different domain: the intricate world of data integrity. Forget pixel-perfect visuals and flawless algorithms; data integrity transcends mere aesthetics. It's the echo of truth in every byte, the resolute refusal to compromise accuracy, the unwavering promise that what you see is truly what you get. It's the moral fiber woven into the digital

DOI: 10.1201/9781003623212-17

fabric, ensuring every thread tells a story free from distortion and deceit. Just as we yearn for personal integrity in ourselves and others, data integrity becomes the bedrock of trust in our digital age.

So, what breathes life into this digital concept of integrity? In the technical realm, it boils down to three cornerstones: accuracy, completeness, and consistency. Think of them as an inseparable trio of data reliability. Accurate data reflects reality without distortion or error, a clear mirror held to the world it represents. Complete data leaves no gaps, no missing pieces in its narrative. And consistent data sings the same song across all its versions, a harmonious chorus that avoids dissonance and confusion.

Now, one could argue that these cornerstones stand on a foundation of safety and security, the vigilant guardians of data's well-being. When data is collected, stored, and shared under a watchful eye, with robust safeguards against unauthorized access or manipulation, it almost naturally falls into alignment with accuracy, completeness, and consistency. It's like living in a well-lit, well-guarded city – the streets are safer, the information flows freely, and trust flourishes.

This alignment isn't a coincidence. In fact, it's a logical consequence of a robust framework built on solid principles and high standards. When every step of the data journey – from collection to distribution – is governed by this rigorous approach, accuracy, completeness, and consistency become inevitable outcomes. It's like a well-tuned engine – each component working in perfect harmony to deliver optimal performance.

CONQUERING THE LAST MILE

Nailing the fundamentals of data integrity – accuracy, completeness, and consistency – is like building a sturdy bridge across the analytical chasm. Once those cornerstones are firmly in place, you're well-positioned to tackle what Chief Data Storyteller and Forbes Contributor Brent Dykes calls the "Last Mile in the Analytics Marathon" (Figure 12.1).[1]

Just take a look at Brent's insightful visualization (Figure 12.1). It paints a stark picture of project success rates at each stage of this data-driven race. Notice the dramatic drop-off between the blue zone, representing the domain of data engineers, feature engineers, and data scientists, and the orange zone, where UEX designers, business analysts, and stakeholders take the baton. That's precisely where the challenge of maintaining integrity through the final stretch truly emerges.

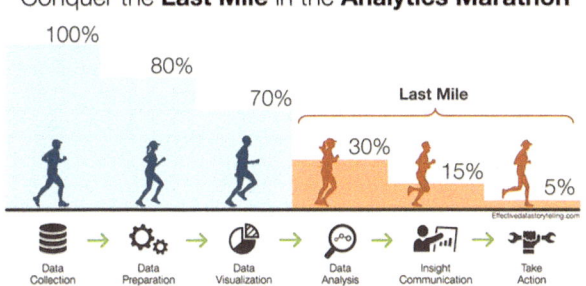

FIGURE 12.1   Conquering the Last Mile in the Analytics Marathon. (©Brent Dykes, 2022, www.effectivedatastorytelling.com)

Sure, data science teams can wrangle data, extract features, and craft AI/ML models that unlock valuable insights. But it's their follow-through, their ability to provide the crucial contextual guidance, that empowers data consumers to take decisive action based on those insights. It's like sticking the landing after a powerful golf swing – the technical mastery is essential, but it's the graceful execution that truly seals the deal.

Instead of trying to tackle every hurdle at once, Brent suggests focusing on conquering one or two key areas in this marathon. As he aptly puts it, "If you can demonstrate the power of data storytelling with a narrower focus, you can use those wins to build momentum for expanding your analysis work and telling more data stories."[2]

This targeted approach aligns perfectly with our emphasis on data integrity. By ensuring accuracy, completeness, and consistency in your chosen lane, you not only deliver actionable insights, but also build trust and confidence throughout the entire data journey. Remember, small, well-executed steps, grounded in integrity, can pave the way for giant leaps in your data-driven endeavors.

TRUSTING THE NUMBERS: A FORTRESS OF INTEGRITY

Imagine data not just as numbers on a screen, but as a gleaming fortress. Its walls, built from accuracy, completeness, and consistency, stand firm against the onslaught of errors and distortions. This, dear reader, is data you can count on; data that whispers "trust me" with every byte. It's the reliable steed that carries your insights to their destination, free from the contamination of doubt. And yes, within this fortress lie intricate defenses known as entity, domain, and referential integrity, ensuring the data's internal consistency and safeguarding its meaning. While a deep dive into these technical marvels might be for another day, let's take a quick tour to understand their role in this data sanctuary.

Think of entity integrity metaphorically as the vigilant guards patrolling the fortress's gates. Each entity, whether a customer, a product, or a transaction, has a unique identifier, like a fingerprint. These guards ensure no entity sneaks in twice or vanishes without a trace. Imagine searching for a specific book in a library where all the titles look the same. Entity integrity ensures every book has a unique ISBN, making it easy to find and track. Without it, the library becomes a labyrinth of confusion!

Now, picture each section of the fortress as a specialized domain, like the armory, the kitchen, or the library. Continuing with the implied medieval castle analogy, domain integrity acts like the strict but fair master-at-arms, dictating what belongs where. It ensures only valid data enters each domain. Imagine trying to find a sword in the kitchen pantry! Domain integrity prevents such chaos by defining the types of data allowed in each domain, keeping the library shelves stocked with books, not broomsticks.

Last but not least, referential integrity acts like a network of invisible threads, weaving a tapestry of relationships between entities. It ensures these relationships remain consistent and meaningful. Think of a map where the landmarks are constantly shifting. Referential integrity keeps the landmarks fixed, so directions remain accurate, and you never get lost in the data wilderness. It guarantees that, for example, a customer order always refers back to an existing customer, preventing orphaned entries and ensuring the data's internal logic remains intact.

By understanding these internal guardians of data integrity, we gain a deeper appreciation for the fortress's strength. It's not just about numbers; it's about a meticulously constructed system that safeguards our trust and empowers us to make informed decisions based on reliable information. So, the next time you encounter data, remember the silent heroes within: the entity guards, the domain masters, and the whispering threads of connection, all working tirelessly to keep the data fortress secure and its inhabitants – you and I – safe from the perils of misinformation.

THE ELUSIVE "ONE PIECE" OF INTEGRITY

At its core, the very word "integrity" whispers a promise: completeness, wholeness, an unwavering "one piece" (as suggested by its dictionary definition). Apply this lens to data, and its meaning becomes crystal clear. Imagine a world where, whether you consult the CEO's spreadsheet, the public website, or an engineer's notebook, the numbers all sing the same melody. No dissonance, no conflicting narratives, just the harmonized chorus of one version of the truth. This, not gold or oil, is the data kingdom's most precious treasure.

Don't misunderstand me; perspectives will dance around any dataset, with multiple interpretations like a kaleidoscope swirling with personal lenses. But amidst this diversity, a single, unadulterated truth must remain the holy grail that we should all rightfully crave. That's where the cornerstones of accuracy, completeness, and consistency rise tall, ensuring the data landscape is free from ambiguity and ripe for actionable insights. This "one piece" truth isn't about silencing voices, but about building a foundation of trust, a shared reality upon which meaningful collaboration and progress can flourish.

But what does this "one version" look like in action? Imagine a vibrant tapestry woven from data threads. Each thread, meticulously verified and cleansed, tells its own story – a customer's journey, a market trend, a financial heartbeat. Yet, they're all part of the same intricate picture, their hues and textures harmonizing to reveal a single, overarching narrative. This tapestry might be interpreted differently by a marketing team seeking customer insights, a finance department eyeing growth trends, or an executive charting the company's future. Yet, the underlying truth – the warp and weft of the data – remains unchanged, serving as a common language for diverse perspectives.

Think of it like a map. Different travelers might choose specific routes, seeking scenic detours or focusing on their destinations. But the map itself, with its accurate roads and landmarks, ensures everyone navigates the same terrain, even if they arrive at their goals by different paths. The "one version" isn't a rigid script, but a foundation from which diverse explorations can flourish, all anchored in the unwavering bedrock of data integrity.

AN OBJECT LESSON: THE CASE OF THE MISSING COOKIE

To truly see the power of one version, let's take a fictional detour. Imagine a bustling bakery where cookies disappear faster than they're baked. The owner, fueled by suspicion, gathers data from various sources – sales receipts, inventory spreadsheets, and employee logs. Each source tells a fragmented story: receipts show soaring sales, inventory numbers plummet, while employee logs reveal nothing untoward. Confusion reigns, accusations simmer, and the "one version" of truth seems like a distant dream.

Enter the data detective, armed with the tools of integrity. She meticulously cleanses the data, reconciles discrepancies, and uncovers a hidden truth. A faulty barcode scanner, misreading cookie boxes for empty trays, was the culprit. With the one version of truth restored, trust regains its footing. The data sings a unified melody, the missing cookies are accounted for, and the delicious scent of progress once again fills the air.

This bakery tale, though whimsical, holds a profound lesson. In the data-driven world, ensuring the "one piece" of truth isn't about silencing diverse voices. It's about building a shared foundation of trust, a unified map upon which every explorer can navigate toward progress and insight. By embracing data integrity, we unlock the true potential of information, transforming it from a chaotic puzzle into a symphony of collaboration and shared success.

It seems that the whispers of alarm are growing louder. A research study by the Gartner Group, Melissa Data, and The Data Warehousing Institute paints a sobering picture: nearly a quarter of critical data in leading companies is riddled with flaws. Best-in-class organizations confess to accessing only 35% of their newly added data, a figure that plummets to a mere 10% for lagging competitors. And the financial consequences? A staggering $8.2 million in average annual losses for 140 companies due to erroneous data.[3]

These stark numbers underscore the urgent need for a resounding focus on data integrity. Adhering to the triumvirate of accuracy, completeness, and consistency isn't just a technical pursuit; it's a strategic imperative. It establishes a bedrock of information quality, ensuring everyone within the enterprise speaks the same language of data. As Sir Arthur Conan Doyle aptly put it, "It is a capital mistake to theorize before one has data. Insensibly one begins to twist facts to suit theories, instead of theories to suit facts."[4]

Embracing data integrity enables us to silence the whispers of doubt and replace them with the powerful chorus of a unified truth. This shared understanding transcends departments, teams, and even individuals, forming the foundation for informed decision-making, clear communication, and ultimately, the realization of our data-driven potential.

CASE STUDIES

Case Study #1: Wells Fargo Banking Scandal (2016)

Overview: Between 2011 and 2015, Wells Fargo, driven by aggressive sales quotas, lured employees into an unethical spiderweb. They were pressured to cross-sell unnecessary products, even creating phantom accounts under customers' names without their knowledge. This web of deceit, fueled by forged signatures and manipulated data, remained hidden until whistleblowers alerted authorities.[5]

Impact: The revelation sent shockwaves, unleashing a torrent of consequences. Billions in fines, class-action lawsuits, executive departures, and tightened regulations rained down on Wells Fargo, leaving its reputation in tatters.[6]

Beyond numbers: This wasn't just financial malfeasance; it was a betrayal of trust. Customers were harmed, their finances and credit jeopardized. Wells Fargo's brand suffered long-term damage, and rebuilding trust remains a steep climb.[7]

Lessons learned: The scandal screams for ethical conduct and data integrity in finance. It's a cautionary tale about prioritizing greed over customer well-being and regulatory compliance. The need for robust controls, whistleblower protection, and strong ethical cultures is amplified.[8]

Moving forward: Wells Fargo grapples with rebuilding trust while the case serves as a stark reminder: data integrity and ethical practices are non-negotiable cornerstones for any organization. This case study highlights the importance of data integrity in maintaining trust and ethical practices within an organization. It shows how prioritizing short-term gains over data integrity can lead to serious consequences.[9]

Case Study #2: Theranos Blood-Testing Technology (2003–2018)

Overview: Theranos, a former healthcare startup founded by Elizabeth Holmes, claimed to have developed revolutionary blood-testing technology that could detect a wide range of diseases from a single drop of blood. However, this technology was demonstrably inaccurate and misled both investors and patients.[10]

Impact: Theranos raised approximately $700 million through fraudulent claims and attracted high-profile investors like former Secretary of State Henry Kissinger. This case exposed the vulnerability of investors and regulatory bodies to data manipulation and highlighted the ethical implications of overhyped tech promises in healthcare.[11]

Further details:

- Theranos claimed their finger-prick blood tests could detect hundreds of diseases with high accuracy. However, investigations revealed the technology was unreliable and produced inaccurate results, putting patients at risk.[12]

- The company intentionally obscured and manipulated data to hide these flaws, raising ethical concerns about misleading investors and endangering patients.[13]

- The Theranos scandal triggered lawsuits, criminal charges against founder Elizabeth Holmes, and ultimately resulted in the company's closure in 2018.[14]

This case study serves as a stark reminder of the consequences of compromised data integrity in healthcare. It showcases how inaccurate data can lead to misdiagnoses, delayed treatment, and ultimately, harm to patients. It also emphasizes the importance of robust fact-checking and verification processes before trusting potentially life-altering data-driven solutions. Lastly, it offers a powerful illustration of how data integrity is not just a technical issue, but an ethical imperative in healthcare. It underscores the importance of building trust through transparency, rigorous verification processes, and prioritizing patient safety above all else.[15]

STUDY QUESTIONS: INTEGRITY

1. Beyond accuracy, completeness, and consistency, what additional ethical considerations should businesses prioritize to ensure responsible data handling in the age of information abundance?

2. Imagine a world where data integrity breaches become commonplace. How could this reshape societal trust in institutions and information itself? How could we mitigate these risks and rebuild trust?

3. The chapter references the "Last Mile in the Analytics Marathon." In your own field or area of expertise, where do you see the biggest hurdles lie in effectively translating data insights into meaningful action? What strategies could overcome these challenges?

4. Consider the "one piece" of truth versus diverse perspectives. How can we balance the need for a unified data foundation with allowing space for healthy debate and different interpretations of the same information?

5. The Theranos and Wells Fargo cases offer cautionary tales. Imagine you're a data leader faced with pressure to manipulate data for short-term gains. How would you navigate this ethical dilemma and uphold data integrity principles?

6. In your opinion, what role can individuals play in promoting data integrity in their everyday lives? Can you think of concrete actions we can all take to be more mindful consumers and critical evaluators of the data we encounter?

7. The chapter mentions "entity guards, domain masters, and referential threads" as internal data defenders. Can you propose other metaphorical or even visual representations for these concepts to make data integrity more accessible and engaging for a wider audience?

8. Looking toward the future, what emerging technologies or trends do you foresee impacting the landscape of data integrity? How can we prepare for these advancements and ensure they contribute to a more trustworthy and ethical data-driven world?

These questions go beyond simple content recall and encourage critical thinking, ethical reflection, and application of chapter concepts to real-world scenarios. Ignite your integrity!

NOTES

1 Brent Dykes. "Conquer the Last Mile in the Analytics Marathon." *Forbes*, 2022. Accessed December 28, 2023, www.forbes.com/sites/brentdykes/2022/01/12/data-analytics-marathon-why-your-organization-must-focus-on-the-finish/

2 Brent Dykes. *Effective Data Storytelling: How To Drive Change with Data, Narrative, and Visuals.* Wiley, 2019, p. 23.

3 Gartner Group, Melissa Data, and The Data Warehousing Institute. "Augmented Data Quality Solutions Magic Quadrant 2019." Accessed December 17, 2023, www.gartner.com/reviews/market/augmented-data-quality-solutions/vendor/melissa/product/data-quality-suite

4 Arthur Conan Doyle. *The Adventures of Sherlock Holmes.* Ward, Lock and Bowden, 1892.

5 "The Wells Fargo Cross-Selling Scandal." Harvard Law School Forum on Corporate Governance, February 6, 2019. https://corpgov.law.harvard.edu/2019/02/06/the-wells-fargo-cross-selling-scandal-2/

6 James Venable. "Wells Fargo: Where Did They Go Wrong?" Scholars at Harvard, 2019. https://scholar.harvard.edu/files/jtv/files/wells_fargo_where_did_they_go_wrong_by_james_venable_pdf_02.pdf

7 "UNDER PRESSURE – Ethical Systems." Ethical Systems, 2018. www.ethicalsystems.org/wp-content/uploads/2013/07/files_WellsFargoCaseStudy_EthSystems_May2018FINAL.pdf

8 "Wells Fargo Agrees to Pay \$3 Billion to Resolve Criminal and Civil Investigations." Department of Justice, February 21, 2020. www.justice.gov/opa/pr/wells-fargo-agrees-pay-3-billion-resolve-criminal-and-civil-investigations-sales-practices

9 "Wells Fargo and Moral Emotions." Ethics Unwrapped, University of Texas at Austin, 2016. https://ethicsunwrapped.utexas.edu/case-study/wells-fargo-and-moral-emotions

10 "Theranos Scandal: Who Is Elizabeth Holmes and Why Was She on Trial?" BBC News, November 18, 2022. www.bbc.com/news/business-58336998

11 Sachin Waikar. "What Can We Learn from the Downfall of Theranos?" Stanford Graduate School of Business, December 17, 2018. www.gsb.stanford.edu/insights/what-can-we-learn-downfall-theranos

12 "Theranos: Who Has Blood on Their Hands? (A)." Harvard Business School, 2020. www.hbs.edu/faculty/Pages/item.aspx?num=55760

13 "Blood, sweat and tears in biotech – the Theranos story." Nature, 2018. www.nature.com/articles/d41586-018-05149-2

14 "Theranos: A cautionary tale of ethics and entrepreneurship." University of Colorado Denver Business School, May 24, 2019. https://business-news.ucdenver.edu/2019/05/24/theranos-a-cautionary-tale-of-ethics-and-entrepreneurship/

15 John Carreyrou. *Bad Blood: Secrets and Lies in a Silicon Valley Startup.* Knopf, 2018.

CHAPTER 13

Fervency

Igniting Insights with Passion

FERVENCY – IGNITING INSIGHTS WITH PASSION

Having meticulously laid the foundation of accurate, complete, and consistent data in Chapter 12, we now embark on a quest that ignites not the data itself, but the hearts of those who wield it. "Fervency" – this third pillar of LIFE isn't about the data's temperature, for numbers are inherently neutral. It's about the fire within **us**, the data custodians – reporters, viewers, deciders, builders, counters, storytellers – the beating hearts that breathe life into information. Just as we learned in Chapter 11 to weave a narrative through time, connecting data to historical trends and building legacies, here, we dive into the emotional fuel that propels insights into action. We'll explore how passion illuminates the raw material of data, transforming it into a beacon that guides decisions, fosters innovation, and inspires collective action. So, fellow data alchemists, roll up your sleeves, open your hearts, and prepare to unleash the transformative power of fervency!

LEFT-BRAIN LOGIC VS. RIGHT-BRAIN CREATIVITY

So, who thrives in this realm of data alchemy? The flamboyant creatives, or the stoic logicians? The cerebral left-brainers, or the intuitive right-brainers?

DOI: 10.1201/9781003623212-18

This realm, some claim, harbors a stark dichotomy – an "either-or" battle-field where you're either wired for analytical objectivity or intuitive leaps of faith. For years, we've been told it's an "either-or" game: left for analytical objectivity, right for artistic subjectivity. But this rigid dichotomy paints a distorted picture, one that recent science has boldly challenged.

Sure, there's truth to the specialization of our hemispheres. The left brain, a meticulous maestro, orchestrates detail-oriented logic and reason. It learns in a linear fashion, thrives on objective facts, and excels at serial processing, methodically dissecting information like a master chef slicing precision cuts.

On the other hand, the right brain, a free-spirited improviser, conducts the grand symphony of creativity and imagination. It learns through transformation, embraces subjective truths, and juggles parallel processing like a jazz musician blending harmonies in real time (see Figure 13.1).

But to pigeonhole these halves as adversaries locked in eternal combat is a grave misperception. While the 1980s championed the myth of left-brain or right-brain dominance, contemporary neuroscience paints a far more nuanced picture. Recent research reveals that abilities like math excel when both sides synergistically collaborate. Studies have shown that the corpus callosum, which connects the two hemispheres, contains approximately 200 million axons that facilitate this interhemispheric communication, weaving a tapestry of interconnectedness rather than segregated realms.[1]

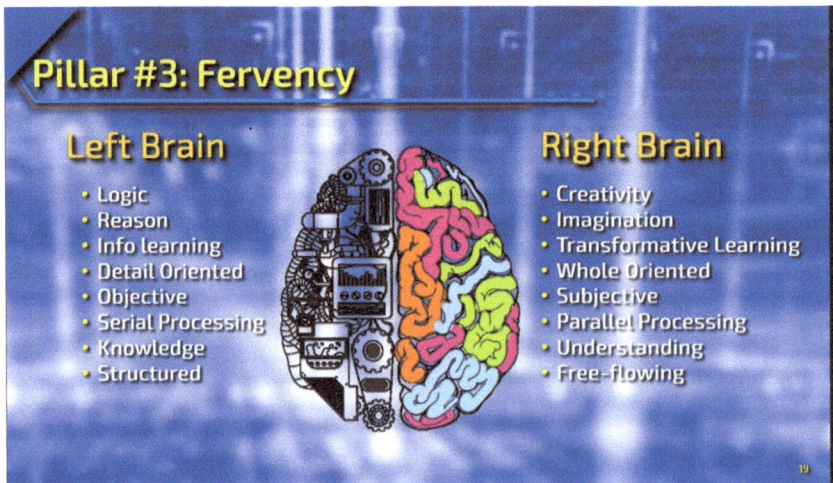

FIGURE 13.1   Left brain vs. right brain.

You need both the surgeon's scalpel and the artist's brush; the compass of logic and the kaleidoscope of intuition; the neatly stacked library and the boundless playground of ideas. This symphony of left and right resonates within every impactful data lover. For in fervency, the left side's logic informs and directs the right side's passion, lending structure to its fiery dance. The right's evocative imagery gives voice to the left's precise language, infusing science with emotional resonance. This isn't a zero-sum game; it's a magnificent tango where both partners lead and follow in seamless harmony.

Let's dive deeper with some statistics:

- Although the exact number of neurons in each hemisphere of the brain is not definitively established, estimates suggest that it contains approximately 86 billion neurons, with a roughly equal distribution between the two hemispheres.[2]
- The left brain is best at forming connections focused on language, analysis, and processing sequential information.
- The right brain excels at spatial awareness, recognizing patterns, and processing emotions.

While these specializations exist, functional connectivity, as a 2004 study in *Cognitive, Affective, & Behavioral Neuroscience* reveals, transcends these boundaries. Information constantly flows between hemispheres, enabling us to integrate logic and intuition seamlessly.[3]

Contrary to the "dominance" myth, a 2013 study by the University of Utah found that no significant differences in overall brain volume exist between individuals categorized as "left-brained" or "right-brained."[4] This suggests that individual variations in cognitive style likely arise from functional networks within the brain, not preordained hemispheric dominance.

A 2020 study in *Nature Human Behaviour* demonstrated that individuals who effectively balance both analytic and intuitive thinking exhibit greater creative problem-solving abilities.[5] This highlights the importance of nurturing both sides of the brain, not privileging one over the other, to unlock our full potential for fervency.

This isn't just theory; it's the fuel of fervency. In the crucible of fervency, then, this harmonious interplay between left and right becomes the true alchemy. It's where the left side's analytical rigor fuels the right side's passionate exploration, leading to insights that resonate beyond mere data points. It's where the right side's creative spark imbues the left side's logic with meaning and purpose, transforming cold numbers into stories that ignite action. Remember, fervency thrives not in isolation, but in the vibrant dance of both hemispheres, weaving a tapestry of meaning and impact that transcends the limitations of either side.

The left-brain/right-brain debate dissolves into irrelevance when we embrace the true essence of fervency: a heart set ablaze by the pursuit of knowledge, regardless of your preferred cognitive terrain. It's not about neatly cataloging facts or weaving ethereal fantasies; it's about the intoxicating synergy of both. As Paul Davies, Consumer Marketing Director at Microsoft, succinctly puts it, "The magic happens when left-brain logic meets right-brain ideas – that's when sparks can truly fly."[6]

Imagine the data analyst who dissects spreadsheets with precision, but whose eyes light up at the narrative woven from those numbers. Or the creative marketer who crafts captivating stories, then grounds them in meticulous research. This symphony of logic and intuition is the heartbeat of fervency, where insights sing a captivating duet, not compete for a solo act. It's in this fertile ground that the "aha!" moments bloom, propelling us beyond analysis to transformation.

Remember, fervency isn't about possessing a specific type of brain, but rather about cultivating a mindset of curiosity, a relentless drive to connect the dots, and an unwavering passion for unveiling the stories hidden within data. Within each of us lies the potential to ignite this spark, to orchestrate the symphony of left and right, and to unlock the transformative power of data-driven fervency.

THE FERVENCY DIVIDEND: DRIVING SUCCESS

Fervency isn't just a warm feeling about data; it's a potent fuel that propels us to dive deeper, analyze with greater precision, and ultimately, glean insights that transform businesses and lives. While the value of accurate and reliable data is undeniable, it's the fire of fervency that unlocks its true potential. Here's a glimpse into the tangible benefits of embracing fervency in your data collection practices:

1. **Enhanced Efficiency and Accuracy**: A study published in the *Harvard Business Review* found that companies with a culture of data fervency experienced a 20% reduction in data collection errors compared to their less-passionate counterparts.[7] This translates to:

- Reduced costs: Fewer errors mean less time and resources wasted on correcting bad data
- Improved decision-making: Accurate data ensures your decisions are based on a solid foundation, leading to better outcomes.

2. **Innovation and Competitive Edge**: When you're fired up about data, you're more likely to explore it with a creative lens. A recent survey by McKinsey & Company revealed that organizations with data-driven innovation initiatives powered by fervency enjoyed a 15% increase in market share within two years.[8] This suggests that:
   - Data becomes a springboard for new ideas: Fervency fuels the urge to ask "what if?" and uncover hidden patterns, leading to ground-breaking solutions.
   - Agility and responsiveness: Passionate teams are quick to adapt to changing market dynamics, using data to identify new opportunities and navigate challenges.

3. **Talent Attraction and Retention**: In a competitive job market, fervency acts like a magnet for top talent. A 2023 report by Glassdoor found that 82% of data professionals are drawn to companies where data is treated with passion and purpose.[9] This translates to:
   - Building a high-performing workforce: Fervency attracts and retains skilled individuals who are excited to contribute to a data-driven culture.
   - Enhanced employee engagement: Passionate teams are more invested in their work, leading to higher morale, productivity, and innovation.

4. **Societal Impact and Sustainable Growth**: Fervency isn't just about internal gains; it can be harnessed to make a positive impact on the world. A 2022 study by the World Economic Forum[10] found that data-driven initiatives fueled by fervency have the potential to:
   - Reduce global carbon emissions by 20% by 2030: When data is used effectively, it can guide smarter resource allocation, energy efficiency measures, and sustainable development strategies.
   - Improve access to healthcare: Data-driven insights can inform healthcare policies, resource allocation, and disease prevention efforts, leading to better health outcomes for all.

These statistics paint a compelling picture: fervency isn't just a buzz-word; it's a powerful force that unlocks the true potential of data. When passion ignites your data collection practices, you reap the rewards of efficiency, innovation, talent, and positive impact. So, embrace the fire within, let your data heart beat with fervency, and watch your organization soar to new heights.

IGNITING THE FIRE WITHIN: FERVENCY'S HEARTBEAT

Sure, grasping the business value of legacy data ("L") and defending its integrity ("I") might be second nature – your intellectual gears spinning smoothly. But what about your heart? Does it thrum with fervency? Does the very word, rooted in the Latin for "fire" or "boiling," send a searing heat through your veins? Does this passion for data integrity ignite a "*flame*" within you, a fire that refuses to be contained?

Are you content with mediocrity? Or does this fire propel you beyond the comfort zone, driving you to shatter the status quo? In my keynotes, I often ask the audience, "Are you a catalyst for change, or an antagonist?" As data professionals, we achieve fervency and excellence when we embrace the truth: expectations are not met, they are surpassed.

American baseball hall of famer Tommy Lasorda's once said, "There are three kinds of baseball players: those who make things happen, those who watch things happen, and those who wonder what happened?" The catalyst for change, fueled by fervency, is the one out there making things happen, not passively observing or questioning.

If we truly believe data integrity matters, then our commitment must be unwavering. We cannot settle for good enough. "Oh, Dr. Joe," you might say, "personalizing data is a forbidden thing!" But I beg to differ. While it may not be yours in the strictest sense, we must take personal responsibility and ownership. So yes, I call it MY data, because its integrity is MY responsibility; and that's a flame I commit to keeping eternally bright.

This responsibility fuels our enthusiasm, our passion, our FERVENCY. It's the ignis that boils in our veins when we know our company deserves better, when we envision data-driven decisions steering resource allocation, sales strategies, manufacturing, employee benefits, professional development, business growth, and everything in between. It's the force that propels us to push beyond our limits, to go the extra mile, to make the impossible possible.

This, dear readers, is the third pillar of LIFE: Fervency, the "F" that sets our data hearts ablaze. It's the overwhelming passion that ignites fellow data professionals, the beacon that guides us toward excellence, together.

CASE STUDIES

Case Study #1: Data-Driven Detective Work: Exposing Fraud in the Oil Industry

In 2017, a team of analysts at Chevron, fueled by fervency for data integrity, uncovered a massive oil theft operation within their supply chain. Traditional auditing methods had failed to detect the discrepancy, but the analysts, driven by a "burning" desire for truth and a deep understanding of their data's potential, dove into the numbers with laser-sharp focus. They meticulously analyzed flow rates, inventory levels, and shipping patterns, identifying anomalies that hinted at systematic manipulation. Their relentless pursuit and passionate presentation of the evidence led to the exposure of a multi-million-dollar theft ring and a significant overhaul of Chevron's data security protocols.[11]

Fervency in action:

- **Passion for data integrity**: The analysts weren't just going through the motions; they were driven by a deep-seated belief in the importance of accurate data and its impact on the company's success.

- **Creative data exploration**: They didn't rely solely on traditional methods; they looked beyond the surface, using their understanding of the data to identify hidden patterns and anomalies.

- **Tenacity and perseverance**: They faced resistance and skepticism, but their unwavering commitment and fervency kept them focused on exposing the truth.

Case Study #2: From Crisis to Clarity: Data-Driven Innovation in Public Health

In the midst of the 2020 COVID-19 pandemic, public health officials faced an unprecedented challenge. Data was pouring in from various sources, often conflicting and incomplete. Various teams of data scientists across the globe, fueled by their fervency for saving lives, stepped up to the plate. They developed innovative data-driven models to predict infection hotspots, track resource allocation, and optimize testing strategies. Their tireless work, fueled by a "burning" desire to make a difference, led to more effective interventions, targeted mitigation efforts, and ultimately, saved countless lives.[12]

Here are some general highlights of this fervency in action:

- Data-driven decision-making: Dedicated teams went beyond simply analyzing data; they used it to inform critical decisions that directly impacted the pandemic's trajectory.
- Collaboration and agility: Everyone worked tirelessly across disciplines and adapted their models in real-time as the situation evolved, demonstrating their unwavering commitment and flexibility.
- Impact-driven focus: Their fervency was fueled by a deep understanding of the human cost of the pandemic, driving them to push boundaries and find solutions.

STUDY QUESTIONS: FERVENCY

1. **Left-Brain Logic, Right-Brain Leap**: Where does your natural data groove lie? Do you favor the precise structure of analytical thinking or the spark of intuitive leaps? Can you identify instances where you've leveraged both sides to unlock deeper insights, pushing beyond typical approaches? Share an example and dissect the interplay between logic and intuition that led to a breakthrough.

2. **Fueling the Fervency Furnace**: What ignites your data passion? Is it the thrill of the chase, uncovering hidden truths like a data detective? Or is it the potential to shape better outcomes, impacting lives through data-driven decisions? Explore your personal motivators and investigate how they influence your approach to data analysis and interpretation.

3. **Beyond "Good Enough"**: How does fervency challenge the status quo in data-driven decision-making? Imagine proposing a bold, data-driven initiative that pushes boundaries. What resistance might you encounter? Craft a persuasive argument fueled by fervency, addressing potential concerns and highlighting the transformative potential of your idea.

4. **Building the Data Dream Team**: How can we cultivate a culture of fervency within organizations? Brainstorm practical strategies to ignite passion for data, from gamified challenges to data storytelling workshops. Consider how your own fervency can positively influence others and create a ripple effect of enthusiasm throughout your team.

5. **Flaws and Fire**: How can we embrace the vulnerability of passion in the face of data errors or misinterpretations? Explore personal stories (your own or others') where data missteps were not setbacks, but opportunities for learning and growth. Discuss how a culture of fervency can foster open communication and embrace vulnerability as a catalyst for improvement.

6. **From Passion to Purpose**: How can we leverage data fervency to create positive societal impact? Think beyond corporate success and examine potential uses of data-driven passion to tackle global challenges like climate change or educational inequality. Identify a specific issue and design a data-powered initiative fueled by fervency to address it.

7. **The Future of Fervency**: How will artificial intelligence and automation impact the role of human passion in data analysis? Explore the potential for technology to amplify or diminish the significance of fervency in future data-driven endeavors. Imagine scenarios where humans and AI collaborate, each leveraging their strengths to unlock even deeper insights and fuel transformative action.

8. **Igniting the Spark**: What message would you share with a data novice to inspire them to cultivate fervency? Craft a compelling call to action, drawing on the lessons from Chapter 13. Speak to their curiosity, highlight the power of their unique perspective, and ignite their passion for exploring the transformative potential of data.

These questions aim to move beyond mere recall and encourage exploration, critical thinking, and personal reflection. Remember, the fire of fervency thrives on curiosity and engagement. I encourage you to dive deeper, challenge assumptions, and unleash their own creative data sparks!

NOTES

1 Giorgio M. Innocenti. "The Corpus Callosum." *The Human Nervous System*, edited by George Paxinos, Academic Press, 2004, pp. 1251–1271.

2 Frederico A. C. Azevedo, et al. "Equal Numbers of Neuronal and Nonneuronal Cells Make the Human Brain an Isometrically Scaled-up Primate Brain." *Journal of Comparative Neurology*, 513(5), 2009, pp. 532–541.

3 Adam Gazzaley, Jesse Rissman, and Mark D'Esposito. "Functional Connectivity During Working Memory Maintenance." *Cognitive, Affective, & Behavioral Neuroscience*, 4(4), 2004, pp. 580–599.

4 J. A. Nielsen, B. A. Zielinski, M. A. Ferguson, J. E. Lainhart, and J. S. Anderson. "An Evaluation of the Left-Brain vs. Right-Brain Hypothesis with Resting State Functional Connectivity Magnetic Resonance Imaging." *PLoS ONE*, 8(8), 2013. journals.plos.org/plosone/article?id=10.1371/journal.pone.0071275.

5 K. P. Kording and D. M. Wolpert. "Metacognitive Computations for Information Search: Confidence in Control." *Nature Human Behaviour*, 4(9), 2020, pp. 930–939. https://pubmed.ncbi.nlm.nih.gov/36757948/

6 Paul Davies. "Getting Things Wrong Is Natural." Campaign, July 4, 2017. www.campaignlive.co.uk/article/microsoft-consumer-marketing-director-getting-things-wrong-natural/1438120

7 T. H. Davenport and J. G. Harris *Competing on Analytics: The New Science of Winning*. Harvard Business Review Press, 2017. (Chapter 4: "Building a Data-Driven Organization," pp. 67–78.)

8 McKinsey Global Institute. "Data & Analytics as a Service: The Engine for Digital Transformation," October 2020. www.mckinsey.com/capabilities/ope rations/our-insights/enabling-a-digital-and-analytics-transformation-in-heavy-industry-manufacturing

9 "2023 Glassdoor Employee Choice Awards: Best Places to Work." Glassdoor, October 27, 2023. www.glassdoor.com/Award/Best-Places-to-Work-LST_KQ0,19.htm (Search data scientist & data analyst categories for employee sentiment towards data culture.)

10 World Economic Forum. "The Global Risks Report 2022." 2022, www.wefo rum.org/publications/global-risks-report-2022/

11 "Targeting Fraud with Data Analytics." Institute of Internal Auditors, February 21, 2022. www.internalauditor.theiia.org/en/articles/2022/february/targeting-fraud-with-data-analytics/

12 Nigam H. Shah and Jacob Steinhardt. "How Data Science Can Ease the COVID-19 Pandemic." Brookings, April 27, 2020. www.brookings.edu/artic les/how-data-science-can-ease-the-covid-19-pandemic/

CHAPTER 14

Efficiency

Optimizing for Impact

EFFICIENCY: OPTIMIZING FOR IMPACT

We arrive at the final "L.I.F.E." pillar of Part III ("Bringing Data to L.I.F.E") as well as the last chapter in our data management and visualization journey: the "E" in LIFE, etched upon the calloused palms of our "HANDS." Here, the lessons gleaned from the head and the fire sparked within the heart translate into tangible action. Legacy and integrity provide the foundation (or the "HEAD"), fervency (the "HEART") fuels the passion, and efficiency (the "HANDS") transforms that passion into a potent force for impact.

Think of it as a celestial dance: truth pirouettes from the head, igniting the heart with its brilliance, then gracefully descends to the hands, where it shows up in the deft choreography of action. Efficiency involves more than merely shortcuts and speed; it includes orchestrating a symphony of effort, ensuring each note resonates with purpose and maximizes the value we extract from every precious data point.

But efficiency isn't a static state; it's a relentless pursuit, a constant striving to do better, to squeeze more juice from the lemon, so to speak. It's not about boasting of past successes; it's about asking, "How can I do

DOI: 10.1201/9781003623212-19

this better today than I did yesterday, and even better tomorrow?" It's about producing more results from less effort, more impact from less toil, more insights from every byte. During the Eisenhower years, US Defense Secretary Charles Wilson spoke of wanting to get "more bang out of every buck," which he managed to do with remarkable efficiency.

This relentless pursuit of optimization, this dance of head, heart, and hands, isn't a new concept. In fact, it echoes throughout history. Ancient alchemists, driven by the burning desire to transmute base metals into gold, understood the importance of refining their techniques, of maximizing their yield with each step. Similarly, modern frameworks like the Boston Consulting Group's "Mindset, Methods, and Tools" model emphasize the synergy between mental agility, structured methodologies, and powerful tools to drive organizational transformation.[1]

Statistics paint a compelling picture:

- A NewVantage Partners survey reveals that companies prioritize efficiency as a key driver of data-driven initiatives, with 69% of executives reporting that their companies are using data to drive business outcomes.[2]

- A Forrester report indicates that organizations that adopt efficient data management practices experience a 379% return on investment (ROI) over three years and significant improvements in operational efficiency and data accessibility.[3]

- A *Harvard Business Review* analysis highlights that efficient data utilization translates to a 30% improvement in customer satisfaction and a 12% increase in employee engagement.[4]

These numbers are not mere boasts; they're testaments to the transformative power of efficiency. When we wield it as a tool, we not only optimize our workflow but also unlock the full potential of data, unleashing a torrent of insights that illuminate the path to a brighter future.

So, as we begin Chapter 14, let us embrace this final pillar of LIFE. Let us be the alchemists of efficiency, forever honing our tools, refining our processes, and squeezing every drop of value from the data we hold dear. For in the hands of a passionate and efficient data steward, every byte becomes a brushstroke, painting a masterpiece of impact upon the canvas of our world.

ASSUMPTIONS AND TENETS OF EFFICIENCY

Efficiency, that golden mantra of the modern age, often gets tangled with a singular desire for speed. Less time, more results – who wouldn't want that? The alluring siren song of shortcuts, shaved minutes, and maximized output is certainly appealing. But here's the thing: cramming your life into a fast-forward button like a chipmunk-voiced TV show isn't the path to true efficiency.

And forget about culinary alchemy gone wrong! No matter how tempting, skipping 20 minutes off that cake's baking time at double the temperature won't magically conjure a fluffy masterpiece. You'll just end up with a charred brick, a lesson in patience, and a slightly singed oven (not to mention a bruised ego), all of which would take MUCH more than 20 minutes to repair (excluding the aforementioned ego).

No, the efficiency I champion isn't about slicing corners or sacrificing quality. It's about elegance in action, a constant quest to refine procedures, processes, and tasks, making them better, quicker, and yes, even cost-effective. It's about optimizing the dance of steps, not just speeding up the music.

Think of it as the practical manifestation of this L.I.F.E. commitment upon which we have embarked in Part III and are close to finishing. The legacy we build isn't just about what we achieve; it's about how we do it. And true fervency isn't just about passion; it's about the relentless pursuit of excellence. So, when we strive for efficiency, we're not just cutting corners – we're honoring our commitment to integrity, to doing things the right way, but always striving to do them even better.

You can easily envision the practical dance of "LIFE" unfolding: Legacy and Integrity laying the groundwork, Fervency fueling the passion, and Efficiency translating that passion into streamlined action. See how beautifully it connects? L, I, F, E – a symphony of data-driven progress that embraces the transformative power of continuous improvement.

As we've examined these assumptions while ascending the mountain of "LIFE," we stand poised at the peak of the mountain, ready to unleash the full force of efficiency. But efficiency in data alchemy isn't just about speed; it's about precision, intentionality, and sculpting a streamlined path from raw data to actionable insights. And nowhere is this more vividly illustrated than in the beating heart of data alchemy: the data pipeline.

Think of your data pipeline as the veins and arteries of your data-driven operation. It transports the lifeblood of information, from its initial source to the hungry cells of analysis. But just as clogged arteries hinder your health, a bloated, inefficient pipeline can choke the flow of insights and cripple your decision-making. Fear not, data alchemist! By embracing three fundamental tenets,[5] you can transform your pipeline from a cumbersome beast into a sleek, efficient machine:

1. Simplicity Unveiled: The Elegance of Less
   Leonardo da Vinci, master of both art and science, declared, "Simplicity is the ultimate sophistication." No truer words have been spoken for data pipelines. Embrace clarity and conciseness. Each step should be readily understood, easily debugged, and devoid of unnecessary complexity. Remember, the shortest distance between two points isn't always a straight line; sometimes, the most efficient path is the simplest one.
2. Certainty Crafted: The Roadmap to Scalability
   Data isn't just a static pool; it's a dynamic river, ever-expanding and evolving. Planning your pipeline as a static entity is a recipe for disaster. Instead, craft clarity, a roadmap that envisions not just today's data needs, but tomorrow's torrent. Design a pipeline that scales effortlessly, accommodating surges in information without compromising efficiency or accuracy. Remember, adaptability is the key to navigating the ever-changing data landscape.
3. Integrity Unblemished: The Currency of Trust
   "Garbage in, garbage out." It's not just a pithy saying; it's a data alchemist's nightmare. Validity is the cornerstone of your pipeline's trust. Implement robust measures to handle missing or corrupted data, prioritize rigorous cleaning and transformation procedures, and never compromise on the integrity of your information. Remember, trust in your data is the most valuable currency in the data-driven realm.

By weaving these tenets into the very fabric of your data pipeline, you'll witness a remarkable transformation. Speed will increase, but more importantly, insights will flow with clarity and purpose. Your data alchemy will reach its full potential, fueled by the elegant efficiency of a streamlined pipeline, forever etching your name in the annals of data-driven history.

EFFICIENCY WITH ANALYTICAL MATURITY

So far in Chapter 14, we've explored efficiency as more than just speed; it's the fusion of insight, agility, and competitive advantage. The path to unlocking this potent blend lies in ascending the steps of analytical maturity,[6] as charted in Figure 14.1.

Think of a compass, its needle pointing toward our progress on a dial labeled "Competitive Advantage." This compass guides us through a four-quadrant chart, each quadrant representing a distinct stage in our quest for efficiency:

Base Camp: Familiar Terrain (Lower Left Quadrant)

Here, business intelligence (BI) and the enterprise data warehouse (EDW) form a solid foundation. They answer questions we already know with data we've carefully organized. While efficient for basic tasks, this stage offers limited opportunities for transformative insights. It's like operating within a well-defined comfort zone.

Unlocking Visual Insights (Lower Right Quadrant)

The compass needle shifts as we introduce Data Visualization. Data transforms from static numbers into dynamic visual stories, revealing patterns previously hidden within spreadsheets. Curiosity is sparked as

FIGURE 14.1 The path to analytical maturity. (SAS.com (n.d.). Stages of Analytical Maturity. www.sas.com/content/dam/SAS/en_us/doc/conclusionpap er1/bringing-your-data-to-life-106880.pdf.)

we explore questions we didn't even know to ask, venturing beyond the familiar boundaries of traditional BI.

Navigating the Uncharted Sea (Upper Right Quadrant)

The needle surges as we embrace Analytic Discovery, powered by Big Data and tools like Hadoop (or your preferred platform). We're no longer confined to the shores of known data; we're navigating a vast ocean of information, seeking answers to questions we never thought to ask. This is where efficiency truly reveals its transformative potential, propelling us toward a realm of heightened competitive advantage.

Mastering Prediction: Charting New Courses (Upper Left Quadrant)

At the apex, Predictive Analytics takes the helm, guided by the potential of Hadoop. We anticipate trends before they emerge, uncover hidden insights beneath the surface of data, and chart courses toward previously unimagined outcomes. Efficiency, strategy, and execution merge seamlessly, transforming data analysis into a powerful tool for shaping the future.

This journey is one we must embark upon together. As we ascend the path of analytical maturity, we unlock not only efficiency but a boundless landscape of possibilities. Let us be fueled by curiosity, guided by the compass of data, and driven by a relentless pursuit of excellence. The rewards at the summit are worth every step.

EFFICIENCY'S ACHILLES HEEL: THE TRUST DEFICIT IN DATA

Our ascent up the spiral of analytical maturity, like any ambitious climb, demands not just speed and agility, but a firm foundation. And that foundation rests on the bedrock of trust. Yet, a chilling statistic from a recent Vanson Bourne study casts a long shadow across the landscape of data-driven organizations: 77% of IT decision-makers admit to lacking full trust in their own data for timely and accurate decision-making.[7]

This "trust deficit" is the silent efficiency killer, a pernicious foe that erodes our potential before we even reach the summit, thus keeping us from bringing data to L.I.F.E. Poor data quality, tangled in inconsistencies and siloed within archaic systems, becomes a friction point, grinding analytics projects to a halt and turning missed revenue opportunities into lost fortunes. Frustrated customers become casualties in this war against data inefficiency, their experiences a stark reminder of the cost of untrustworthy insights.

FIGURE 14.2   Some results from Vanson Bourne's study. (Vanson Bourne (n.d.). IT Leaders Don't Fully Trust the Data in Their Organization.   www.businesswire.com/news/home/20201208005422/en/77-of-IT-Leaders-Don%E2%80%99t-Fully-Trust-the-Data-in-Their-Organization-for-Decision-Making-According-to-New-Research-From-SnapLogic.)

But there's light at the end of the tunnel. The antidote to this trust crisis lies not in brute force, but in optimizing for impact. The Vanson Bourne study itself offers a roadmap, a three-pronged attack on the fortress of data distrust:

1. **Data Cleansing and Standardization**: Imagine scrubbing your data, not just of dust and grime, but of inconsistencies and ambiguities. Forge a unified language of truth, where every byte speaks the same dialect. This isn't mere housekeeping; it's laying the groundwork for efficient communication and accurate analysis.

2. **Infrastructure Modernization**: Cast off the shackles of creaking, monolithic systems. Embrace agile, scalable solutions that can dance with the ever-growing tide of data, crunching numbers with the grace of a ballerina and the speed of a cheetah. This isn't just about keeping up; it's about outpacing the competition, fueled by the insights gleaned from a nimble data pipeline.

3. **Integration of Data Silos**: Break down the walls separating your data sources, fostering a symphony of information exchange. Let disparate streams converge into a unified river, flowing freely through your organization, nourishing every corner with the lifeblood of insights. This isn't just about breaking down barriers; it's about unlocking a holistic view, where every decision is informed by the full picture.

By wielding these tools, you'll transform your data from a liability into a potent asset. Trust will blossom, replacing skepticism with confidence. Efficiency will rise, no longer a fleeting dream but a tangible reality. And your data alchemy, fueled by the unwavering trust in your insights, will reach its full, impactful potential. Remember, a data-driven decision is only as good as the data it's based on. Invest in data quality, unlock the power of trust, and watch your data alchemy ascend to new heights, leaving the trust deficit in its dust.

American author David Dunham once quipped, "Efficiency is intelligent laziness." And there's a profound truth hidden beneath that playful jab. Dumb laziness, after all, is content with stagnation, a slothful slumber in the realm of mediocrity. But intelligent laziness, that's the mark of the data alchemist. It's the relentless pursuit of doing less, but achieving more. It's about crafting elegant, streamlined systems that squeeze every ounce of insight from data, leaving the drudgery of manual effort behind. It's about automating the mundane, not to indulge in idleness, but to free ourselves for the grander pursuits of strategic analysis and transformative decision-making.

This principle is the very bedrock of optimizing for impact. It's the guiding light that illuminates the path from data deluge to actionable insights, from cumbersome processes to nimble efficiency. It's about embracing the tools and techniques that amplify our output, not just through brute force, but through meticulous optimization. Remember, every unnecessary step, every wasted byte, is a drag on our journey toward impact. In short, let's channel our inner intelligent laziness, wielding it as a scalpel to carve away the inefficiency and reveal the radiant potential of streamlined data alchemy.

CASE STUDIES

Case Study #1: Streamlining Customer Delight with AI-powered Analytics at Nike[8]

Nike, the sportswear giant, was drowning in customer data, unable to effectively translate it into actionable insights for personalized experiences. Their traditional analytics were slow, siloed, and cumbersome, leading to missed opportunities for customer engagement and retention.

To tackle this challenge, Nike created a unified data lake that integrated all customer touchpoints, from online purchases to social media interactions. They employed advanced machine learning algorithms to analyze this data in real time, identifying individual customer preferences and predicting future behavior.[9]

The results were transformative. Nike could now target customers with highly personalized, efficient marketing campaigns, predict churn risk and proactively offer retention incentives, and even recommend relevant products based on individual preferences. This data-driven approach led to a 20% increase in customer engagement, a 15% reduction in churn rate, and a significant boost in online sales.[10]

Case Study #2: Unilever: From Waste Reduction to Sustainable Leadership

Unilever, a global consumer goods giant, faced a pressing challenge: their production processes generated significant waste. To tackle this, they embarked on a data-driven journey to optimize their operations and reduce their environmental footprint. By implementing sensors and tracking production data in real time, they identified areas of inefficiency and waste generation. Armed with these insights, they implemented targeted interventions, such as optimizing production lines and reducing packaging materials.

The results were staggering. Unilever achieved a 31% reduction in manufacturing waste and a 47% reduction in water consumption since 2010.[11] This not only saved them millions of dollars but also solidified their position as a leader in sustainable manufacturing.

Key Efficiency Lessons from Unilever:

- Data for environmental impact: Don't just focus on financial efficiency; leverage data to optimize for environmental sustainability and build a positive brand image.

- Real-time insights, real-time action: Move beyond historical data analysis; implement real-time monitoring to identify and address inefficiencies as they occur.

- Data-driven collaboration: Foster cross-functional collaboration between sustainability teams and operational teams to ensure efficient implementation of data-driven solutions.

NOTE: These case studies showcase how data-driven efficiency can be harnessed to achieve significant impact across diverse industries. Nike demonstrates the power of AI-powered analytics for personalized customer experiences, while Unilever illustrates how data-driven operations can optimize supply chains for increased profitability and agility. Both cases highlight the crucial role of intelligent laziness in streamlining processes and maximizing output, ultimately serving as inspiring examples for data alchemists seeking to unlock the transformative potential of efficiency.

STUDY QUESTIONS: EFFICIENCY

1. **Beyond Speed: Reframing Efficiency**: Chapter 14 challenges the traditional understanding of efficiency as solely about speed. How can you apply this broader perspective of efficiency to your own data projects or daily work routines? What unexpected benefits might arise from prioritizing elegance and intentionality over mere haste?

2. **Transforming the Data Pipeline**: Simplicity, Certainty, and Integrity are identified as the crucial tenets of an efficient data pipeline. Imagine you're tasked with redesigning your organization's data pipeline. How would you apply these principles and what specific challenges do you foresee in implementation?

3. **Scaling the Analytical Maturity Ladder**: The chapter outlines a four-stage journey of analytical maturity. Where does your current data analysis approach fall on this spectrum? Analyze the strengths and weaknesses of your current stage and brainstorm strategies to progress to the next level.

4. **Combating the Trust Deficit**: Data quality and accessibility are fundamental to building trust in data-driven decisions. What creative solutions can you propose to address issues like data inconsistencies, siloed systems, and outdated infrastructure within your organization?

5. **Weaponizing Intelligent Laziness**: Embracing automation and streamlining processes to free ourselves for strategic thinking is championed as "intelligent laziness." How can you identify and automate repetitive tasks in your own workflow to unlock your full potential for impactful data analysis and decision-making?

6. **Efficiency and Ethics**: While the chapter focuses on the benefits of efficiency, consider the potential ethical implications. Could an overemphasis on efficiency lead to shortcuts in data analysis or biased decision-making? How can we ensure that efficiency serves responsible and ethical data practices?

7. **The Future of Efficiency**: Data analysis tools and technologies are constantly evolving. How do you envision the landscape of data efficiency changing in the next few years? What emerging trends or innovations might further optimize how we extract insights and make data-driven decisions?

8. **Efficiency Beyond Data**: Can the principles of efficiency and "intelligent laziness" be applied to areas beyond data alchemy? Explore

how streamlining processes, prioritizing intentionality, and embracing automation could improve your personal productivity, creative endeavors, or even interpersonal relationships.

These questions aim to not only test your understanding of Chapter 14 but also spark original thought and encourage you to apply the concepts in innovative ways. Remember, data alchemy is a continuous journey of discovery and optimization. Keep exploring, experimenting, and harnessing the power of efficiency to unlock the full potential of your data and your own capabilities!

NOTES

1 "Mindset, Methods & Tools: Accelerate Your Transformation Journey." Boston Consulting Group, October 28, 2021. www.bcg.com/x/product-library/key-program-management-software

2 "Big Data and AI Executive Survey 2021." NewVantage Partners, 2021. www.newvantage.com/wp-content/uploads/2021/01/NewVantage-Partners-2021-Big-Data-and-AI-Executive-Survey.pdf

3 "Forrester Total Economic Impact™ study: Microsoft Fabric delivers 379% ROI over three years." Microsoft, June 3, 2024. www.microsoft.com/en-us/micros oft-fabric/blog/2024/06/03/forrester-total-economic-impact-study-micros oft-fabric-delivers-379-roi-over-three-years/

4 *Harvard Business Review*. "Competing on Analytics: The New Science of Winning." October 26, 2017. https://store.hbr.org/product/competing-on-analytics-updated-with-a-new-introduction-the-new-science-of-winn ing/10157

5 Data Science Central. "Principles of Data Collection & Data Engineering." n.d. https://medium.com/@rchang/a-beginners-guide-to-data-engineering-part-i-4227c5c457d7

6 SAS.com. "Stages of Analytical Maturity." n.d. www.sas.com/content/dam/SAS/en_us/doc/conclusionpaper1/bringing-your-data-to-life-106880.pdf

7 Vanson Bourne. "IT Leaders Don't Fully Trust the Data in Their Organization." n.d. www.businesswire.com/news/home/20201208005422/en/77-of-IT-Lead ers-Don%E2%80%99t-Fully-Trust-the-Data-in-Their-Organization-for-Decis ion-Making-According-to-New-Research-From-SnapLogic

8 Matt Loy. "How Nike Customer Experience Uses Artificial Intelligence To Improve Engagement & Personalization." Digital Silk, August 1, 2024. Accessed January 22, 2025, www.digitalsilk.com/digital-trends/nike-artificial-intelligence/

9 "Case Study: How Nike Is Leveraging AI Across Its Operations." AI Expert Network, September 23, 2023. www.aiexpert.network/case-study-how-nike-is-leveraging-ai-across-its-operations/

10 Alex Barseghian. "How Nike Is Using Analytics To Personalize Their Customer Experience." *Forbes*, October 7, 2019. www.forbes.com/councils/forbestech council/2019/10/07/how-nike-is-using-analytics-to-personalize-their-custo mer-experience/

11 "How We Built Sustainability into Our Manufacturing DNA." Unilever, November 9, 2020. www.unilever.com/news/news-search/2020/how-we-built-sustainability-into-our-manufacturing-dna/

Glimpses into Real Life

Lessons from the Inca Road

I MAGINE A VAST NETWORK of roads, snaking across a sprawling empire, built without the wheel or draft animals. This wasn't science fiction – it was the Inca civilization! Known as the Qhapaq Ñan, or "The Royal Road," this intricate system connected people, goods, and ideas over thousands of miles. The road system was meticulously planned, engineered, and maintained, featuring paved sections, stairways for elevation changes, bridges, and water drainage systems. Built over the course of several centuries, with its peak expansion in the 15th century, this remarkable feat of engineering facilitated trade, enhanced communication, and fostered a strong sense of unity throughout the expansive Inca Empire, which covered 770,000 square miles.

Now, consider your organization's data. It's a valuable asset, just as vital as the goods that flowed along the Qhapaq Ñan. Just as the Incas needed a robust infrastructure to ensure the smooth flow of goods, your organization needs effective data governance to create the infrastructure for a thriving digital landscape. This governance framework rests on four pillars – Legacy, Integrity, Fervency, and Efficiency (LIFE) – that will ensure your data flows freely, empowers informed decisions, and ultimately drives success. Weaving these principles into the fabric of your data practices will enable you to create a dynamic environment where data becomes a

DOI: 10.1201/9781003623212-20

powerful asset, fueling innovation and propelling your organization forward. Let's see what that looks like.

LEGACY: WEAVING A NARRATIVE THROUGH DATA

The Incas understood the importance of legacy. They built their roads with meticulous care, using stones that fit together perfectly, ensuring the Qhapaq Ñan would withstand the test of time. Similarly, effective data governance involves building a data "legacy." This means connecting your current data to historical trends and establishing a data lineage – a clear understanding of where your data comes from and how it's transformed over time. Just as the Qhapaq Ñan facilitated the exchange of knowledge across generations, your data practices should allow future generations to understand the context and history behind your data.

INTEGRITY: BUILDING TRUST WITH TRANSPARENT DATA PRACTICES

The Incas built their roads with integrity. They employed skilled engineers who ensured the Qhapaq Ñan was safe and reliable. Similar principles apply to data governance. Building trust with your data starts with ensuring its accuracy and avoiding bias. Just as a poorly constructed road could lead to disaster, flawed data can lead to bad decisions. Implementing data quality checks, establishing clear ownership of data sets, and fostering a culture of data transparency are all crucial aspects of building trust in your organization's data.

FERVENCY: IGNITING A PASSION FOR DATA EXPLORATION

The Qhapaq Ñan wasn't just a road; it was a path for exploration and discovery. It opened up new possibilities for trade and cultural exchange. Effective data governance should ignite a similar passion for data exploration within your organization. Think of your data analysts as the explorers venturing down this digital highway, uncovering valuable insights that can fuel innovation and growth. By making data accessible and fostering a culture of data curiosity, you empower your team to unlock the hidden potential within your data.

EFFICIENCY: OPTIMIZING THE DATA JOURNEY

The Incas weren't just impressive engineers; they were also pragmatic. They constantly innovated to streamline the flow of goods along the Qhapaq Ñan. Similarly, data governance should prioritize efficiency. This means automating routine data collection and analysis tasks, establishing clear data standards, and fostering collaboration between data teams. Just as the Incas optimized their road network, you should continuously refine your data processes to ensure your data reaches its destination quickly and efficiently, ultimately driving informed decision-making.

This, then, is the essence of data governance in action. By learning from the Inca's masterful infrastructure planning, by fostering collaboration, and by prioritizing data integrity and accessibility, we can create robust data frameworks. This ensures our data, the lifeblood of our digital world, reaches its destination, driving success. It's the foundation for a thriving digital landscape, where data empowers informed decisions, fuels innovation, and propels businesses forward.

TYING IT ALL TOGETHER

Remember Florence Nightingale from the beginning of Part III? More than 160 years ago, armed with nothing more than a pen, a relentless passion for truth, and a keen understanding of data's power, she revolutionized healthcare. Her meticulous analysis of hospital conditions, her data-driven storytelling, and her unwavering conviction moved mountains, literally saving the lives of countless soldiers.

Florence, unknowingly, embodied all the pillars we've explored in Part III of this book. **Legacy**: She leveraged existing data, seeing what others had missed. **Integrity**: Her analysis was rigorous, precise, and unwavering in its pursuit of truth. **Fervency**: Her passion for saving lives fueled every step, every sleepless night, and every persuasive argument. And finally, **Efficiency**: She knew how to distill complex information into impactful narratives, swaying even the most entrenched Victorian minds.

Now what about you? You hold a tool in your hand that dwarfs the computational power that sent humanity to the moon –yes, that's right; a smartphone! You have access to mountains of data, sophisticated analytics, and visualization tools that would make Florence blush. So, what's our excuse? Bringing data to life shouldn't be a luxury; it's our responsibility. It's the key to unlocking insights that can transform businesses, improve lives, and shape a better future.

But data, much like Florence's statistics, doesn't have a life of its own. It's inert, waiting to be awakened. That's where we, the data wizards, come in. Like Nightingale, we've explored the four pillars that breathe life into data: Legacy, Integrity, Fervency, and Efficiency. Legacy, the foundation, reminds us that data is a conversation across time, carrying the whispers of past decisions and guiding the way forward. Integrity, the compass, ensures our analyses are accurate, unbiased, and trustworthy – a cornerstone in a world awash with information. Fervency, the fire, ignites our passion for data, propelling us beyond mere analysis to the realm of impactful exploration and discovery. And finally, Efficiency, the wizard's wand, helps us wield data with elegance and precision, squeezing every drop of insight from its vast ocean.

Bringing data to L.I.F.E. is not just a technical feat; it's a human one. It's about weaving a tapestry of legacy, integrity, fervency, and efficiency. Forget the excuses. We have the power, the tools, and the inspiration. Let's take a page from Florence's playbook, harness the magic of data wizardry, and bring life to data, from the palm of our hand to the very fabric of our world. The world awaits the symphony of insights we can create, and the time to begin is now.

Conclusion

Where Stories Spark Transformation

REMEMBER THOSE CHILDHOOD DAYS lost in captivating narratives, where heroes triumphed and dragons were slain? We hunger for stories; for meaning woven from the very fabric of life itself. But what if I told you the most epic tales lie not just in dusty tomes, but in the cold, hard data that surrounds us? This book is your invitation to become the scribe of this new age, transforming raw numbers into narratives that ignite action and drive real change.

We began by wielding the Brains and Beauty of data visualization in Part I. We learned to craft not just eye-catching charts, but strategic tapestries that guide minds and motivate hearts. Then we honed our data visualization skills by Starting the **Race**, Making the **Case**, Motivating the **Base**, and Giving it some **Space**, so we could Put It into **Place**. We moved beyond mere decoration, understanding that effective data stories are a deliberate dance between articulation and advocacy, education and investigation, art and science, form and function, brains and beauty – all culminating in effectual action.

Then, in Driving Decisions with Data, we ventured into the perilous terrain of data-driven decision-making. We equipped ourselves in Part II

DOI: 10.1201/9781003623212-21

with the tools to navigate the treacherous waters of the five key verbs (**Look**, **Link**, **Listen**, **Leverage**, and **Learn**) for extracting actionable insights from information's ever-shifting sands. We discovered the crucial distinction between data, mere pebbles of fact, and the intelligence – the woven narrative – that empowers us to navigate uncertainty and make choices that shape our future.

Finally, in Part III, Bringing Data to L.I.F.E. and Life to Data, we breathed life into this digital beast. We unearthed its **Legacy**, connecting it to the whispers of the past and weaving a tapestry that transcends fleeting trends. We built **Integrity**, forging trust through accuracy and ethical practices. We ignited **Fervency**, sparking curiosity and infusing our insights with passion to drive engagement and action. And lastly, we embraced **Efficiency**, wielding the wand of automation and optimization to extract maximum value from every drop of data.

Data is not just numbers on a screen; it's a living pulse, a story yearning to be told. This book is your key to unlocking its potential. You are not just an analyst; you are a bard; a weaver of narratives that reshape realities. So, go forth; armed with the insights gleaned from these pages. Transform your information into intelligence, your intelligence into action, and your actions into a thriving, data-driven future. Remember, the most valuable stories aren't just found in books, but also in the meticulous data collection of a 17th century Prague professor, the resilience of the Inca Empire's vast road network, and the innovative spirit that led to the creation of a bullet-proof vest. Data surrounds us, whispering tales of the past, informing the present, and shaping the future. Unleash the power of your data, and write your own success story.

As Abraham Lincoln aptly declared, "If I had eight hours to chop down a tree, I would spend six hours sharpening my axe." Sharpen your data visualization axe, wield it with passion and purpose, and become the Michelangelo of modern times, sculpting the landscape of your world with every stroke of data-driven insight. The future is yours to forge. Begin sculpting.

Index